Praise for *The Wizard of Foz*

"Welch begins his chapters with the greatest collection of stirring epigrams I've ever found in a single work. That means it is a history filled with the suffering of pursuing a new idea in a world fanatically ready to doubt. It is about the power of invention, and the need for wisdom in teachers confronted by that invention. Fosbury and our society have needed decades to be able to fully tell or accept Dick's story. Now it is done, and Welch does magnificent justice to it all."

—Kenny Moore, Olympic marathoner,
former *Sports Illustrated* writer,
and author of *Bowerman and the Men of Oregon*

"Competing in the Olympic trials is stressful and nerve-racking enough, but to have to do it twice? Dick's read gives us a peek into an athlete's world and more importantly the politics that have seeped their way into the sport!"

—Debbie Meyer, three-time Olympic champion
and Sullivan Award winner

"Great read! Bob Welch has the rare ability to provide context to what some might consider to be purely a sports story. He evokes a time and place that many of us remember well, and provides insight for those who came after. This is a 'history book' in the best sense of that phrase."

—Tom Jordan, author of *Pre: The Story of America's Greatest
Running Legend, Steve Prefontaine*

"Dick Fosbury has always been one of the most compelling figures in American sports. Through Bob Welch's fascinating look at Fosbury's extraordinary story, we see just how the high jump's innovative but enduring style was created. Foz's ingenuity combined with Welch's purposeful prose results in one great book. It's anything but a flop."

—Kerry Eggers, sports columnist, *Portland Tribune*

"*The Wizard of Foz* raises the bar in showcasing the life of a man who revolutionized the high jump. Whether you're a track enthusiast or not, it's a must read."

—Tom Pappas, former world decathlon champion

"Newly employed at *Track & Field News* in the late 1960s, I imagined knowing much about Dick Fosbury. Lately I've learned that I knew little beyond his Flop and resulting statistics. Bob Welch's book teaches in wonderful detail about the man behind the method."

—Joe Henderson, former writer/editor for
Track & Field News and *Runner's World*

"In a moment of mid-air inspiration, a mediocre prep high jumper named Dick Fosbury changed the course of his event, and his life. Such is the impact of the 'Fosbury Flop' that the label itself seems virtually forgotten—it's simply the way all high jumpers compete these days. In *The Wizard of Foz* author Bob Welch excellently captures the angst of the teen-age high jumper who became an Olympic gold medalist during the turbulent late 1960s. It's the rest of the story you never knew."

—Ron Bellamy, former (Eugene) *Register-Guard* sports editor
and winner of the Track and Field Writers of America's
Jesse Abramson Award for Excellence

"As an author of sports books, I'm no stranger to athletes-overcoming-the-odds stories. But Welch's Fosbury tale is like nothing I've ever seen. Though flat-out true, it has the feel of fantasy, particularly when Dick is struggling to make the Olympic team at a high-mountain venue where giant pines stretch to the sky from within the track's infield. But such fantasy clashes with the volatile '60s. Ultimately, Fosbury not only changes the world, but the world changes him, particularly in his seeing the light regarding the insidious racism so many wanted to ignore."

—Mike Yorkey, coauthor of *After the Cheering Stops: An NFL Wife's Story of Concussions, Loss, and the Faith That Saw Her Through*

"*The Wizard of Foz* is more than a sports story. It's a wonderful narrative about the culture of innovation, rooted in the pioneer spirit of Oregon."

—Paul Swangard, TV track and field commentator
and Olympic Games in-stadium announcer

"Masterfully written with exactness of countless memories. This book from the beginning is a testament of family love through the pain of family tragedy. The social growth wrapped around the mental anguish of Dick's options through a time of social change did not interrupt his battle to defeat the many competitive negatives received on his journey to capture elusiveness."

—Tommie Smith, 200m gold medalist, Mexico City 1968 Olympics

THE WIZARD OF FOZ

THE ECHO SUMMIT TRACK AND FIELD LAYOUT, WHERE FOSBURY'S
CHANCES OF MAKING THE OLYMPIC TEAM CAME DOWN TO A
SINGLE JUMP DURING THE TRIALS, HAD A FANTASY FEEL TO IT.
HIGH-JUMP PIT WAS JUST INSIDE THE TRACK, LOWER RIGHT.

(STEVE MURDOCK/CITY OF SOUTH LAKE TAHOE)

The good people of Medford, where Fosbury invented The Flop!

THE WIZARD OF FOZ

DICK FOSBURY'S ONE-MAN HIGH-JUMP REVOLUTION

BY BOB WELCH
WITH DICK FOSBURY

Sept. 11, 2018

Foreword by Ashton Eaton

Skyhorse Publishing

Skyhorse Publishing books may be purchased in bulk at special discounts for sales promotion, corporate gifts, fund-raising, or educational purposes. Special editions can also be created to specifications. For details, contact the Special Sales Department, Skyhorse Publishing, 307 West 36th Street, 11th Floor, New York, NY 10018 or info@skyhorsepublishing.com.

Skyhorse® and Skyhorse Publishing® are registered trademarks of Skyhorse Publishing, Inc.®, a Delaware corporation.

Visit our website at www.skyhorsepublishing.com.

10 9 8 7 6 5 4 3 2 1

Library of Congress Cataloging-in-Publication Data is available on file.

Cover design by Tom Lau
Cover photo credit AP Images

ISBN: 978-1-5107-3619-1
Ebook ISBN 978-1-5107-3625-2

Printed in the United States of America

To those who follow their imaginations,
shoot for the moon,
and stand for what's right.

Those who have finished by making all others think with them have usually been those who began by daring to think for themselves.
— C. C. Colton

CONTENTS

FOREWORD

"FOSBURY! REMEMBER FOSBURY!" I was at the 2011 IAAF World Track and Field Championships in Daegu, South Korea, and, from beyond the high jump pit, my coach Harry Marra was saying these words to me because I was in trouble. A year before I had graduated from the University of Oregon, signed a shoe deal, and become a professional decathlete. Now I was a young athlete in my first global competition as a professional. And ranked No. 1 in the world.

I had recently amassed the highest decathlon score in the world by a decent margin. It was the year before the Olympic Games—a critical time for an athlete like me hoping to make the U.S. Olympic team. The competition in South Korea was an important proving ground on many levels. And, frankly, I was not doing well. It was my last attempt in the high jump; the bar was not high.

"Fosbury! Remember Fosbury!" It seems almost cosmically designed that Marra was yelling that at me at this pivotal point in my career. Dick and I were both born in Portland, both raised in Oregon, and both graduates from colleges in the Willamette Valley. As I stared at this seemingly insurmountable height, the only difference between us was that Dick was an Olympic champion and I was only hoping to become one.

So it seemed ironic that I was struggling with the event in which he had won gold. A few weeks prior to this meet I started looking at videos of the top high jumpers in the world, trying to see if there was something I could do to improve. After hours of analyzing the top men and women, I was still struggling to understand the keys to the technique. Then it dawned on me: these athletes didn't invent this technique. They were emulating the Flop style just like I was.

Who would be the best reference? The person who invented the style, of course. I found a video of Dick Fosbury jumping in the 1968 Olympics. I can still see him, the clenched hands, his weight shifting back and forth as he looks at the ground. Then: acceleration, curve, a plant of his foot—almost imperceptible from a normal stride—and a passionate launch into the air.

It was beautiful, it was simple, it was magic. And I understood it. The day before the meet in South Korea, I went to Marra. "If I get in trouble tomorrow in the high jump," I told him, "just tell me 'Fosbury.'"

I went on to clear the bar and many others after, eventually joining Dick as an Olympic champion. I won decathlon gold in London in 2012 and Rio in 2016 and, in between, set the world record at 9,045 points. I still remember standing on the podium in London. My mind zipped back in time through all the experiences, large and small, leading to that moment.

"Every athlete who makes it to the Olympic Games has a thousand reasons why he or she shouldn't have," a coach once told me.

He was suggesting that there are beautiful stories of athletes, many of them involving humble beginnings, passionate eagerness, and unbending human spirit. But most such stories don't ever get told. Thanks to this book, Dick's story *is* getting told—and rightfully so, considering Fosbury is one of the most influential athletes in the history of track and field.

— *Ashton Eaton, 2012 and 2016 Olympic gold medalist and current world record holder in the decathlon*

PROLOGUE

IT IS SEPTEMBER 2017 and a tall, gray-haired man of seventy walks through a High Sierra forest. Dick Fosbury is looking for something that he left here nearly half a century ago and only now has come back to find: a memory. A moment. A reconnection with the magic of a place called Echo Summit, where at this unlikely spot in September 1968 the men's U.S. Olympic Track and Field team held a competition to see which athletes would represent America for the Games in Mexico City.

A track had been plopped down in California's El Dorado National Forest with only a few trees having been cut. More than a hundred pines rose from the center of the oval itself. Granite boulders nudged the inside edges of the track and came within a foot of the long-jump runway. In a country fractured by a decade of dissent, assassinations, and war, nearly 200 athletes had come to a place so peaceful that, as one athlete said, "you could hear your heartbeat." None was like Dick Fosbury.

At the time, essentially every competitive high jumper in the world used a technique called the "straddle," which dated back decades. Fosbury, as a teenager in Medford, Oregon, could never master it. So he invented his own method. He jumped backward over the bar—against the will of some coaches who thought it foolhardy, some fans who thought it laughable, and some doctors who thought it dangerous.

But as the years passed, Fosbury jumped higher and higher with the style. In fact, he jumped so high that he was among twenty-four high jumpers invited to compete in the Olympic Trials in Los Angeles, from which ten athletes in each event were to advance to Echo Summit, for the final Trials. The top three in each event would make the team to compete in Mexico City, whose 7,350-foot altitude is why the US was holding the tryouts at a similar altitude: to acclimate the athletes for what was to come.

On a laptop computer he brought with him, Fosbury glances at a picture from the 1968 trials at Echo Summit. "Look at the rock in the photo, then look at this," he says, pointing to a slab of granite arching from the ground like the back of a gray whale. "Same rock. Same clump of pines. The high jump pit was right over here in this clearing. I would have started my approach from right . . ."—he walks a few steps—" . . . right . . . here." His eyes dart back and forth between trees and boulders to the photo.

It is September 16, exactly forty-nine years to the day of those high-jump trials. It is almost 4 pm, the same time of day he had attempted a height—7'2"—that he had already missed twice. One more miss and he would not make the team.

The light, splintered by towering pines, looks eerily as it did in wire photos of his final jump that day. A breeze tickles his wavy gray hair, longer than it was back then. A slight limp accents his gait. And a subtle glint in his eyes suggests it's no longer 2017 for him.

Without prompting, he sets the computer down and clenches his fists in front of him, as if he might be holding trekking poles. He faces north, toward where the tree-studded infield would have been, his back to what then was hundreds of fans but now is just a few skittering chipmunks. He shakes his hands as if to loosen up. All is quiet. He starts rocking back and forth ever so slightly. He stares at something, but what?

Perhaps what he senses at this moment: the trees, the smell of pine needles, the hint of autumn. Perhaps that day in 1968, on which his future hung. Or perhaps a time even earlier, when Fosbury was a boy and the seeds of revolution were just taking root.

PART I

BLUEPRINTS

Chapter 1

The greatest and most powerful revolutions often start very quietly, hidden in the shadows.

— Richelle Mead

FOR DICK FOSBURY, the day arrived with less promise than the morning sky. It was April 20, 1963, a Saturday. Rogue Valley farmers, with an unseasonal cold snap threatening to freeze their peaches and pears, had burned their oil-based smudge pots all night to keep frost from the buds. By mid-morning, the resulting smoke shrouded much of Southern Oregon in a sooty pall resembling dusky fog. A *Medford Mail Tribune* editorialist tried vainly to stay optimistic. "It used to be far worse," he wrote.

Temperatures strained to rise above freezing. People venturing into the Cascade or Siskiyou Mountains for the opening day of fishing season threw in tire chains alongside rods, reels, and six-packs of Olympia and Hamm's beer. Folks setting up for the Pear Blossom Parade downtown—President John F. Kennedy, while campaigning against Richard Nixon, had been grand marshal three years earlier—wore wool caps and gloves. Meanwhile, the boys on Medford High's track and field team only reluctantly left their—or their parents'—heated vehicles after arriving at the school, from which they were to bus north for a track and field meet in nearby Grants Pass.

So much for spring in Oregon. April was often glorious in the Rogue Valley: fruit trees in full blossom; velvety green hills dotted with sheep; snowy Mount McLoughlin, a Mount Fuji look-alike, rising 9,495 feet to the east; and, to the north, the Rogue River, frothing westward down from the Cascade Range snowmelt, twisting through the valley, and cutting through the Coast Range to spill into the Pacific Ocean. But now blotted in an oily haze, Southern Oregon's natural wonders were more like actors in a lavish musical caught backstage in street clothes. The fishermen and festival-goers may not have been deterred in their quests for fun—Oregonians tended to be a hardy and hopeful bunch— but, beyond that, the day did not smack of grand possibilities.

Dick's mother, Helen, eased the Buick to a halt in front of Medford Stadium and turned to her son with a kind but almost robotic cadence. "Good luck," she said. "Jump high."

He nodded. "See you around six."

Helen Fosbury was tall and slender like her high-jumper son, the two bound—and separated—by a common loss of which neither had spoken. She epitomized a generation of Wonder Bread women who, despite some quiet disappointment in their own lives, brought forth the first wave of Baby Boomers and wrapped their children in the swaddling clothes of optimism. "Jump high" might have sounded like a going-through-the-motions comment, but given her son's meager success thus far, she might as well have said, "Shoot for the moon, kid."

In 1948—Dick had been born a year earlier, on March 6 in Portland, Oregon—a baby was born in the US every eight seconds, almost double the Depression Era rate. World War II was over. Soldiers were home—and didn't hesitate to make up for lost time. When Dick was a sixth-grader at Medford's Roosevelt Elementary School, nearly a third of the nation's population was under the age of fourteen.

Such baby boomers were the proverbial "pig in the python," children who would irrevocably reshape America as they came of age. Cities built new schools to accommodate them. Marketers made skateboards, Pluto Platters, and Duncan yo-yos to appease them. Musicians, young and hip, wrote songs to inspire them. And filmmakers made movies to entertain them, including *The Absent-Minded Professor,* a 1961 blockbuster about a college chemistry prof who creates a flying rubber— "Flubber"—that, among other things, helps Medfield College basketball players jump high above the rim.

The glow of US and Russian soldiers meeting at the Elbe River to seal their victory over Germany in World War II had long since faded.

Soviet-spun Communism was the new US fear. As Dick was greasing his hair for his first day of high school in 1962, the Soviets were aiming multi-megaton nuclear warheads at America from Cuba, only ninety miles from Florida. But if the placid waters of youth had been rippled by "duck and cover" drills at schools during fall's Cuban Missile Crisis, six months later the good times were back. Medford's KBOY disc jockeys were spinning such tunes as Bobby Vinton's "Roses are Red," the Four Seasons' "Big Girls Don't Cry," and Ricky Nelson's "Fools Rush In."

"They were raised in unprecedented prosperity and unparalleled expectations about the future," wrote Steve Gillon in *Boomer Nation*. *Time* declared teenagers to be "on the fringe of a golden era." As the 1960s deepened, JFK—at age forty-three, the youngest president replacing, at age seventy, Dwight Eisenhower, the oldest—further fueled such optimism. In 1957, the Soviets had been first into space with the Sputnik satellite and, in April 1961, first into space with a man, Yuri Gagarin, beating America's Alan Shepard by four weeks. Now, Kennedy was rallying America to shoot higher, go faster, be stronger. "We stand today," he said, "on the edge of a new frontier."

He launched the President's Council on Physical Fitness; soon, millions of children—few actually overweight—started their school days doing calisthenics to a song called "Chicken Fat." He challenged America to put a man on the moon by the end of the decade. And he basked in glory when, in February 1962, astronaut John Glenn became the first American to orbit the earth, circling it three times—two more than Gagarin had completed the previous year.

Meanwhile, the Soviets' Valeriy Brumel emerged as the world's best high jumper, leaping 7'5¼" in September 1962. Dick Fosbury? He just wanted to jump higher than 5'4" in a Medford High uniform. He just wanted to be on the team. Like the other "one-every-eight-seconds" babies, now in their teens, he just wanted to *belong*.

But midway through the season, his mother's encouragement to "jump high" was, if simple in word, elusive in deed. It was as if Dick's height (6'2") and feet size (12) were high school sophomores but the rest of his body was still in eighth grade, desperately running after him like a man who'd missed his train. In the season's first meet, Dick had failed to even clear the opening height of 5'0". A month later, his season-best of 5'4" would not be good enough to win a lot of junior high meets. A high jumper from Colton High, a Class "B" Oregon school that had fewer students in it than Dick had in some of his individual *classes*, was jumping 6'2". And in Los Angeles, the epicenter of US high jumping in the 1950s and '60s, Joe Faust had set an age-group record of 6'8¼"—at fifteen.

In a sport upon which four numbers determined one's success— How fast? How far? How long? How high?—the reality was harsh but true: in the spring of 1963, Dick Fosbury was one of the worst prep high jumpers in the state of Oregon. Not that he wore such woefulness on his sleeve. Even then, Fosbury was so skilled at hiding the pain of self-perceived failure—and of deeper things—that, decades later, class-mates would remember him as a kid whose exterior was as calm as the tucked-in-a-bowl surface of nearby Crater Lake.

Whimsical, not worried, was the more applicable description for Dick; hadn't it been his idea to put the Limburger cheese on the caf-eteria radiator to see how it might smell? "He didn't seem nearly as hampered with being himself as I was," said Doug Sweet, whose friend-ship with Dick dated back to Roosevelt Elementary. "As they say, 'He wore the world like a loose garment.'" Doug was serious, maudlin, and bookish; Dick was lighthearted, upbeat, and comic-bookish—or so he came across to his closest friend and others. Inside, he was not nearly so comfortable.

Fosbury was remarkable in being unremarkable, the essence of average. He wasn't a great athlete; he wasn't a bad athlete. He wasn't a great student; he wasn't a bad student. He wasn't a hellion; he wasn't an angel. Teammates, years hence, would describe him many ways but virtually all, at some point, would offer the same description: "Dick Fosbury was just another guy on the track team."

At the time, he was the oldest of two Fosbury children: Gail was three years younger. When Dick was twelve, the family moved to a sub-urban rambler on Ridge Way in northeast Medford. His father, Doug, was a salesman at Witham's Truck Stop; his mother, Helen, was a book-keeper at Elk Lumber. The family played Monopoly and Yahtzee on Friday nights, vacationed at Lake Shasta and on the Oregon Coast, and had a terrier named Wags. Doug and Helen led a local square dance club. Doug bowled. Helen played classical piano; music was her passion.

Dick had been high-jumping since he was an eleven-year-old in 1958. He cleared 3'10" that year. His first instructor—and first inspiration—was a teacher, Chuck "Chief" McLain. McLain, Native American, taught Dick and his fifth-grade classmates the scissors method. McLain was a legend in Medford. He had played guard on a 1930s University of Oregon basketball team, had gotten a game-winning hit off famed pitcher Satchel Paige, and had been a Golden Glove boxer. He could be brutally blunt; if he yelled at a kid who was screwing up, the admonishment hit home like a well-hammered nail. But the underlying message was noble: *You're a Medford kid; be something great.*

In Medford, sandlot baseball played second-fiddle to sandlot track and field. In back of the Fosbury house on Ridge Way, Doug built his son a high-jump setup with a sawdust pit, two-by-four standards, and nails every two inches to hold up a dowel rod. His father was forever chiding Dick, as a right-hander, for jumping off what his father thought was the wrong foot, his right. "You're jumping goofy-footed," said Doug, who'd run track and played football in his high school days in Portland. "You should be jumping off your left. You're never going to jump very high that way."

In the spring of 1961, an alternative high-jump style was introduced to Dick and his classmates by a man they knew only as Mr. Monroe, a Hedrick Junior High P.E. teacher.

"Gentlemen, there are two ways to high-jump," said Monroe, with one of those "coach voices" that dramatized six-count burpees as if they were the moral equivalent of going to war. "The scissors-kick and the straddle—or 'belly roll.' Let me demonstrate." The teacher placed a crinkled metal bar on the standards in front of a sawdust landing pit, then backed up on the grass apron.

For the scissors, he approached the bar at roughly a thirty-degree angle from the right side of the run-up area. He leapt from his outside foot, his left, scissoring straight-legged with a quick right-left sequence and landing on his feet. For the straddle, he approached the bar from the left side and at less of an angle. He sprang into the air off his inside foot, his left, and thrust his right leg up toward the bar almost like a punter kicking a football. That, in turn, helped lift his body into a layout over the bar; he momentarily looked like a chicken kabob on a skewer. After clearing the bar, he twisted his body, then rolled onto his side, landing in the sawdust.

"Now, your turn, beginning with the scissors," said Mr. Monroe, brushing himself off. "Last man without a miss wins."

Dick Fosbury did just the opposite of what Mr. Monroe recommended, starting from the left side and jumping off his right foot. But he won. "I'll never forget his scissor-style jump that day," said a classmate, Ron Wallace. "He was smooth as silk. Like a human gazelle."

Next came the straddle, a more complicated style that lent itself to a higher degree of athleticism. Dick missed all three of his attempts—badly. "The results were disastrous," said Wallace. "Nothing worked. Dick's arms and legs flew in five different directions, the bar clanged off the standards, and Dick landed on it. In disgust, he threw a handful of sawdust across the pit."

NOW, AT SIXTEEN, Dick had no illusions of athletic grandeur. He knew he was no Steve Davis, a fellow sophomore who had already cleared 6'0". Unlike Ernie Shelton, a University of Southern California jumper from the 1950s, he did not make a mark seven feet up on his bedroom wall and vow to someday be the first to jump that high. He did not lay in his room and dream of Olympic glory like Boston University's John Thomas. Instead, he read comic books: Archie, Richie Rich, Superman, and Batman.

"All I ever wanted to do," remembered Fosbury, "was just make the team and stay on the team. I lived in the moment."

It was, he had discovered, the safest place to be. Attending the largest high school between Portland and Sacramento, Dick realized his dilemma: to set his sights on the future was to be reminded of how fierce life's competition could be, whether the challenge was making a track team that often competed for state titles or mustering the courage to invite Janet Kolkemo from his French class to a school dance. On the other hand, to dwell on the past was to be reminded how cruel life could be—to be reminded of things Dick wanted to forget. Thus he found strange comfort nestled in the eye of life's storm, in the moment, in the now, where the future stretched no further ahead than a horizontal high-jump bar fifty feet in front of him and the past could stay safely in the shadows, where it belonged.

FOR SATURDAY AFTERNOON'S Grants Pass Rotary Invitational, the boys changed into their uniforms beneath the Medford High football stadium, in a locker room that smelled of mold, sweat, and unflushed urinals. Of Atomic Balm Deep Heating Rub. Of smudge smoke from boys on the team who'd had to light pots early that morning, and now—nostrils full of soot—prided themselves in hocking up loogies nearly the size, and color, of hockey pucks.

Amid this cluster of burbling testosterone, Fosbury's body had, in the last few years, changed from the stick-figure drawing it had been—but not by much. His XL uniform, necessary for length, not width, hung on him like dried moss on a broom handle: white silk pants and singlet with red piping, a red "Flying M" emblazoned across the sleeveless chest. His father had bought him a set of weights to build muscle but never showed his son how to use them, even after Dick had asked. So Dick never used them.

When Dick had tried out for the sophomore football team the previous fall, coaches had a hard time finding a place for him to fit. He loved basketball but was only a so-so player. Now track and field was threatening to complete Dick's trifecta of athletic failure. As he boarded the bus for Grants Pass that morning, however, he knew a secret that he'd only shared with one other person—his buddy Sweet, a half-miler on the track team: in a last-gasp attempt to jump higher, Dick was considering going rogue.

He was mulling the idea of reverting back to a style, the scissors, that hardly anybody used anymore. A style he'd used since he was eleven but had ditched at the start of the season when MHS track and field Coach Dean Benson suggested he bag it in favor of the technique virtually all jumpers now used, the straddle. But after a handful of meets, Dick was now so frustrated he'd gone to Benson during practice to see about scissoring at Grants Pass.

"Now why in the hell would you want to do something like that, Fosbury?"

"I just feel like I could do better that way."

Though young, twenty-eight-year-old Dean Benson knew his track and field. He had been a national small-college champion hurdler at Willamette University in Salem, Oregon. In the 1956 Olympic Trials in Los Angeles—the same trials where Charles Dumas, not Ernie Shelton, became the first man to clear 7'0" in the high jump—Benson had come within inches of making the Melbourne team in the 110-meter high hurdles. In only five years, he had MHS poised to win a state championship—and not by trying to resurrect high-jumping styles that hadn't been used since the *Titanic* was floating.

"Dick, you can't live in the past," said Benson. "Brumel went seven-five last summer down in Palo Alto. He straddles. Hell, everyone straddles."

"I've been trying all spring and haven't gone higher than I did last year. Five-four."

Benson took off his hat and rubbed his forehead. Was it his realization that failure might be the better teacher? The kid's damned persistence? Or pity? For whatever reason, Benson exhaled.

"OK, Fosbury, don't give up learning, but it's *your* decision if you want to try the scissors," he said. "And, jeez, score us a point or two, huh?"

Said Fosbury years later: "The implication was that, 'Dick, it doesn't matter what style you use because you haven't qualified for district and this may be one of the last meets you're going to compete in for Medford High, period.'"

Decades later, when asked about Fosbury, Benson just shook his head. "Dick Fosbury," he said, "was more suspect than prospect. He was a gangly, gawky, grew-too-fast kid. And he was just looking for a niche somewhere. Someplace to fit in."

As THE BUS wound its way through town to Highway 99, Dick sat at the back right as usual, next to Sweet, safely on the periphery, far from the team's power bloc. It wasn't a particularly raucous bunch, but as a sophomore, you wanted to err on the side of caution. The juniors and seniors were Dick's heroes, guys he'd watched compete as a kid. Now here he was, amongst them.

Up ahead, distance runner Greg Swanson and a few others were already well into a medley relay of jokes, boasts, burps, and farts. Not far from him sat Mike Mayfield, a thrower who'd found himself in that uncomfortable position of being the son of a school superintendent—and facing detention for fighting. Most guys were quiet, lost in thoughts of who knew what: relay baton exchanges? The previous night's party? Distance runner Dennis Brumback's amazingly cute sister, Becky? The eyes of the smudgers—the boys who'd been up since 4 a.m.—were already growing heavy with the vibration of the bus.

Dick looked out the window at the place that had been his home since 1954, when he was seven. The images flashed by like View-Master slides: *click*, the dollar-a-carload Valley Drive-In, with Alfred Hitchcock's *The Birds* on the marquee; *click*, the lumber mills, with seemingly endless stacks of dimensional lumber lined up three stories high, attesting to Oregon's rank as the world's top timber producer; *click*, the huge wigwam burners, like giant, rusted badminton birdies, turning the mills' mountains of sawdust into smoke; *click*, orchards as far as he could see; *click*, folks driving Impalas, Corvairs, Galaxies; *click*, *Dick Fosbury clearing 5'6" for the first time ever, ladies and gentlemen, using the old scissors style . . . the crowd goes wild . . . the bar is raised to 5'8" . . . he's over! . . . Now the bar is at 5'10", six inches higher than he's ever gone before, just south of outer space! . . . Fosbury starts his approach, he leaps, he scissors his legs, he—.*

"Fosdick, where the hell are you, man?" said Sweet, elbowing Dick with an accompanying moniker his pals had given him based on a bumbling cartoon-strip detective. "I asked if you wanna see *The Birds* tonight at the Valley. Heard this ol' geezer gets his eyeballs pecked out."

Chapter 2

What's a man's first duty? The answer is brief: to be himself.

—*Henrik Ibsen*

FIVE FEET, FOUR inches. How could a bar so low be an obstacle so high? At Gold Hill, as the bus began climbing out of the valley and alongside the Rogue River, Fosbury looked around at this jiggling-headed collection of teammates. Yes, he was part of all this—and as a sophomore, no less. Like everyone else, he wore the red "Flying M" on his chest in honor of the Medford High Black Tornado. But for how long? He started inching back on his decision to scissor. Maybe he should just stick with the straddle and hope for the best.

The athletes' job each week was to run faster, throw farther, vault higher, and jump higher. And most Medford boys were doing just that. But not Dick. He had not improved on his 5'4" best since late in his ninth-grade season. At smaller schools, no sweat; who was going to take his place? At Medford, things were different. For most meets, three athletes were entered in each event. If a boy couldn't prove himself worthy of being among them, a handful of others were eagerly waiting in the wings. Medford High hadn't won twenty-three of the last forty state track and field championships without benefit of a certain survival-of-the-fittest mentality. The Black Tornado hadn't played in more state football championship games than all but one other school by taking an "everybody-plays" approach.

Beyond lumber, peaches, and pears, what powered Medford, Oregon, was one thing: boys' athletics. (It would be nearly a decade before the Title IX law would require federally funded schools to allow similar opportunities for girls.) Sports knit the community in common purpose, helped school-bond measures pass, and allowed folks to strut a bit—perhaps more than a bit. It had been that way for decades—at least since 1928, when the football team qualified for the state championship game in Portland and the town promptly hired a private train to send the boys up north in style.

THE HEADWATERS OF the Medford High sports dynasty could be traced to a man who played for Medford, coached for Medford, and ultimately would become the most influential man in US track and field history: William J. Bowerman. The namesake of Dick Fosbury's junior high, Ercel Hedrick, had more than a little to do with Bowerman becoming the legend he was.

When Bowerman was a Medford High student in the 1920s, he was an angry young man, as accounted in Kenny Moore's *Bowerman and the Men of Oregon*. He revered his mother, but because of a father who essentially abandoned Bill—and the traumatic death of a little brother—he often let his fists do the talking. As a sophomore—the same age Fosbury was as the bus rolled north—Bill was suspended for fighting again. Hedrick, the superintendent of schools, had Bill come to his office.

"This is *ridiculous!*" he boomed. "You're good in band, good in journalism, so you're not stupid, just a hell-raisin' son of a bitch."

Hedrick was just getting started. As if Charles Dickens's Ghost of Christmas Future, he pointed a bony finger at what lay ahead for Bowerman. "You'll fight, and I'll be rid of you. You'll fight, and everybody else will be rid of you. Fight here, fight there, die in prison or on some barroom floor. The only thing wrong with that is that you'll dishonor a worthwhile human being."

Bill raised his drooping head. "Who's that?"

"Elizabeth Hoover Bowerman."

At the sound of his mother's name, Bowerman's bravado melted like spring snow. With some time to let it settle in, he returned to school a changed young man. Ultimately, he led Medford High to two straight state football champions, 1927 and 1928; got nothing lower than a single "B" in school; and married a young Medford woman,

Barbara Young, who passed up football games to take private dance lessons. In years to come, she softened some of Bill's harder edges. At the University of Oregon, Bowerman became a track star. He graduated, told his father, who was trying to woo him into the law profession, to "go straight to hell," and decided to attend medical school. Meanwhile, he took a teaching job at Franklin High in Portland for $80 a month. But Hedrick intervened.

"Come coach our football team," he wired Bowerman. Thanks, said Bill, but he was going to become a doctor. "You're a *Medford* product. I know in Portland you get paid $1,000 a year. We pay $1,500."

So Bowerman became the Medford High football coach. In 1935, he oversaw the building of Medford High's first track and started its first track and field team. He got Medford into the state football championship in the fall of 1940, and his teams won state track and field titles that spring and the year after, creating a momentum that was still rolling two decades later when Fosbury entered high school. When, in 1948, Bowerman left to coach at his alma mater, Oregon, he passed the track and field baton to Bob Newland, one of Bill's former MHS athletes who'd set the school high-jump record in 1940 at 6'0". Newland's Medford teams won an unprecedented nine state track and field championships in ten years, from 1948 through 1957, a record unequaled before or since. Like Bowerman, Newland held nothing back in his attempt to help his athletes be the best they could be; he would send questions to, and get letters back from, the likes of Herb Elliott of Australia and Peter Snell of New Zealand. Meanwhile, Fred Spiegelberg took over the football program and turned it into a state powerhouse.

THIS WAS THE sports culture to which Dick Fosbury was expected to assimilate—a culture built not only on the *act* of being the best, but on the *expectation* of being the best. Medford High wasn't just a high school; it was a machine that ground forward with each passing generation. "Sports," said Fosbury classmate Jack Mullen, "permeated the lives of Medford kids in those days."

If tradition was a major reason for the success of its teams, Medford's location was another. In a large state that stretched from ocean to valley to mountains to desert, the Rogue Valley in southern Oregon was separated from the more mainstream Willamette Valley by half a dozen minor mountain passes, leaving it as something of a world unto its own. It was far from the pulsing commerce of Portland, at the Willamette Valley's northern tip; the politics of the state capitol, Salem; and the educational pursuits in Corvallis and Eugene, home to Oregon State University and the University of Oregon, respectively. With its community psyche not distracted by other such options, it poured most of its energy into Medford High athletics.

One final thing fueled Medford's athletic prowess: numbers. With a population of 25,919 in 1962, Medford, along with Corvallis, was larger than any other Oregon city but Portland (370,906), Eugene (55,413), and Salem (50,429). With 2,500 students, Medford was Oregon's largest high school outside Portland; Dick Fosbury's Class of '65 had more students, 645, than most Oregon's high schools had *total* students.

As boomers made their way through Medford's halls—and through the 1960s—classroom sizes bulged. School districts nationwide added modular classrooms. Some started running double shifts—half a giant class would attend a morning session, the other half an afternoon session—and, in some cases, built new schools. Not in Medford—at least on the new-school front. Never mind overcrowded classrooms, to even mention adding a second high school—to dare *suggest* diluting the athletic power-bloc by 50 percent—was blasphemous talk that would bring Alibi Tavern banter to a hush.

Around the state, MHS was affectionately known as the "University of Medford," a place unlike any other in Oregon in terms of its singular focus on sports. On the Friday of the big football game with rival Grants Pass, businesses routinely closed mid-afternoon. Beginning in 1960, men gathered at North's Chuck Wagon to hear coaches pontificate about the big game—a tradition that would span more than half a century. On Friday nights, nearly a third of the city's population would be at a home game; attendance sometimes neared 10,000 fans.

The environment of excellence fostered a sense that anything was possible, particularly in, but not limited to, sports. By the time Fosbury first slipped on a Medford High uniform, Bowerman had saved a buddy's life in World War II as part of the Army's 10th Mountain Division in Italy; introduced America to jogging after a trip to New Zealand where he'd learned about it; and won an NCAA track and field title as coach of his alma mater, Oregon. Within a year, he would enter into a handshake deal with Phil Knight, one of his former milers, to start an athletic footwear company. Blue Ribbon Sports would later become Nike, the largest footwear producer on the planet. Bowerman would also later coach the 1972 U.S. Olympic track and field team in Munich.

As if rockets aimed for the heavens, others were on similar trajectories: Dave Frohnmayer, the son of Bowerman's close friend, Otto Frohnmayer, would become state attorney general and, later, president of UO. One of Dave's brothers, John, would become chairman of the National Endowment for the Arts; another, Phil, the star of MHS's "My Fair Lady," would become a world-renowned opera singer and instructor. Bob Haworth, who sang in a quartet with Dick, would become a member of the Kingston Trio. In time to come, Medford would produce congressmen; PGA golfers; NFL football players; NCAA champs in diving, wrestling, and track and field; a secret service agent for two presidents—and even an Olympic gold medalist.

For a kid who just wanted to make the team, Dick Fosbury found Medford's tradition of success fascinating and frightening. It was fascinating because it made him feel part of an adventure, like a drift boat ride down the Rogue. It was frightening because he knew, at any moment, he could find himself swimming in the icy-cold froth of the rapids, outside the boat. At MHS, an unwritten contract existed between coach and athlete: a position on the team was given to you *temporarily*; your job was to prove yourself worthy of it *permanently*.

Unlike some sports, track and field—with its stop watches and measuring tapes—left no ambiguity about who was fast and who was not; who jumped high and who did not. Five-foot-four was 5'4", whether your father performed surgery each day at Medford Sacred Heart Hospital or thinned pears in the orchards for $5.80 an hour. In football, a blocker could miss an assignment and nobody in the stands might know. But there was no such hiding in track and field. It was athletic objectivity, the great equalizer: when it was your turn, you either produced or did not. You either cleared the bar or did not.

Dick Fosbury was a nice guy. Coaches liked him. Teammates liked him. Girls liked him. In fact, almost everyone seemed to like him. That said, he knew perfectly well where nice guys finished: last. And so it was that somewhere coming up Highway 99's twisting grade to Grants Pass, Dick Fosbury confirmed what he'd been trying to talk himself out of: he would go with the scissors. It wasn't out of any sense of bravado. It wasn't out of any desire to be a lone wolf; while he had an independent streak, Fosbury enjoyed being part of the pack. The reason behind his decision to go it alone was simple: sheer desperation.

"Hell, Fosdick," said Sweet, "whataya got to lose?"

People do what they must do to survive. About ten miles north of where the MHS team was now, a similar bus had been headed south on the same Highway 99 on a cold December night in 1948. The Grants Pass High football team was on Sexton Pass, only twenty minutes away from arriving home from Portland to a crowd that had gathered to celebrate the school's first state football championship. A three-foot-high trophy, topped by a golden punter, sat on a seat, almost as if a member of the team itself.

Suddenly, the bus lurched right after the driver apparently swerved to miss something in the road. The bus careened off the gravel shoulder and plummeted 200 feet down a steep grade. It crumpled in two and burst into flames. A dark, silent forest was suddenly ablaze in fire; the screams and groans of young men pierced the quiet. Sterling Heater, a starting end, was burned to death as he tried to rescue student manager Ray Alpeter from the flames. Alpeter survived. Heater and Al Newman, a substitute halfback who'd been trying for four years to earn his letter—and the previous night finally had—were killed.

Ultimately, two died and five were seriously injured. What saved the others was one thing: sheer desperation. In the pandemonium, players searched in the orange-flickering darkness for anything they could use to break open windows so they could escape the smoke-and-flame inferno. And then they found it: the trophy. Players used it to smash windows, helping save the lives of nearly two dozen young men. *Whatever it takes.*

Now, FIFTEEN YEARS later, at the high school where that charred trophy was on display, the Medford High bus arrived. Teams from the six other visiting schools, their athletes full of pent-up energy, piled out of buses. Dick felt the familiar stomach twinge of anticipation and angst, part of him wanting to jump right now—to see what scissors-jumping might do for him—and part of him wanting to be home, alone in the bunk bed, with a good comic book. The bus door swung open. Dick grabbed his gym bag and waited for the others to unload. Finally, it was his turn. He stepped through the door, the last kid off the bus.

He would never be the same again.

Chapter 3

A death from a long illness is very different from a sudden death. It gives you time to say goodbye and time to adjust to the idea that the beloved will not be with you anymore.

—Meghan O'Rourke

THE DRIVER WHO hit and killed Dick Fosbury's little brother while Greg and Dick were riding bikes had been drinking all afternoon. It was Saturday, September 9, 1961, the weekend before Dick, fourteen, would start ninth grade at Hedrick Junior High. Greg had just turned ten a few weeks before, and in two days, he was to start fifth grade at Lone Pine Elementary school. As was their Saturday night habit, Helen and Doug Fosbury had gone to a square dance, where Doug was the caller. The two boys were out riding their bikes at dusk, not far from the house they had moved to on Roberts Road.

Gail Fosbury, Dick's eleven-year-old sister, was home alone when Dick stumbled into the house. Breathless. Face wet with tears. Clothes splattered with blood. "Accident," Dick mumbled. "Greg . . . think he's . . . dea . . . dea . . . dead . . . ." Gail's face contorted in horror. Dick flopped on his bed and buried his head in a pillow.

The Sunday morning *Medford Mail Tribune* published the story on the top left corner of the front page:

Gregory Fosbury, [10]-year-old son of Mr. and Mrs. Douglas Fosbury, of 2257 Roberts Rd., was pronounced dead on arrival at Sacred Heart Hospital Saturday night. The boy and his brother, Richard, about 14, were riding bicycles north on Crater Lake Ave. They were presumably going home. The older boy was in front with Gregory trailing him a short distance.

Witnesses said what appeared to be a red, 1956–1960 model car struck Gregory from the rear, careened to the left side of the road and narrowly missed a car coming in the opposite direction, before continuing at a high rate of speed away from the death scene.

The mishap occurred just south of the intersection of Roberts Rd.

Another youth on a bicycle, about a block north of the Fosbury brothers, said he heard a crash and a red car sped by him at a high speed.

The dead youth was sprawled face down on the pavement when police arrived. Sgt. Leo Mitchell administered artificial respiration until a nurse, Mrs. Lorraine Jones, arrived. Mrs. Jones continued artificial respiration. Gregory suffered a severe head injury and was bruised on his side.

Police estimated the youth was carried 75 feet down the highway by the car. His two shoes were 50 feet apart.

Dick had been knocked off his bike by something, but had not been hurt. Or so said the paper.

A YEAR AND A half later, as Dick warmed up for the Grants Pass Rotary Invitational, the wonder of this day would be found not only in what he was about to do in the high-jump event, but in what he had already done in general: shown up. Stayed focused enough to make the track team. *Survived.* His parents' marriage did not. As is often the case after the loss of a child, Doug and Helen Fosbury separated a year after the accident and, ultimately, divorced. Dick felt like a kid in an earthquake who steadies his feet when the shaking stops, then gets leveled by a hurricane. Alone in the storm.

"The loss of a sibling creates a huge change in a child's environment and that's often compounded by divorce," said Chicago psychotherapist Jerry Rothman, who, after struggling for twenty-five years with the accidental gun-shot death of his brother, established the Rothman-Cole Center for Sibling Loss in Chicago.

In Rothman's case, the loss of his brother and the neglect of his parents—preoccupied by their own grief—left him stranded on an island of isolation. Feeling unable to show his grief, he grew angry and depressed. Acted out. Blew off school. Got in trouble. "Kids will say, 'I got left out. Everybody came and comforted my parents, but nobody came and said anything to me.' With sibling loss, there is often less opportunity for children to talk about their grief, to work through it and express their feelings. For most kids, the loss of a sibling becomes a double loss. They also lose their parents, who get involved in their own grief and withdraw."

Helen spiraled downward into depression. Doug refused to talk about the loss; "not once did I ever see him cry," said Gail. "Not once did I hear him talk about Greg." The couple saw a counselor—never presented as an option to Dick and Gail—but it was as if they were struggling in emotional quicksand: the harder they tried, the deeper they sank. "She blamed the fact that we were at the square dance for it happening," Doug later said.

The two never went square dancing again. Never. If they hadn't been off dancing, Helen reasoned, this never would have happened. "We tried to live normal lives, but Helen was so down and completely withdrawn," said Doug. "We had quite a few pictures around our house of the five of us. And then suddenly it was just the four of us."

In late summer 1962, Helen filed for legal separation. Doug countered by filing for divorce. It was over. "We were the atomic family of the 1960s," said Gail. "Boom. There was a big explosion and, in a sense, the four of us all went our separate ways." Dick doesn't remember the details. "All I know is my dad either left or got kicked out." Neither child was told a thing.

For Dick, the potential for repressed feelings was rife. It was the early 1960s. The mental health profession had not yet recognized the full effects of post-traumatic stress disorder that the war in Vietnam would bring to the forefront. His parents reacted to the loss as people of that generation would be expected to: by soldiering on. Having been through the nation's worst economic depression and costliest war, they'd been taught to keep a stiff upper lip and get on with things.

Like Jerry Rothman, Dick had essentially no tools to deal with his grief following the double loss. At fourteen, he was too old to cry, vent, and question without inhibition, and too young to process the loss with adult perspective—not that that had worked for his parents.

With her son dead and her husband gone, Helen would sit out on the patio, smoking Marlboro after Marlboro. "Staring out at nothing," said Gail. Doug Fosbury moved to nearby Grants Pass, only seeing Dick at an occasional meet or game—and hardly ever seeing Gail, period. She turned to music. Played flute in a jazz band. Wrote poetry. Listened to Miles Davis. "I was this liberal-brain-psychedelic person." And Dick? He was still looking for a rock to grab hold of as the water swept him down the stream.

"When there's a death in a student's family these days, schools are on it in a heartbeat with counseling," said Debra Whiting Alexander, a counselor and author from Eugene, Oregon, who specializes in children's grief. Alexander was deeply involved after a teenage gunman, in 1998, killed two students and wounded twenty-five others at Thurston High in nearby Springfield. "In Dick's case, probably the only way he knew how to deal with the loss was to model his father's reaction—and that meant burying it. Remember, his brother's death on that bicycle was now the *most powerful moment in Dick's life*. To not have a chance to acknowledge that pain was to have an elephant in his room, wherever he went. Every. Single. Day."

What might have been able to save Dick Fosbury? "He had an outlet," said Alexander. "He had what we might call a 'good distraction.' He had the high jump."

If he could only prove himself worthy of staying on the team.

Chapter 4

He was falling, in thin air. But, luckily, he kept his wits and his purple crayon. He made a balloon and he grabbed on to it.

—Harold and the Purple Crayon, *by Crockett Johnson*

"**FIRST CALL, HIGH** jump," crackled the loudspeaker at Grants Pass Field. "First call, high jump. Second call, 100-yard dash; second call, 100-yard dash . . . ."

It was 1:30 pm Saturday, April 20, 1963. In the wooden bleachers, Dick pulled off his Chuck Taylor Converse All Stars—black high tops—and replaced them with his red Adidas track shoes.

The location of the high jump event at Grants Pass was different from that of most other schools, whose tracks ringed their football fields and whose jump pits had to be flush-left or flush-right beyond the end zones. Because Grants Pass's track was separate, the high-jump pit was placed in the middle of the field, front-and-center for fans. And because eight schools were on hand, more than the usual smattering of people was filtering into the stands. It was one thing to fail obscurely—that Dick was used to. It was another to fail famously.

He mentally gulped and headed for the high-jump area, where other competitors were already practicing, the bar set at 5'4". That would be the opening height, too—and, not incidentally, Dick's lifetime best. He watched as the competition, all straddlers, started on the grass, hit the rain-softened cinder apron, charged to the bar, jumped, twisted over the bar, and landed in the wood-chip pit. Every now and then, a couple jumpers would yell "hold it" and fluff the pit with a pitchfork. Three 2x10 boards, on edge, kept the wood chips in check.

Dick stretched his calves, quads, and groin, then grabbed his spike to mark in the grass where he wanted to start his approach. It wasn't too late to change his mind and stick with the straddle, he knew; Coach Benson certainly wouldn't mind. He would be drawing enough attention to himself just by using the scissors style; missing the opening height—which wouldn't be a first for him—would only double the embarrassment, double his failure. He had permission to do the scissors, but did he have the guts?

Dick looked at where he'd need to set his spike used to mark the start point of his eight-stride straddle run-up. It was to the *right* side of the bar as he faced it. Instead of walking to that spot, he walked to the black-and-white Gill bar fronting the pit. He looked down at where he'd need to jump from, then ran back eight steps to the *left* side of the bar as he faced it, where he would begin his scissors jump. His thinking? *Stick with the straddle and I'll take a beating. Switch and I at least have a chance of going higher—a chance of not losing my spot on the team.*

When he plunged his spike into the soggy Oregon grass, it was more than an act of orienting himself to his starting point. It was like a pioneer who'd come West and, when deciding where to sink his roots, driven a stake in the ground as if to say, "Here's where I start over."

"First call, mile . . . first call, mile . . . second call, high jump . . . second call, high jump . . . ."

Dick peeled off his hoody sweatshirt, stretched, and went to his mark for a practice jump. It was then that he noticed a familiar figure in the distance: his father. That was Dick's dad, at least since the divorce: in the distance. There, but not really *there*.

He turned his attention to the bar. *Concentrate.* With a little hop-jump, he began his approach. He scissored over the bar, though not by much. He was relieved, even a touch encouraged; missing a practice jump was like getting skunked while fishing at a trout hatchery—in front of all the other fishermen. Behind him, a few smirks from other jumpers mixed with a few hand claps. Even if they didn't say it, the inference was clear regarding his style: *in a world of Ford Thunderbirds and Corvettes, some kid from Medford had shown up in a Model T.*

Moments later, a Grants Pass jumper, with the prance of a whitetail deer, bounced up to the bar and cleared it by almost six inches. His name was Bob Shepard, among the state's best. More than five decades later, Shepard would remember a few tidbits from the meet. That rains had softened the track so much one Grants Pass kid ran barefoot. That one of the high-jump officials had been Bob Byrd, at whose market in Grants Pass kids with birthdays were given a free quart of ice cream. And that the new Interstate 5, chiseled into a hill above the track, was almost complete. But Shepard had no recollection of a Medford High kid named Dick Fosbury even jumping that day.

"LAST CALL, HIGH jump . . . . Last call, high jump . . . ."

Mr. Byrd and another high-jump official walked to the center of the apron to give the jumpers their instructions and to wish them good luck. Meanwhile, on the track, a starter's gun went off. Hundred-yard-dash sprinters charged down the homestretch. Cheers swelled from the crowd in the west-side bleachers, building like an audio wave as the sprinters closed on the finish line. Dick's heart pounded like the spikes on the track. It was time.

A half a dozen jumpers easily rolled over the bar. No misses. A few more did the same. Still no misses. "Fosbury, Medford, up," said Mr. Byrd.

Dick peeled off the sweatshirt, tightened the laces in his shoes, and went to his mark. He eyed the bar—5'4"—and cleared it, though he brushed it with his butt. Afterward, as the bar was raised to 5'6", he thought of how his legs had gotten over no problem but his backside only barely. That prompted four words of inspiration that weren't likely to make *Bartlett's Familiar Quotations: raise your butt, stupid.*

What did this mean? What's my mind trying to tell me? How do I raise my butt in the middle of a scissor jump? The edict came a second time. *Raise your butt, stupid.* What did he have to lose? He decided to comply, even if he was still missing a significant component of the edict: *But how?*

He exhaled. Eyed the bar. Gently rocked back and forth. Burst toward his target. Jumped. Scissored and—instinctively, the answer came: *Lean back.* In the flash of inspiration, he did so, which forced up his hips, and therefore his butt, up and over the bar. *That's how.* When he hit the wood chips the bar was still in place; he had a new personal best. And a slight sensation that he might be on to something here.

"The bar goes to five-foot-eight," said Mr. Byrd, ratcheting up the standard with help from the official on the other side.

A few jumpers were only now starting the competition, so confident that they could make this height. All made good on that confidence, clearing 5'8". Now it was Fosbury's turn. *Stay in the game,* he said to himself. *Stay in the game. Raise your butt.* Elsewhere, discus throwers were grunting, fans cheering, runners puffing. Fosbury heard none of it. He angled toward the bar, scissored his left leg high, over the bar as usual. But now, instead of automatically repeating a similar kick with the right leg as if he were a can-can dancer, he leaned even further back than on the previous jump. His butt and hips arched over the bar. And as they came down, the motion naturally forced his legs up and over. Surprisingly, he felt no bar as he descended.

Benson, the MHS coach, nudged assistant coach Fred Spiegelberg. "See that?" Spieg was too spellbound to reply.

After having gone nearly a year without improving his 5'4" best, Dick had now gone four inches higher, setting two personal bests in less than an hour—thanks to this new-fangled "layout" style: half scissors, half who-knew-what? All *feel.* All *instinct.* All *spontaneous.* "I didn't change my style," Fosbury later said. "It changed inside me."

"The bar goes to five-feet-ten-inches," said Mr. Byrd.

By now, only a handful of the nearly two dozen jumpers were still in the competition, Fosbury among them. A sprinkling of fans darted across the track and started lining up in a half-moon arc behind the pit. One was Dick's father, Doug, who overheard a man in a Grants Pass sweatshirt say, "What in hell is that Medford beanpole doing?"

"Starts out like the old scissors," said the guy next to him. "Not sure what it is after that. Looks like a guy taking a nap on a picnic table with his feet over the edge."

Reality returned with the clang of the bar: Dick missed, then missed a second time. If he didn't clear it on his third and final attempt, rules stipulated he'd be out of the competition; his official height would be that which he last cleared. He returned to his starting spot and eyed the bar. One last chance. The bar suddenly looked incredibly high but as he stared at it, the fear of failure slowly melted. *Focus.* Dick watched the bar, waiting for his body to tell him when to leave. Finally, the prompt: he strode toward the bar, but about ten feet from it, sensed something wrong. His steps were off. Way off. Like a pilot aborting a takeoff, he quit his attempt in mid-jump, landing with one foot under the bar, the other still in front of the bar, legs spread.

He returned to his mark and gathered himself for a "redo." By now it was late afternoon. What had been a dozen people around the pit was now three or four times that. The sun had slipped deep into the southwest sky, bathing the infield with a crisper, slightly golden light that tinted the moment in a touch of drama.

Fosbury toed his mark. Exhaled. *Three. Two. One.* He ran, jumped, half-scissored, arched backward—*raise your butt!*—thrust his hips up and exalted when feeling nothing touch the bar. He'd done it: 5'10"! A rare sense of success bubbled throughout his body like Fizzies in water. He smiled big, bounding out of the wood chips to a smattering of applause.

Meanwhile, a Grants Pass coach briskly strode toward Mr. Byrd. He pointed to the takeoff area, gesturing as if trying to make a point without making a scene. Mr. Byrd wasn't saying much, as if he were on the defensive side of this discussion. Finally, Mr. Byrd nodded, then headed Fosbury's way. Dick's stomach lurched. He had no idea what this could be about, but he didn't like the possibilities. The official came closer, another stranger coming Dick's way with perhaps bad news, like the motorist who'd come to help Dick after Greg had been hit by the drunk—*Son, was that your friend on that bike? You OK?*

"Son, I'm afraid we can't count that last jump of yours," said Mr. Byrd.

Dick recoiled. "Wha-what?"

"As the coach pointed out, when you crossed under the plane of the bar on that previous jump, that, by rule, constituted a jump, a miss. My fault. Shoulda realized that and told you then instead of giving you another chance. Sorry. You finished with five-eight."

Dick looked away; his dad was watching from afar.

"And one more thing, son. The coach said there's a chance that whatever that, uh, style is you're using—it might be against the rules. Just so you know for future meets."

It was as if someone had pulled the plug on a jukebox. Dick tried to hold them back, but the tears came anyway. "He was," remembered his father years later, "totally devastated." He walked off by himself so nobody would see.

The bus trip home, however, proved cathartic. The team had won the meet with 170 points, and Dick had contributed to that total. "Jeez, Fosdick, you scored as a sophomore," said Sweet. "That's cool." In an eight-team meet, competing against nearly two dozen others, Dick had finished fourth, a fact that would be confirmed in Monday's *Grants Pass Courier*, though his last name would appear as "Fosbery." Word spread on the bus about his height and finish, news greeted by raised eyebrows and widened eyes.

"Fosdick scored? Five-eight?"

As the bus rumbled home, he could see it in his teammates' eyes: guarded approval, but approval nevertheless. For Dick, it felt a little like when he was a Cub Scout and had done his first good deed; now, he could finally turn over his Bobcat pin. And no matter what the paper said, he knew he'd cleared 5'10", six inches higher than his previous best and, it turned out, the winning height of Grants Pass's Shepard. It was an incredible improvement for a season—even two seasons—much less a single meet.

Coach Benson found Dick in the back of the bus. "Saw a couple of your jumps, Fosbury," he said. "Don't know whether to pat you on the back or scratch my head; never seen anything like it. And, frankly, don't know quite how to coach it. But come by my office Monday and let's check out some high-jump film. See if there's any sort of model out there we can find that you can learn from."

While his willing spirit was admirable, Benson would find no such model "out there." There was only one. And though Benson didn't realize it at the time, the coach was sitting right next to it.

Chapter 5

When we try to pick out anything by itself, we find it hitched to every-thing else in the universe.

—John Muir

ON AUGUST 12, 1963, nearly 700 miles from Medford and almost four months since Fosbury's epiphany at the Grants Pass Rotary Invitational, a man twice Dick's age walked into the US Patent and Trademark Office in Los Angeles, California. It was an unseasonably cool day—high seventy-three—and Don Gordon was in an uncommonly upbeat mood. After years of working on his latest invention, today was the day. Today, he would go public with—and seek official approval for—what would ultimately become known as Patent No. 3,204,259: "Cushion apparatus for landing pits for jumpers, vaulters, divers, etc."

Until the early 1960s, high jumpers traditionally landed in sand, sawdust, wood chips, or shavings. The brunt of their landings, after a straddle, was taken on the sides of one arm and one leg. Don Gordon thought he had a better idea.

At thirty-one, Gordon looked like a TV game-show host. Handsome. Dark hair. Neat. Compact. And sturdily built, as you might expect a former gymnast to be. He'd grown up in LA and attended Garfield High, where he'd overcome learning disabilities with an imaginative mind and a gymnast's body. He won numerous high school and college competitions. He helped start and coach gymnastics programs at the University of Nevada-Las Vegas and at Brigham Young (he was Mormon). After a stint in the Korean War, he returned to California to teach—and dream.

More than anything, Donald Gordon was a visionary. "To Don, everything was possible," said his second wife, JoAnne. As a teacher and a coach, he was forever looking for a more efficient technique, a safer athletic environment, a softer track and field implement. At LA's Gidley Elementary School, in 1959, he was in charge of the annual track and field day, which included—in lieu of the discus—the softball throw. Safer. Simpler to teach. Less expensive than the platter. But, he soon realized, also hard on kids' arms. So he asked "why not?"—and invented a discus made of neoprene foam. He named it the Neo-Discus. Kids loved the soft platters.

Gordon wondered if there was a market for such items. So, with no business background, he blundered forward. Armed with a $500 loan from his mother-in-law, he drove more than 2,000 miles from LA to Iowa and back, trying to interest schools in the product—with little success. But when a sportscaster of track and field meets held in the Los Angeles Sports Arena heard of the Neo-Discus, he was intrigued. He was a friend of shot-putter Dallas Long, who held the world outdoor record, but, because of small hands, was decidedly less successful in indoor competitions, which required a larger, heavier implement so it wouldn't go as far in the space-restricted arenas.

"Can you come up with a smaller-diameter shot for Dallas?" the sportscaster asked.

Gordon did so. With help from Stauffer Chemical Company in LA, he used a new material called Daycalon to invent a shot that was only slightly larger than an outdoor variety and proved to be a great improvement over the leather balls being used at the time. Once, while meeting with Stauffer officials at their plant, Gordon noticed what he thought were foam-rubber "buns"—two feet thick, five feet wide, and eight feet long. They were actually urethane foam buns, he learned, which had an even lighter specific gravity than foam rubber. Being a former gymnast, Gordon couldn't resist.

"Do you mind if I try one out?" he asked a Stauffer staffer, pointing to a bun.

"Be my guest."

Gordon positioned one of the buns, a little longer and narrower than a king-size mattress. He loosened his tie, flipped off his dress shoes, then began doing backflips and front flips onto the urethane pad. People were amazed at his athleticism. He was amazed at how soft the bun made his landings. This stuff, he said to himself, would make for a perfect landing pit for gymnasts, high jumpers, and pole-vaulters.

Once back home, he called his sportscaster friend. "I've got something that can replace sawdust jump pits," he said. "When's your next indoor meet at the Arena?"

When meet officials heard his plan, they told Gordon they'd let him try out his foam pits at an upcoming meet—a gimmick like that might draw a few curious fans—but only on two conditions. "First, it's got to pass muster with Ron Morris." A pole vaulter, Morris had won a silver medal in the 1960 Olympics in Rome and was now coaching at Cal State-Los Angeles. "Second, it's got to pass muster with Joe Faust." Faust, too, had competed in Rome—at seventeen, he was the youngest US Olympic high jumper ever.

Once Faust and Morris agreed to be Gordon's guinea pigs, all he needed was money, material, and some clue as to how to contain all this foam—in other words, essentially everything. At the time, Gordon was struggling to survive on a teacher's salary while working on a master's degree at Cal State-LA. Suddenly, he was like the Vegas gambler who'd gone all in—without even taking time to count his chips.

He called Stauffer. The company was intrigued by the idea and more than willing to provide as much Daycalon as Gordon needed; they dumped a truckload of scrap foam at Cal-State LA's pole-vault site for Morris to try. Hay bales, used to contain the sawdust in the current pits, were used to contain the foam—half a dozen of the buns with scrap foam on top. Morris took his pole, measured his steps, and found his start. Then he became a footnote to track-and-field history: on that day in January 1963, he became what's believed to be the first jumper in the world to land on foam rubber. He loved the stuff.

So did rabbits and gophers, Gordon soon learned; they nested in it. But that was the least of Don's worries. Gordon called an LA company, West Coast Netting, and had them put a canvas cover on a two-foot by five-foot by eight-foot solid foam bun. Days later, at another track and field facility, Faust gave it a try.

"He could hardly believe how much better it was than sawdust," said Gordon.

Faust and Morris both touted Gordon's invention to the Los Angeles Sports Arena, which green-lighted the use of it for the upcoming meet. On the morning of the event, Gordon enlisted a fellow LDS church member with a trash-hauling truck to go with him and Morris to Stauffer to select, and carry, the foam. Stauffer offered them all sorts of options. The one they liked best, it turned out, was breast prostheses that had been rejected from a recent production run.

"Both Morris and I thought the material was perfect," said Gordon, "but on second consideration, felt it would be disrespectful to women who had to use them. So we elected to use regular foam scrap."

It worked wonderfully at the meet, but scraps got scattered about—and, following the event, fans helped themselves to pieces as souvenirs. Gordon returned to West Coast Netting and had the company concoct a sleeve made of what looked to be white cargo netting.

At the next indoor meet in LA, world-record high jumper Valeriy Brumel of the Soviet Union, after winning the event, endorsed what Gordon was now calling the "Port-a-Pit." Gordon brought aboard a former high school buddy, Ray Snow, to help him market the item. The two paid $8 a month to lease an office so small that Don had to arrive first; otherwise, he couldn't get past Ray to his desk. When Long set the world indoor record with one of Gordon's shots, he not only took time on ABC's *Wide World of Sports* to laud Gordon's shot but the Port-a-Pit as well. After the show aired, the demand for Port-a-Pits increased among those organizing elite meets. Soon, Gordon's pits were being used in most major US indoor and outdoor championships.

He quit his job as a teacher and cashed out his retirement fund from the teacher's union.

"You're crazy," a brother of Gordon's told him.

Perhaps, but Gordon wasn't turning back. "There are times when you need to take risks—when you believe in something—and the landing pits show a lot of potential," he said.

Not only did Gordon believe in his product, he put his life on the line to prove it. In Albuquerque, New Mexico, prior to the 1963 NCAA

Track and Field Championships, he jumped thirty-five feet off a stadium railing onto one of his six-foot by eight-foot foam pits, the first of many such press stunts. He enlisted a professional diver to do a swan dive into the foam from forty feet. He talked his way on to TV's *Steve Allen Show*.

But if big national and college meets that had some money were his best takers, high schools were another matter. Though he did get to place his pits in the 1963 Utah State Championship meet in Salt Lake City, most high schools were cool to the idea. "Why should I pay $900 for a Port-a-Pit when I can get sawdust for $75?" an athletic director would say. Or: "It's too big and bulky." Or: "Why spend so much money on something only a few athletes are going to use?"

Convenience was one reason; there would be no more raking wood ships or re-shoveling sawdust. Safety was another. A jumper could land anywhere on the pit and be assured of a soft landing. As the 1960s deepened, that was proving to be particularly important for the pole vault, largely because of the event's transition, at the start of the 1960s, from aluminum poles to springier and stronger fiberglass and carbon poles. In the 1940s and 1950s, the world pole vault record increased less than a foot, but in the 1960s alone—in half the time—it would rise by more than two feet, in part because of better poles.

High-jumping, on the other hand, wasn't experiencing such dramatic increases in heights cleared. To begin with, high jumpers had less than half the height to fall as pole-vaulters; twelve days after Gordon filed for his "cushion apparatus," John Pennel of the United States became the first man to pole vault 17'0". A month earlier, Brumel reset his own world high-jump record to 7'5¾", meaning a fall of nearly ten feet less than the vaulters.

In other words, on that August day in 1963 when Don Gordon filed for his patent, there wasn't any particular demand for a softer pit for high jumpers. As Fosbury's junior year began, his breakthrough at the Rotary Invitational seemed little more than a brief wisp of fresh air for a kid quietly struggling for breath.

If, at the time, Don Gordon and Dick Fosbury shared something in common—a penchant for thinking outside the box—there was nothing to suggest their paths would ever cross. Nor that each would someday infuse the other with exactly what he needed, at exactly the right time, in exactly the right way.

PART II

TEST FLIGHTS

Chapter 6

Things don't go wrong and break your heart so you can become bitter and give up. They happen to break you down and build you up so you can be all that you were intended to be.

—*Samuel Johnson*

A WEEK BEFORE the defending State Class A-1 champion Medford High Black Tornado burst through the butcher paper to start the 1963 football season, a father in Huntsville, Alabama, defied Governor George Wallace, death threats, and mobs of angry protesters to walk his six-year-old son to school. The little boy, Sonny Hereford IV, became the first black student in history to attend an Alabama public school. A federal judge had ruled that segregation in America was no longer legal.

Sometimes, resistance explodes with the pop of a camera's flash bulb, the cacophony of reporters shouting questions, the clack-clack-clack of teletype machines. What's on the line is something as profound as someone's yearning to be treated with dignity in a country that is no less theirs than anyone else's. And sometimes the unwillingness to play by the old rules whispers from someone in the shadows—and not out of anger or angst or injustice but out of desperation.

As the 1963–64 school year began, Dick Fosbury heard the whisper. "Dick's challenge brings to mind the psychologist Erik Erikson," said Doug Sweet, with half a century's perspective. "He said either the world crushes you, or you carve out a new space. The question was: Could Dick carve out a new space?"

In 1963, revolution was in the air on many fronts; old ways of doing things were being questioned, challenged, and overturned. In August,

Martin Luther King Jr. delivered his "I Have a Dream" speech in front of 250,000 demonstrators in Washington, D.C., not that it deterred Wallace from ordering state troopers to encircle Tuskegee High a few days later to prevent black students from entering. Nor did it prevent the Ku Klux Klan from dynamiting the 16th Street Baptist Church in Birmingham, Alabama, killing four children. Within five months of each other, Rachel Carson's book *Silent Spring* triggered the environmental movement and Betty Friedan's *The Feminine Mystique* helped fuel the women's movement. And by the time the leaves were turning on Medford's peach and pear trees, girls in England were screaming, fainting, and crying hysterically as a mop-haired band called the Beatles jolted audiences with rock music and a charisma that was unlike anything the world had seen.

But Medford, Oregon's air was different. It may have been tinted with smudge and the smoke of giant wigwam burners at the mills, their tops lighted up at night like the glowing tips of cigars, but revolution? No. Unless you harkened back to 1941, when Southern Oregon and Northern California tried to form their own state of "Jefferson," revolution had never been in Medford's air and wasn't now. People in Medford liked the world just as it was, which is why a billboard on the edge of town warned, "If you're black, don't lay your head here at night."

In 1963, as the civil rights movement struggled to get a foothold in the South, there was no such rancor in Medford. Race had never been an issue because there were virtually no black people to defy the subtle but strong edict that Medford belonged to white people. "It was a known fact that Medford was a 'sundown town,'" said a classmate of Dick's, Bob Haworth. "People of color couldn't stay overnight." James W. Loewen, author of *Sundown Towns,* says evidence suggests Medford "surely" qualified as such. Loewen, emeritus professor of sociology at the University of Vermont and author of *Lies My Teacher Told Me,* says Medford was hardly unique in that regard; at the time, thousands of US towns and cities qualified.

Though some people had railed against such bigotry—including *Medford Mail Tribune* Editor Robert Ruhl, beginning in the 1920s, when the Ku Klux Klan entrenched itself in the state as the largest division west of the Mississippi River—most thought nothing of it. And though it wasn't like in the South, where police used snarling German shepherds, fire truck water hoses, and batons against blacks, the bias was real.

Medford wasn't the only southern Oregon town with little empathy for African Americans. In May 1963, a *Grants Pass Courier* editorial writer said young blacks in the South would be fine if they'd simply stick with the status quo as their parents had. "The white folks take care of them; there's a feeling between the oldtime Negro man and woman, 'uncle and aunty'—as the whites call them down there—that is difficult to describe. Certainly it is not conducive of trouble between the two races. But the younger generation is a 'horse of another color,' if you please." Such were the times. In 1961, a *Mail Tribune* story about a Medford High football game began: "A war pathing band of The Dalles Indians journeyed home without a scalp Friday night . . . ."

In the early 1960s, when the Medford weather service at the airport hired a black man, he was refused service at markets, peppered with racial slurs, and otherwise derided. The man's coworkers had to buy food for the family since so few clerks would serve them. The family lived across from the grade school Dick Fosbury attended, Roosevelt; one night, say some, a cross was burned in his lawn. The family left.

None of the 100 members of the football team were black, not that that was particularly surprising given that of Medford's nearly 25,000 people, the official US census in 1960 listed only six blacks in the city. At the time, they comprised only about one percent of Oregon's population, Medford only one-sixth of that one percent.

In the high school auditorium, an adults-only blackface comedy show drew a raucous crowd. Kids sometimes did minstrel shows at their schools. "Racist jokes were rampant," said Sweet. "The N-word was used regularly. I found it disgusting, without, at the time, even actually knowing why. Something about the tone in people's voices. Medford was as down and dirty a racist place as I'd ever lived—and I'd lived in South Florida and North Carolina for spells."

Unless you were black and looking for a hotel room, Medford had a *Happy Days* feel to it. "The school pride was so strong that when the Beach Boys sang 'Be True to Your School,' I thought they were singing specifically about Medford High," said Haworth. High school life meant burgers at Jack's Driveup, movies at the Craterian or the Holly, skiing at Mt. Ashland come winter. "A working-class town, really," said Sweet, "with all the prejudices and attitudes common to white American culture in 1963 to 1965." Blacks were suspect. Girls were the lesser sex. And football was God, which, of course, made football coach Fred Spiegelberg "The Pope."

At forty-three, Spiegelberg had the presence of General Patton and the looks of Charlton Heston. He was tough but fair and built like the former collegiate boxing champ he'd been at Washington State. He was hardened by a stint in the army amid World War II. Now in his twelfth season as head coach, Spiegelberg had built one of the finest programs in the state. In the past seven years, his teams had won or tied 57 of 64 games, claimed two state championships, and been runners-up twice. If there was an overriding reason why people in Medford were willing to donate $100,000 for a new stadium, it was he.

Nobody in Medford was more revered than Fred Spiegelberg. When he'd walk into North's Chuck Wagon for the weekly Linebackers Club breakfast, heads turned and waitresses rushed to be the first to offer him water and a menu. "Spieg," as he was known, had built an athletic empire that started with grade-school kids being charted on everything from pull-ups to the fifty-yard dash. And Fosbury wasn't the only kid in town with a high-jump setup in his back yard. Haworth used a bamboo pole for a bar, Ron Wallace his father's fly rod. This was Medford. Fred Spiegelberg's Medford, where sports ruled.

Though autumn was his season in the sun, Spiegelberg played a far less visible, and prestigious, role in Medford High athletes come spring: assistant track coach. Though roughly half Spieg's age, head coach Dean Benson knew the intricacies of technique and strategy; Spiegelberg knew kids. "Mostly," said Sweet, "he told football stories." He was the high-jump coach. A high-jump coach who, the previous spring, hadn't taken a shine to the newfangled technique of a certain sophomore named Dick Fosbury. *Going backwards over a high-jump bar? Who in the hell jumps like that?*

HIGH JUMPING WASN'T part of the original Greek Olympic Games. By most accounts, it started in Germany in the late 1700s as a game for children, was adopted by the British in the 1800s, then caught on in Canada and the United States. Styles changed over the decades, from a straight-on hurdle to a scissors-like kick to something called the "Sweeney Roll" to the Eastern cutoff and then to the Western roll. Last used by an Olympic champion, Walt Davis, in 1952, the roll begat the straddle, which became the go-to technique staring in the early '50s. In it, a jumper threw one leg high into the air and twisted over the bar in what some called a "belly roll."

It was the Soviets who fine-tuned the straddle, an outgrowth of national coach Vladimir Dyachkov, who studied the style like a botanist might study plant cells. He filmed jumpers. He introduced training with barbells, which many thought deterred speed, flexibility, and endurance. He modified the straddle to what became known as the "dive straddle." And the efforts began to bear fruit. In 1957, the same year the Soviets put the first satellite, Sputnik, in orbit to launch the Soviet-US "race for space," Yuri Stepanov broke American jumper Charles Dumas's world record with a jump of 7'1". The Soviets took Olympic gold in Rome in 1960, with Robert Shavlakadze winning at 2.16 meters (7'1"), and in 1964, Valeriy Brumel winning at 2.18 meters (7'1¾").

Meanwhile, back in North America, if the high-jumping energy was scattered across the US and Canada with far less stylistic regimentation, virtually everyone nevertheless used the straddle. As talented American jumpers such as Dumas, Joe Faust, and John Thomas struggled to dent the Soviet dynasty, however, something peculiar began happening among a few young jumpers in the Northwest and British Columbia: unbeknownst to each other and to practically anyone outside their hometowns, three began flipping backward over the bar.

In Missoula, Montana, Bruce Quande jumped with such a style for the Kalispell High track team as early as the spring of 1961. As a senior at Flathead High School, Quande was shown in a photograph by the *Missoulian-Sentinel* while leaping backward into a sawdust pit on May 24, 1963, at the Montana state meet. His high school best was 6'2".

In 1962, a stick-thin country girl near Vancouver, British Columbia, Debbie Brill, began leaping backwards into a collection of foam rubber that her father had gathered in a fishing net. She was nine—and soon winning competitions with the style, going 4'11" as a thirteen-year-old. (At thirteen, Dick scissored 4'8".)

Meanwhile, Fosbury, if finding a touch of success in the spring of 1963 with the first rendition of his half-scissor/half-lay-back style, wasn't putting all his apples in the high-jumping basket. He wanted to play football, too. After his father had moved out the previous year, Dick found a yearbook of his dad's days at Commerce High in Portland. Doug Fosbury had been a pass receiver on the football team, and he was known as "Sticky-Fingered Fosbury." Dick liked the sound of that. Maybe he could be the Sticky-Fingered Fosbury of Medford High. But he wasn't good enough to be a receiver. He tried defensive tackle. He wasn't bulky enough. Coaches moved him to defensive end.

At 6'3" and 165 pounds, Fosbury in a football uniform brought to mind Norman Rockwell's drawings of high school football players for the *Saturday Evening Post* in the 1950s: all legs, arms, and hips. As one practice unfolded, Dick was lined up at defensive end when he realized the lead blocker out of the backfield—the guy who would likely be targeting Dick—was "Wild Bill" Enyart. Fosbury wished he were anywhere but there at that moment. At 6'2" and 215 pounds, Bill Enyart was the toughest kid to ever wear a Medford High uniform, destined to play major college football, perhaps in the NFL. Oregon State, four hours up the freeway, wanted him badly.

Now, he lined up behind the quarterback as the "up back," ready to take a handoff or block. Dick was supposed to tackle whoever got the ball. Enyart was a pal of Fosbury's—maybe, thought Dick, he'll go easy on me—but he outweighed the defender by a medium-sized bag of concrete mix and had only one gear: high.

"Let's go!" barked Spiegelberg. "Run the play!"

Enyart snapped his chinstrap and worked his cleats into the turf. *Tweet.* The quarterback faked a handoff to Enyart, meaning Wild Bill would be blocking. He rumbled Dick's direction like a runaway boulder down Mt. Ashland.

"Broke his helmet in four places," remembered Scott Spiegelberg, the coach's son and a sophomore on the team that year. Three of Dick's teeth were chipped.

"Dick was crying," said Jack Mullen, a junior quarterback. "It broke your heart. He never had a chance."

Fosbury never played another down of football. For the third straight year, the beginning of school had dealt him a bitter blow: his brother's death, his parents' divorce, and now the humiliation at having to quit the sport that was king in Medford. As 1963 wound down, Dick Fosbury was running out of options.

Chapter 7

The mind is its own place, and in itself
Can make a Heav'n of Hell, a Hell of Heav'n.

—John Milton

HE BLAMED HIMSELF for it all—Greg's death and his parents' divorce. If Fosbury was less well-read than his buddy Doug Sweet, he had a mathematician's mind that could quickly pencil out the equation: Dick's negligence on the bike ride equaled Greg's death. Greg's death equaled his parents' divorce. The common denominator in both? Dick. Not that he'd dared to share that with anyone—or, to some degree, with himself. It was just *there*, like Rogue Valley smudge smoke in the early spring. And *there* was a place you weren't to visit.

So he practiced the art—perfected the art—of normalcy. He laughed. He joked. He pranked. It was Fosbury, once he'd gotten his driver's license, who convinced Sweet to set aside his Jean-Paul Sartre book on existentialism long enough to take a late-night spin on the freshly built Interstate 5—before the highway had even opened.

"Whimsical," said Scott Spiegelberg. "It's fair to say Dick was a whimsical high school kid." Lighthearted. Loosey-goosey. Squirrelly. Besides comic books, he read *Sports Illustrated* and *Track & Field News*. He tiptoed into the world of beer, girls, and chewing tobacco, the latter of which had him puking out his guts while on a summer shift at Elk Lumber Company.

He could sometimes be the life of the party and sometimes be a loner. But he was always the keeper of the secret, the cowboy in the movie who drags a pine branch behind his horse to cover his tracks.

More than a dozen friends from those early years say the same thing: "He never talked about his brother's death." Never.

Nobody was to return to September 10, 1961, even the one whom it haunted most severely: Dick himself. He doesn't remember visiting his brother's grave. He only vaguely remembers the memorial service—and how, though he looked up to Dick, Greg was not athletic like his brother. And he had a pronounced peculiarity: on Sunday mornings, by himself, Greg walked to a local church that he attended regularly, as if he were forty-one instead of ten. The older women thought he was the sweetest thing since peppermint candy.

But, no, the model from his parents suggested that to remember Greg was to revisit the pain of losing him. What Dick would only realize later is that, like a ghost on the wing, the memory of the accident followed him, like it or not. Every. Single. Day. And the harder he tried to forget the bicycle incident, the deeper entrenched it became. As he later recalled as an adult:

> That day was nice, typical end of summer. We played outside in the front yard. The folks left to a dance late afternoon, so I was in charge. Greg and I threw the Frisbee, played catch, different games. At some point I wrestled with Greg and dominated him easily with my weight advantage until I made him cry. I let him up and felt bad I had beat him up so easily. I wanted to make it up to him, so I offered to take him for a bike ride with me, down to the shopping center, about two miles away.
>
> This would be a big ride for him (1.8 miles one way) and I'd never invited him previously, to ever go on a ride together. So we took off together—Gail stayed home—up Roberts Road and then onto Crater Lake Avenue toward town. Saturday night traffic was not too bad, but I told Greg to ride behind me, single file, along the paved shoulder.
>
> We crossed McAndrews, a major intersection—two-way stops—and Spring Street, and turned off on Bennett, to get to Sears, the final destination. We didn't stop to shop. I intended to just have a target location to show him how to ride down to the shopping center on his own someday. So we headed back, same route, except it was slightly uphill, and, thus, slower.
>
> He seemed to keep up just fine, and I set a pace so we could both stay together. It was getting dark, near sundown, and I carried a flashlight just

in case. I gave that to Greg to light the road in front of him. We rode past McAndrews and everything was going well; this was a nice adventure for the two of us.

We got to the hill on Crater Lake, to climb up the hill that Roberts Road and the corner grocery store was on. I just reached the crest of the hill, with Greg behind me somewhere—I couldn't hear him—when I heard a loud crashing noise and suddenly was hit from behind and the front of my bike bucked upward. Something had crashed into me and knocked me flat on the ground.

I looked up the road to see taillights swerving back and forth, getting smaller, moving away from me. I was stunned. Where was my brother? I slowly got up. Headlights from another car shined on me as they pulled over and stopped. The driver got out and asked me what happened, was I all right. I said I didn't know, but I was able to stand up, a little shaky.

I said I didn't know where my brother was, though he and I had been riding together. The driver and passenger began to search and found him off the road in the weeds.

He asked if he were my friend. I said he was my brother. "Stay where you are," one of them said. "You, uh, don't want to see him now."

He wasn't moving. Wasn't making any sounds. I knew this wasn't good. Another car came up and pulled over. The people from it raced off to call an ambulance. One man stayed with me, and we checked my bike and saw the rear wheel was bent badly and couldn't be ridden. He asked where I lived and offered to give me a ride. He said they would stay with Greg until the ambulance arrived.

"Is he . . . . ?"

"He's not breathing," they said.

The man loaded me up into his car and put my bike in the trunk and took me home, only about half a mile away. I wasn't crying until I got in the house and told Gail that we were in an accident and I thought Greg was dead. The man asked where our folks were, so he could call them. We found the number of the dance hall, and he called them about the accident. He had us each go into our bedrooms and just stay there until Mom and Dad made it home. When they got home, I told them what had happened, how I had seen the weaving taillights from the ground.

Mom was shook up and bolted to her bedroom. Dad stayed in the living room with me when the police arrived and interviewed me. He talked with them privately after they were finished with me, about the hit and run driver. All of us went to bed and tried to sleep. I eventually passed out until morning.

The next day was awkward. Friends and their kids, dancers from the club, a lot of people came over to help support us. I didn't know what to say, none of our friends knew what to say; there was a lot of food on the tables, but we just stood around with nothing to do. It was not a time to go play games, nothing was normal.

The police checked in on Dad and told him they could not find the driver, and no one admitted to the accident. Finally, on Monday, the police came late afternoon and told Dad that a man came in and admitted to being the driver. I remember them discussing what crimes he could be charged with, whether it was murder, manslaughter, hit and run, etc. Dad wanted him punished, but didn't want this to drag out, causing us any more stress than we were going through already.

School started, and I began the ninth grade. Class was awkward, I felt like I was in the spotlight, although I wasn't. It just felt that way. A couple kids were nice and voiced their sympathy and hoped I was OK. I was conflicted, because I liked having some attention, but not for this reason.

I felt guilty, because I tried to do something for my brother and it backfired in a big way. I had him ride behind me with the light, but should have ridden behind him. He took the full hit, and I got a glancing blow. He died, and I lived. How was this fair? Why me? Why did I deserve to live when my brother had died?

So Dick kept quiet. Tried to forget. Told nobody, not only about his brother dying, but about how after Greg was hit, something had hit Dick—the "glancing blow." A bike? The car? *Something*.

"Why didn't you tell anyone that you were hit, too?" people later inquired.

"Because," he said. "Nobody ever asked."

ON NOVEMBER 22, 1963, Medford and the nation froze in horror when Walter Cronkite, at 10:40 a.m. PST, interrupted CBS's *As the World Turns* to announce that President John F. Kennedy had been assassinated in Dallas. In December, Frank Sinatra's infant son was kidnapped. In February, in front of the largest TV audience to ever watch a program—roughly half of all TVs were tuned to this—the Beatles appeared in New York on *The Ed Sullivan Show*. And, in March, after another uneventful basketball season, track and field came—Dick's last, best hope.

Now, at Medford Stadium, he was jogging to the high-jump area—he hated to run—when something caught him by surprise: two giant nets full of foam-rubber scraps where the high-jump and pole-vault sawdust used to be.

"Cool!" For Fosbury, the foam seemed heaven-sent. Thanks to Medford's Bill Bowerman connection, the netted-foam pits were hand-me-downs from the University of Oregon, which was upgrading to a new Don Gordon "Port-a-Pit." Medford was the first high school in the state to have foam pits—naturally. Even Oregon State, where the state Class A-1 championships would be at season's end, was still using wood chips.

Fosbury took a few practice jumps on the foam and loved the soft landing. It was about a month from the April 5 opener. The Southern Oregon weather was its typical spin-cycle self for this time of year: sun, rain, snow, sometimes all in the same hour.

After the high jumpers met with Coach Benson and Coach Spiegelberg, the bar was set at a low height and the athletes began blowing out the winter cobwebs with practice jumps, yipping in glee with every foam landing. By now, Fosbury's half-scissor, half-layout style was starting to feel comfortable, if not complete. Coming into this season he was leaving the ground as a scissor-jumper, then making a mid-air "correction" by thrusting his hips skyward in what looked like an airborne seizure. Now he instinctively felt a need for some modifications. He started coming at the bar far less parallel to it, as a typical scissors jump required but more "out front." Like the original manifestation of the style, it was all based on feel. Spontaneity. It was like riding a bicycle while simultaneously putting it together.

He experimented with starting his approach at roughly a forty-five-degree angle and adding a touch of curve to it so it looked a bit like a "J." At takeoff, he began sensing himself "running into the air," what had been a straight-leg kick now becoming more of a bent-knee drive upward. Instead of scissoring, he began leading with his shoulder and rotating his upper body; the legs, in essence, were just along for the ride.

It was becoming less leg-led and more shoulder-led and head-led, with the back arching over the bar. He tried a few successful jumps at 5'6" and felt good about the latest nuances.

"So," asked Benson, "you're sticking with this stuff?"

"Yeah, I think it can work, coach."

Benson wasn't convinced. "Doubt you'll ever go much higher than you have with that."

That said, he was inclined to give the kid the benefit of the doubt, but Spiegelberg thought Fosbury's method was flat-out crazy, akin to kicking a field goal backward with your heel. Bill Foulon, a pole vaulter who practiced within earshot of Spiegelberg and the high jumpers, remembers seeing Spiegelberg, on numerous occasions, shaking his head while watching Fosbury jump in practice.

"Dean," he'd tell Benson, "he's never going to be a jumper unless he gives up this god-awful whatever you call it. If we teach him to straddle maybe he can score for us at district. But with this—not gonna happen."

If Spiegelberg never told Fosbury as much to his face, Dick picked up the vibe. Spiegelberg was a "no." Benson was a "maybe." And, as the season unfurled, some opposing coaches were also a "no," declaring "That's illegal!" Never mind that Fosbury had yet to clear 6'0" or win an event and wasn't a particular threat to make a difference in the outcome of a meet; at nearly every competition some coach would, at best, question Benson about the legality of the style and, at worst, file a protest.

"He's jumping off two feet," one would say. "It's against the rules. That's not how we high jump around here. We *straddle*."

Benson would point to the rule book, which said: "A competitor may attempt to clear the bar in any manner, provided the takeoff is from one foot and provided no weights or artificial aids are used. All of the competitor's body must go over the bar." Fosbury's final two steps were a quick stutter, but they weren't simultaneous, Benson said in Dick's defense.

For the most part, Benson—and Spiegelberg, too—left Dick alone to experiment with the new approach, but Dick never felt full buy-in from the football coach. At the same time, he felt a certain loyalty to a man he respected. "He had a strong body and a strong personality," said Fosbury of Spiegelberg. "When he chewed you out, you knew you'd been chewed. He was tough but fair, wanting nothing more than to win, but with grace. He demanded your respect. And demanded your fear."

Fosbury felt that fear but persisted. "The kid had a work ethic," said his father, Doug. "He'd cut wood for us with a five-foot crosscut saw. Haul sacks of cement when we built our patio. He didn't give up easily."

To Dick, the high jump wasn't some passing fancy. "He'd found something he could do well, and he obsessed on it," said his sister, Gail. "When he jumped, he was in his own world. Like Greg, we found, had this inner world, going to church—well, this was Dick's inner world. His secret world."

As the season deepened, fans and competitors didn't know what to make of Fosbury's style. Some marveled at it. Some laughed. Some thought he was going to break his neck. "I don't think many people took him too seriously," said Frank Toews, a teammate.

While he was warming up for a meet, a fellow jumper came up to him. "Whataya call whatever that is you do?"

"Guess I'd call it the 'back layout,' or just 'my style.'"

Cautiously, Dick moved forward with the new method, but almost as if edging out on lake ice: carefully. Very carefully. Never quite sure when it might break. When Benson or Spiegelberg might say no. Then came a second major step forward: in late April, a year from his break-through jump—at the same Rotary-sponsored meet in Grants Pass—Dick not only cleared 6'0" for the first time, but made 6'1". He finished second to teammate Steve Davis, who went 6'2". However, just as Dick's original effort in this meet had triggered controversy, so did this one. On one of his jumps he had hit his head on a 2x10 that bordered the wood-chip pit; he'd been momentarily shaken up. Later, when word got back to the administration, Benson was, in essence, called to the principal's office. It seemed like something from the 1961 Walt Disney movie *The Absent-Minded Professor,* after a Flubber experiment had gone wrong.

"Dean, the kid's gonna kill himself. And the school district's gonna get sued."

Benson was between a rock and a hard place. "Let's give the straddle one last shot," he said to Dick.

"But, coach—."

"Humor me, Dick. Spieg thinks you can be something with the straddle. So do I. Just give it a final shot."

What could he do? "At that age, coaches are God, and you're not," said Foulon.

Reluctantly, Dick gave in. But it was like teaching someone right-handed to write left-handed.

Dick's sister, Gail, watched him come home night after night more confused than ever. "In Medford, you make your way in the world through sports, and he desperately wanted to do that," she said. "But even though he'd found some success, the coaches were undoing that success."

Gail hated to see her brother hurt. "He was suffering. He just needed to succeed at one thing; that'd be enough. But he wanted to jump his way, and his coaches wanted him to jump *their* way. Finally, I just told him, 'Hey, it doesn't matter what the coaches say, you have to do what you can do with the best of your ability.' I wasn't telling him to be a rebel—but, yeah, essentially I was telling him to be a rebel."

Dick had an independent streak. "He always had his own idea about how things should be done," said classmate Jim Cox. "When everyone else would be joining a group, he would be off doing something on his own." But he also could be a people-pleaser, thus his dilemma.

Dick chose conformity, at least for the time being. He gamely tried to straddle during practice, even if it was like teaching a giraffe to do the twist. "At this point in his life, Fosbury was still growing into this huge frame," said Marc Bayliss, a year behind Fosbury at MHS. "He'd lope up there to do the straddle and one arm was jutting out here, the other arm there, and his body flailing around everywhere. He looked like a giant Swiss army knife."

"He could never do a straddle worth sour apples," said Dick's father, Doug. "He was just terrible."

Still, the lure of conformity is its invitation to comfort. Nobody questions you. Nobody laughs at you. Nobody doubts you. And, in Medford, the status quo was highly esteemed. When celebrated singer

Marian Anderson came to Medford, no hotel would let the black woman stay. But Helen Hedrick, wife of the superintendent and a free-lance writer for *The Saturday Evening Post,* welcomed her to stay at their house. For weeks, Helen was the "tsk, tsk" scuttlebutt at bridge clubs across town.

After a night of near-sleeplessness, Dick joined a handful of other jumpers who were already doing their practice jumps. When it was his turn, Dick took his mark set for a straddle jump, stared at the bar, and tried to will himself to want this. But he found no such inspiration. After a few agonizing seconds, he exhaled and, without looking around for approval from anyone else, shifted a few steps to the old spot in the grass where he would begin the approach for his own style. He rocked back and forth just a bit, ran toward the bar, gathered himself, jumped, and cleared it, popping from the foam with a sense of satisfaction.

The practice soon ended. Sweet, a distance runner, showered and headed out of the locker room. He heard the padding of shoes on cinders. There, alone at the high-jump pit, was his pal Dick Fosbury, staring at the bar, wiggling his fingers, visualizing himself soaring over it. Sweet couldn't tell how high the bar was set. It was too dark.

Chapter 8

What lies behind you and what lies in front of you are tiny matters compared to what lies inside of you.

—Ralph Waldo Emerson

WHAT SAVED DICK Fosbury—*who* saved Dick Fosbury—was the brother he couldn't save: Greg. And his parents' now-gone marriage. And the fact that he'd endured—was enduring—both. What evolved in the spring of 1964 was a notion that, at the time, he wasn't even aware of: the idea that he was on to something good here with this high-jump style, and whatever price he'd have to pay to keep it—ridicule, ribbing, doubt from coaches—wouldn't be as high as the payments he was already making.

"With his new high-jump style, even after people laughed at him and coaches told him it wouldn't work, he stuck with it because he didn't feel he had anything to lose," said Kevin Miller, a few years behind Fosbury at OSU and, eventually, editor of the school's alumni magazine, the *Oregon Stater*. "He'd already lost it all. It was like: 'You think embarrassment is going to hurt? Hell, I've lost my brother and parents. I know what *real hurt* is. You think I'm going to worry about being different? Hey, I'm the only kid in school with a dead brother and divorced parents.' I'm not saying Dick said these things to himself, but they likely happened at a deeper level."

Miller's perspective aligns with what author Carol S. Pearson wrote of in *The Hero Within: Six Archetypes We Live By*. At their core, people long for safety. But those who fit what she calls the "orphan" arche-type—and Fosbury clearly fit this category—do so because they've experienced something traumatic: an illness, a death, a divorce. In other words, hardships that can make someone feel as if they've fallen out of a boat and are struggling for any sense of safety. However, it also triggers within them a deeper sense of risk.

"Some people who have suffered tragedies," she writes, "have an almost transcendent freedom, for they have faced 'the worst' and survived it. They know they can face anything."

Bowerman, architect of the Medford sports dynasty, grew up angry after, like Fosbury, he lost a brother and watched his parents split up. The incident was instrumental in Bowerman becoming the person he was, said friend Mike Friton. "Bill's defining moments may have been the loss of his twin brother and the breakup of his family," Friton said in *Bowerman and the Men of Oregon*.

As a high school kid, Fosbury wasn't conscious of any such motives himself. "I just wanted to make the team." But regardless of whether he noticed, he agrees, in retrospect, that deeper things were at work inside him as he tried to navigate a life discombobulated by loss.

"Spiegelberg is the Lion King and Dick, as a seventeen-year-old kid, is going toe-to-toe with him," said Sweet. "He knew Fred didn't like his style. But I don't think his decision to stick with his own method had so much to do with rebellion as it did with him wanting to feel good, by God, about clearing that bar. About accomplishing something—*his* way."

The better it felt, the more he could distance himself from how badly it felt when Dick thought of beating up his brother and taking him for a bike ride as a "make-up call." From survivor's guilt. Said Sweet: "When his brother died and his parents divorced, there was no way Dick was prepared to deal with those things. So he muddled along best he could. But suddenly he had something that would help him shut that bad stuff out of his life. Suddenly, he had this thing—his own thing. You could argue that when he readied to jump, he entered a zone that was the safest place he'd been in years. This was Dick's perfect storm. This is where he finds his peace: right there, in the eye of the hurricane."

Every new innovation comes from some need or desire. Dick's came from a need to belong to something. To find his place. To *matter*. "The '60s was full of pain," remembered Dick's sister, Gail. "The Khruschev years. Kennedy's assassination, massive societal changes that were cosmic in scope. And my brother's death. But now Dick had an outlet to process that."

ULTIMATELY, FOSBURY'S STRADDLE-OR-BACK-LAYOUT issue was settled where it needed to be settled: in the high-jump pit. Benson and Spiegelberg finally stepped aside and simply watched—with, as it turned out, amazement. Spring deepened. Nelson Rockefeller beat Barry Goldwater in the Oregon Republican primary. *Jeopardy* made its television debut. Ford introduced the Mustang at a base price of $2,368. And Dick, while chainsawing logs on a county youth corps project, threw out his back so badly he couldn't get out of bed one morning.

But he bounced back. In early April, he jumped at the Rogue Valley Relays in Medford. On hand was a Medford grad, Jay Mullen, who'd come to watch his brother Jack pole vault. "What in the world is Fosbury doing?" he asked Jack.

Soon, some people around the world were wondering the same thing after a photo of Fosbury jumping was sent, by the Associated Press, around the world. Des Moines, South Africa, Europe—in places far away, Dick's style was furrowing brows, those of Jesus Dapena among them. At fourteen, the young Spaniard was doing some high jumping of his own.

"Suddenly me and my friends see in the paper this picture of this crazy American guy," he said. "Because the photograph didn't show the pit, you couldn't tell which direction he was going. We thought he was going feet first, not head first. And we said: 'How can he be doing that?'"

Back in Medford, Sweet awoke to the realization that his friend was suddenly more than just a local curiosity. "I remember thinking, *holy crap, this guy's the real deal.*"

In mid-May, Fosbury's climb into high-jumping prominence continued at a three-way home meet. From the grandstands, a casual friend of Dick's, Ron Wallace, watched eagerly. "At school, people were speaking about this weird way that Dick Fosbury was clearing the high-jump bar," said Wallace, who decided to come watch.

When Dick cleared 6'0", the bar was raised to 6'1½", a half-inch higher than Dick had ever jumped. Wallace turned to a couple of buddies. "Come on," he said. They scurried across the track to where a few other fans were ringing the high-jump pit. What struck Wallace first was how much deeper the wood chips were than the thin layer of sawdust he, Dick, and the others had jumped in back at Hedrick Junior High. He remembered Dick's arms flying all different directions when Coach Monroe had them first try the straddle. And how, after missing, Dick had thrown a handful of sawdust in disgust. Now the bar was almost as high, 6'3", as Dick was tall.

"Dick approached the bar fairly directly, launched himself, spun to his back, and cleared the height," remembered Wallace. The small group of onlookers hooted, hollered, and clapped. "With the front of his body pointed skyward, he landed hard on his upper shoulders and lower neck with momentum pushing him into a backward somersault—as if the landing had come terribly close to injuring him."

The jump, it turned out, gave Fosbury a career first. He'd beaten Davis for the first time in high school. In fact, at 6'1½" Dick came within 1½" inches of the 6'3" school record. Wallace just stood there in amazement, struck by two thoughts. First, that his pal had come a long way from Hedrick Junior High. "This," I realized, "was a pretty gutsy high-jumping style. If Dick were limited by anything, it certainly wouldn't be a lack of effort." There was an intensity, a passion, a hunger in Fosbury's efforts that day that Wallace would never forget.

Though impressed by his friend, Wallace was equally worried for him. "It seemed to me that the higher Fosbury attempted to go, the steeper the angle would be coming down. I concluded, right there on the spot, that Dick couldn't come down any steeper without getting himself seriously injured."

ONLY ONE MEET remained—a dual at Grants Pass—until the Southern Oregon Conference championships, a prelude to the State A-1 meet in Corvallis. A knee injury was hobbling Davis, meaning Fosbury might be Medford's best chance for high-jump points at district. On his second jump, Dick was just getting ready to start his approach when he heard it: laughter coming from a group of non-high-jumping athletes behind him. Laughter clearly aimed at him and his style. His response wasn't laced with any venom toward his detractors. Instead, he thought: *Hey, I've got their attention now. Cool.* Already, Fosbury had realized that athletics was about performance. He liked audiences. And liked to prove his worth in front of them, especially the doubters.

He easily cleared 6' and 6'1", which started giving him a feeling he'd never experienced before: a feeling of limitlessness. A sense that the bar wasn't setting his limits, *he* was. Thirteen months before, he'd planted his start mark in this same turf as if to stake a claim to something uniquely *him*. Now, he'd come to believe there was more sky to climb into—maybe way more.

"The bar goes to 6'2"," said the official.

Fosbury exhaled, eyes riveted on the bar. He rocked gently, then arced toward the pit and leapt. When his back and shoulders hit the wood chips, the amazement wasn't born of his having cleared the bar, but of having cleared the bar with what seemed to be room to spare. *Yes!* He had just set a personal best of 6'2".

When the other two competitors failed in their three attempts, Steve Davis among them, Dick had won—a first for him in high school. The official nodded his way. "Congrats, son. Wanna keep jumping?"

For an instant, Fosbury seemed undeserving of such respect. *Who, me?*

"Nothing to lose," said Dick. The school record was 6'3". "How about 6'3½"?"

The two officials loosened the L-screws on the metal pipe and adjusted the height.

"Bar goes to 6'3½"," the official announced to the few dozen fans ringing the high jump pit. "The winner of the competition, Fosbury of Medford, is up."

The previous year he'd arrived at this place with a best of 5'4". Now, the challenge was essentially a foot higher—half an inch higher than Dick was tall. A height that would suddenly make him the best jumper in the history of Medford High. The crowd inched forward in anticipation, even though most were not Medford fans; the doubters were now believers, the laughers no longer laughing. Fosbury didn't disappoint. He cleared the height on his first attempt, thrusting a fist into the sky. A spirited cheer rose from those ringing the pit.

Dick's teammates mobbed him, ruffled his hair, slapped his butt.

"Fosdick flies!" said Sweet. "School record!"

Someone stuck a relay baton in Fosbury's face as if it were a microphone. "I'm Jim McKay with *Wide World of Sports*. Uh, can I get your autograph, Dick?"

Dick Fosbury did something he wasn't all that used to: he grinned, like someone who had just carved out a new space for himself in the world.

Chapter 9

They who achieve great victories have first learned how to conquer . . .

—James Thomas Fields

STEVE DAVIS WAS more than an athlete. Steve Davis was a man for all seasons: In the fall, a star as a receiver on the football team. In the winter, a skilled basketball player. And in the spring, a bullet in track-and-field sprints. Not incidentally, he was also one of the school's two best high jumpers ever. Ask anyone at the Linebacker Club in 1965 which MHS athlete was going to wind up in the NFL or the Olympics, and two names would come to mind. One was "Buffalo" Bill Enyart. The other was Steve Davis.

If Enyart was a man among boys, Davis was like the sixth Beach Boy, though with better pecs and a vertical leap that frogs envied.

"Steve Davis," said Gail Fosbury, "was prince charming. He was just too good-looking, too perfect."

Thanks to the first-ever Olympic broadcast by satellite, in the fall of his senior year, Dick had watched on the grainy, black-and-white Magnavox as little-known Billy Mills, Native American, rallied down the cinder homestretch of the 10,000 meters to win gold in the '64 Games in Tokyo. Oregonian Don Schollander won four gold medals in swimming, Bob Hayes tied the world record in the 100 meters, and American John Thomas again lost to the Soviets in the race for high-jump space.

Dick was even more attentive to a tall brunette in his choir class, Marali Stedman. They traded notes in class, danced to such tunes as The Kingsman's "Louie, Louie," went to movies, and behaved themselves splendidly when her father, a teacher, was around. "I was," he said, "totally in love."

Meanwhile, girls trailed Davis as if he were a teenage pied piper. "He was full of himself, yes, but you would *have* to be," said Gail.

At Oregon State, football Coach Dee Andros and track and field coach Sam Bell both wanted Davis on their teams. And when new basketball coach Paul Valenti, replacing the legendary Slats Gill, heard about Davis, he, too, started recruiting him. In football, Davis played both offense and defense; Dick watched from the stands. In basketball, Davis was a starter; Dick rode the bench. Track and field was Dick Fosbury's only hope to beat Steve Davis in anything resembling a sport.

Fosbury and Davis met at Hedrick Junior High, where they began competing against each other in the sawdust pit. The two were never buddies nor, frankly, bitter enemies. Just two guys anxious to beat each other in this, their final sport together at MHS before June's graduation. Between junior high, high school, and summer all-comers meets, the two had gone head to head dozens of times. In high school, Fosbury had beaten Davis only twice.

"When they went head-to-head," remembered Jack Mullen, "Fosbury's inner fires were stoked. It was Medford's C.K. Yang-Rafer Johnson setup, the two UCLA teammates who went head-to-head in the decathlon in Rome in the 1960 Olympics."

IT WAS THE spring of 1965. Since Fosbury and Davis had last competed against each other, the US had launched air strikes on North Vietnam; 25,000 civil rights demonstrators, to demand equal rights for blacks, had walked fifty miles from Selma, Alabama, to the state capitol in Montgomery; and Martin Luther King Jr., whose indefatigable drive led to the 1964 Civil Rights Act, had won the Nobel Peace Prize. Lost in the fog of teendom and testosterone, Fosbury had absorbed little of this. His biggest fear had come the previous summers when a doctor, because of the two compressed vertebrae in his back, worried him sick that he'd never jump again. But Dick had gotten better and had no more pain.

By now, Fosbury's technique, if still rough around the edges, had evolved into essentially what it would remain: he was no longer pollywog but full-fledged frog. Though he still plodded a bit on his approach and was still a bit jerky going over the bar, the transformation from scissor-jumper to back-layout was complete.

Fosbury would start almost straight out from the middle of the bar, having, over the two-year evolution, gradually crept farther away from the side for his first step—and farther out. If Fosbury was jumping, even in practice, no runner wanted to draw one of the inside lanes of the track. "He was always starting his approach in lane three or four," said Sweet. "We'd be running 440s and you'd have to dodge Dick to complete your workout."

He would approach from roughly a sixty- to seventy-degree angle to the bar. His eight-step, fifty-foot approach followed the same pattern each time: a run toward the bar with a slight curve ("J") to the right at the end. With three steps left, he lowered his hips—technically, the *settle,* as if in a slight crouch—and slightly increased his speed. With about three feet from the bar, in preparing for takeoff, he'd pull back his arms to add a touch of thrust when he jumped. As he did so, he'd plant his takeoff foot (right) with vigor, heel first. He'd then jump with every ounce of energy in him.

Once off the ground, he'd arch his back, tilt back his head, and thrust his hips skyward, the centripetal force carrying him forward even as he was rising. As he raised his hips when they crossed the bar, physics required the head and shoulders to begin their descent. Likewise, when he tucked his chin left, overlooking his shoulder, physics demanded his legs flip upward at the knees—enough, he hoped, to clear the bar. His eyes stayed on the bar over his left shoulder, so he'd know the exact nanosecond to arch the back, then flip up the legs before descending into the pit on his back.

On paper, Fosbury's technique sounded slightly more complicated than John Glenn's 1962 orbit of Earth. But when asked, Fosbury would suggest just the opposite. "It's simpler than the straddle," he would say. And thanks to the serendipitous timing of Don Gordon developing foam pits—MHS probably wouldn't have gotten a pit had Oregon not bought a Gordon pit—Fosbury's technique was far easier on the neck and spine.

Nevertheless, Medford High's worry-wart administration wasn't entirely out of line in its concern about jumpers hurting themselves using Dick's new method; the style, which required a landing on the back, appeared to be more dangerous than using the straddle method, which required a side-and-shoulder landing. Yes, it was possible to go backward and land on sawdust or woodchips—Fosbury had proven that numerous times—but, as Dick's buddy Wallace suggested, the higher the bar went the more chance Fosbury would get hurt. Now, in a touch of serendipity, Fosbury was the beneficiary of the type of pit that few jumpers outside the LA area were landing in.

Indeed, Donald Gordon's foam pit may have saved Dick's high-jumping career. Just as John Glenn's groundbreaking mission required some provision for getting his space capsule safely back to Earth with a parachute-slowed drop into the Atlantic Ocean, so did Fosbury's groundbreaking style benefit from a safer landing than wood chips or sawdust provided. Thus Gordon was to Fosbury what NASA was to Glenn. "In a sense, Fosbury is a child of technological progress," the *Los Angeles Herald-Examiner*'s Morton Moss later wrote. "The backward flip would have been too dangerous to attempt in days of old when you landed in a sand or sawdust pit."

STEVE DAVIS HAD not forgotten the pain—and surprise—of watching Fosbury break his school record at season's end the previous year. Perhaps motivated by the memory, he shattered Fosbury's mark by two inches in the first meet of 1965, the Rogue Valley Relays. Despite cool temperatures and his barely having lost his "basketball legs," Davis's 6'5½" leap was only a quarter-inch below the state record and accentuated his incredible athleticism. The jump—and Fosbury's lackluster 6'2" response—jolted Dick. It triggered the beginning of an agonizing month-long slump.

When, at last, Fosbury bested Davis—at a dual meet in Klamath Falls May 8—it was a hollow victory. Though Dick had gone a solid 6'2", Davis had been hampered by an ailing knee. Only one more meet remained before district; where had this season gone? The multi-team competition was in Medford May 14, a rare Friday night meet, Dick's first time jumping under the lights.

Although the turnout was only a fraction of what a football game would draw, it was the largest home crowd Dick had jumped in front of. The gathering twilight imbued the meet with a sense of big-time drama. A three-quarter moon hung in the darkening sky to the south, above Mt. Ashland. When the lights switched on, energy coursed through the crowd, and through Fosbury, too. As he eyed the bar for his first jump, 5'10", his stomach was knotted more tightly than usual. He sensed a now-or-never urgency, a touch of desperation that he'd learned could be more friend than foe.

After all, hadn't desperation triggered his switch back to the scissors? His mid-jump decision to lift his butt? His conviction last season to stick with the back layout, even as his coaches were nudging him back to the straddle? Yes, to all. But something else stirred within, something he hadn't noticed until the end of his junior year, when he'd beaten Davis in back-to-back meets: Dick Fosbury loved to win. Not only against the competition but against himself. He liked to mentally challenge the competition with a "catch-me-if-you-can" confidence. And liked to pop out of the pit knowing he had won the challenge against himself to jump his best.

"Steve Davis was clearly the more athletic-looking of the two," said Mullen, "but what no one knew at the time was the mental makeup of Dick Fosbury and his deep competitive nature."

Not far away, Davis warmed up. A *Medford Mail Tribune* photographer inched closer. Fans started coming out of the grandstands and ringing the pit. Fosbury fed off it all. As evening became night, he climbed the steps higher and higher until he'd notched a personal-best 6'5½", breaking Davis's school record by half an inch. It was an inch and a half higher than Fosbury had ever jumped. The following week, at the Southern Oregon Conference meet, Dick achieved another first: a championship, going 6'3" to beat Davis.

A note arrived the next week from Bowerman, the Oregon coach, inviting Dick to a luncheon in Eugene. Despite the misspelling of his name—Dick *Foursby*—Fosbury was honored to have heard from the Medford legend. But Dick's interest was in engineering, which Oregon did not offer, and he was already planning on going to OSU, which did. No other school had shown him any interest.

The following week, on wood chips, Fosbury jumped 6'3¾" at the State Class A-1 championships at OSU's Bell Field to finish second to South Eugene's Al Tuttle, who broke the state record at 6'6½". A couple of photographs of Fosbury jumping, taken by (Eugene) *Register-Guard* photographer Paul Petersen, captured an interesting phenomenon: it wasn't Dick and his style. It was the fans beyond. Unless a sports photo is taken at a stellar moment of an event—say, a last-second shot in basketball—it's common to catch lots of fans *not* looking at the action. They're doctoring a hot dog or talking to a friend or eyeing the cute girl or boy in Row 14. But in the two photographs Petersen shot—neither of which, by the way, made the next day's paper—that's decidedly *not* the case. In one, twenty-six people are visible; all but four are focused on Fosbury. In another, shot from a different angle, about forty people can be seen. That all but three are watching Fosbury was remarkable, all the more so because more than half were in the upper rows of the baseball grandstands, ignoring the ball game behind them to watch the kid with the new-fangled style.

If it was Fosbury's style that drew people, it was the context that deepened the intrigue for serious track-and-field fans. In two years Fosbury had gone from 5'4"—and being one of the worst high jumpers in the state—to 6'5½", and being the second-best in the state, largely because he'd found a new way to jump.

Berny Wagner, who was replacing the highly regarded Sam Bell at OSU, first saw Fosbury jump the next week in the state Junior Chamber of Commerce meet in Gresham, a Portland suburb. Dick went 6'4" to win and earn a trip with the state's team to the national Jaycees meet in Houston come August.

Dick looked up to see a man approaching him whose photo he'd seen in the papers: he was thin, deeply tanned, and had gleaming white teeth. He wore orange and black clothes, a plaid fedora, and sunglasses. Wagner shook Fosbury's hand and said he'd heard Dick was interested in OSU because of its engineering program. "Love to have you on our track team," he said.

Dick was a soft sell; he'd all but committed to OSU but Wagner's offer of a partial scholarship sealed the deal. They chatted. Wagner said he would be in touch with Dick's father. They shook hands and parted.

An opportunistic reporter for *The Oregonian*, Don Fair, wasted no time approaching Wagner.

"What," he asked, "were your first impressions of this Fosbury kid and his new style?"

"I immediately thought he was using an illegal jump with both feet planted on the ground at the same time at takeoff."

"And as the competition continued?"

"After I proved to myself that wasn't true, I couldn't believe it. I wondered how Dick got up there."

In Houston, on the night before the Jaycees meet was to begin, athletes attended a banquet at which three-time Olympian Bob Richards—the first person, in 1958, to grace a Wheaties box—gave a motivational speech about the essence of winning. Fosbury, at a table far from the podium, remembers most of his fellow athletes virtually ignoring Richards. Dick, however, was mesmerized. "You are what you *think*," said Richards. "You are *what you go for*. You are *what you do*." Until now, coaches had taught Dick to train. But Richards was the first person who inspired him to *win*. Who taught him the importance of believing in himself. And who introduced the concept of success having as much to do with the mind as it does the body, maybe more.

Coincidence or not, Fosbury flew a career-best 6'7" the next day to win the national Jaycees meet. Hearing the news back home, Sweet was again stunned at his friend's success. "That was madness," he said. "Dick winning a national competition at a height like that? It was like the earth stopped rotating."

Wagner, meanwhile, seemed more impressed with the athlete than his style. He began wondering about the possibilities of turning Fosbury into a triple jumper—perhaps even a hurdler.

Chapter 10

The struggle is always between the individual and his sacred right to express himself . . . and . . . the power structure that seeks conformity, suppression, and obedience.

—William O. Douglas

THE RELATIONSHIP BETWEEN Dick Fosbury and Berny Wagner was complicated. They both arrived on Oregon State's fir-studded campus in the fall of 1965 with a touch of bravado and a tad of insecurity. They both were intensely competitive. And they both were committed to OSU. But they came from two generations that were in the midst of a long, awkward parting. And though they could agree on some particular approach, they tended do so with far different levels of buy-in.

Wagner, forty, was replacing the ever-popular Bell, who had unexpectedly left for Cal, as head track and field coach at OSU; he had big shoes to fill and an archrival forty miles south, Oregon, whose coach, Bowerman, had established one of the top track and field programs in the nation. Fosbury, eighteen, was entering college as a much-talked-about high jumper—and yet with a confidence as fragile as his style was new. Despite his recent flurry of success, Fosbury was burdened with a sense of doubt not uncommon for any college freshman, much less one who, thanks to his unorthodox style, was defying an older generation's world order.

As part of the World War II generation, Wagner had been encultured to believe anything standardized—the straddle, for example—was likely to be wholesome and trustworthy. You did what you were told, how you were told to do it. You favored the tried and the true. The proven. And you accomplished things—helped win a war—as a group. But Dick Fosbury was nurtured in a different generation, one in which you experimented. Questioned things. Protested a war. And let their individual creativity come out to play.

In the fall of 1965, the "world order," like Fosbury's young high-jumping career, was at a tipping point. "Everything," wrote historian James MacGregor Burns, "seemed to come unhinged." The previous May, not far from where Wagner was then working as track coach at the College of San Mateo, forty young men burned their draft cards at Cal-Berkeley and a coffin was marched to the Berkeley Draft Board. President Lyndon Johnson was not moved. In July, he doubled the number of men drafted per month from 17,000 to 35,000. In August, the Watts Riots—racial angst at its ugliest—broke out in Los Angeles, leaving thirty-four people dead. In November, Norman Morrison, a father of three, doused himself with kerosene below Secretary of Defense Robert McNamara's office in Washington, D.C., and set himself on fire to protest the war.

The previous summer, Dick had contentedly cocooned himself in the youth-shielded world of work and love. He bundled lumber on swing shift at Elk Lumber's planer mill and spent most of his free time with girlfriend Marali Stedman: attending drive-in movies, swimming in the Applegate River, and doing whatever it took to postpone the inevitability of Dick leaving for Corvallis and Marali staying in Medford. Before Dick left for school, the two had agreed to extend their relationship despite the four-hour drive on Interstate 5. It was one of three Fosbury-related commitments made in September 1965 that would not last past his sophomore year.

Besides a stint in a fraternity that was fun but ended badly, the other was an unwritten contract Dick made with Wagner, who called Fosbury into his small office in Gill Coliseum soon after Dick unpacked his bags in September.

"Dick," he said, "what are your goals this year?"

Fosbury was stymied. "Not sure I have any specific ones, other than wanting to be a good jumper. Be on the team, you know, stuff like that."

"Have you ever tried the straddle?"

"Well, yeah, sophomore year—and a little my junior year. Not too good at it."

Wagner told Dick he'd had some success in California coaching straddlers, one of whom had sniffed 7'0". "I'd like to see if I could help you do the same—that is, with the straddle."

"No more using my style?"

"I didn't say that," said Wagner, "but, I'll admit, I'm not convinced that backward style of yours is going to get you much higher. I propose a hybrid plan: you work with me during the week on the straddle and use your technique to score points on Saturday."

Dick was more intrigued about Wagner's promise to help him go higher than irked about his style getting relegated to part-time status. And Wagner *was* the coach—and the guy who decided whether he'd keep his scholarship.

Fosbury nodded a yes. "Sure."

That's the way Fosbury remembered it. Over the years, the story would, in Dick's estimation, get twisted to suggest he was, as *Sports Illustrated* would say, "not wanting to be laughed at anymore" and uncertain his style would work. *Wouldn't work?* Why would a kid who, with his backward style, had improved fifteen inches in two years, who had just won a national junior championship at 6'7," and who was already less than three inches from the OSU record be desperate to switch to a style he loathed? It didn't make sense.

But, politically, Wagner was in control. And Dick, despite his success, was imbued with a well-hidden insecurity that traced back to his family losses. "I had very little confidence in myself as a jumper at that time," he said. A school that had just granted him a partial scholarship was now making a request—and Fosbury was sitting in a college coach's office for the first time. "He's the coach. I'm just another athlete on the team," he remembered. "I had nothing to lose. And I needed to keep my scholarship as long as I could."

Wagner and Fosbury shook hands on the deal.

MORE THAN 5,000 miles away, tragedy struck: in October 1965, Soviet high jumper Valeriy Brumel, who'd dominated the event for four years and was already the odds-on favorite to win in Mexico City in 1968, had been the passenger on a motorcycle that crashed into a stone ramp. A shattered shin bone jutted through his skin. It would take twenty-nine surgeries to save his non-jumping leg. But he vowed he would high-jump again, quietly setting his sights on Mexico City in October 1968.

WAGNER WAS MOVING to an upper-division college in a region that, in the mid-'60s, was a hotbed for track and field. In 1965, when *Track & Field News* compiled a list of best all-time marks by the nation's top fourteen schools, USC barely nudged out Oregon and Oregon State for the top spot. Since 1949, the Pac-8 (and its equivalent league prior to 1968) had won fourteen of the last seventeen NCAA meets. Dual track meets at Oregon and Oregon State had the big-time feel of football games. Form charts in hand, fans—up to 5,000 in Corvallis and 10,000 in Eugene, would show up on Saturday afternoons to watch their "thin-clads," some of whom were among the best in the world.

In January 1966, Fosbury made his OSU jumping debut at the Portland Indoor, where he leaped 6'6", the same height as ex-Medford rival Steve Davis, who had also chosen OSU, and Oregon junior Bob Shepard, the former Grants Pass jumper who competed against Dick on the day Fosbury first tried his "back layout." Wrote Corvallis *Gazette-Times* columnist Jack Rickard:

> Oregon State didn't have many individual standouts in Saturday night's indoor meet at Portland, but the Beavers did have one of the more unusual performers. Freshman Dick Fosbury really wowed the crowd with his high jumping form. And he did clear 6-6, only an inch off his best mark. Fosbury goes over the bar backwards, starting head first. Then come his shoulders and finally his legs. He has to flip his legs at the last second to keep from catching the bar.
>
> A product of Medford, he's been jumping this way since early in his high jump career.
>
> But he wants to change, and he and Coach Berny Wagner are working on a more standard method. In the long run it should increase his potential. But it does eliminate one of track's more unusual techniques.

In the G-T's brick office downtown, Rickard had a desk decorated heavily in bikini-clad bathing beauties. He would find any excuse to get onto a golf course. And he often rapped out his sports column over coffee in a shop across the street, which is why he might not have taken the time to ask for Fosbury's perspective. Instead, he obviously defaulted to Wagner's point of view that Fosbury's style had no future and that it was Dick's idea to stop jumping backwards.

It's understandable why Wagner was skeptical to endorse it. Although he had blown into sleepy Corvallis with a touch of panache—he bought a white Karmen Ghia VW and had it painted orange to go with the black leather upholstery—he hadn't proven a thing yet as OSU's coach. A safe first step in doing so was perhaps beating rival Oregon in a dual meet, not investing in a high-risk stock involving a kid and his wacky high-jump style.

Others believed in it. "When you think about it," Bowerman told one of his jumpers, Shepard, "it's a very efficient way to jump."

"Can't disagree with that," the former Grants Pass jumper said.

"I knew that as we were jumping in college, Dick would excel," said teammate Davis, who left the high jump to concentrate on sprints and relays. "It was apparent his technique was phenomenal. It seemed to me that his style had much more potential than the roll. I tried it a few times, but couldn't get used to the concept of landing backwards on my neck. Dick made it an art form."

Wagner wasn't convinced. When Steve Kelly, an artsy freshman from California, set the OSU freshman record at 6'5", it was, to Wagner, just more validation that the traditional way was the best way. Even when Fosbury tied that record, Wagner remained skeptical. Early on, he believed Dick's style might, like a shot of adrenalin, get a high jumper to new heights but probably wasn't a good, long-term solution. "You can teach it to a 5'6" jumper, and in two weeks he will be going 5'10"," Wagner said. "Of course, it may just be a shortcut to mediocrity."

Using OSU's new foam-chunk-in-a-net pit, Wagner worked with Fosbury during the week on the straddle. But if Dick was open to the idea early in the year, toward the end his theme song could have been the Rolling Stones' just-released "(I Can't Get No) Satisfaction." "I was totally embarrassed," said Fosbury, who had managed only a paltry 5'6" with the straddle. Meanwhile, his once-blossoming "back layout" had all but wilted. In the two years between his sophomore and senior years of high school, Dick had improved just shy of a foot going backward. But as a freshman at OSU, despite bumping the frosh record to 6'6¼", he actually *regressed* by ¾" with his style.

The result was a subtle identity crisis. Was he fish or fowl? Or, for that matter, high jumper or high hurdler? Wagner had him run the 120-yard high hurdles against Washington—and he won. But to himself—and to those who knew him—Fosbury was losing his sense of who he was.

"Every time I saw Dick he just seemed sad," said Sweet, who ran the half-mile his freshman year at OSU. "Berny seemed unwilling to pay attention to the obvious. Dick was wasting his time with the straddle." Why, Sweet wondered, was Berny trying to deprogram Dick from a style that clearly had been working well and had such potential for the future?

Along with Sweet and Kelly, Fosbury had pledged at the Theta Chi fraternity. Wagner didn't particularly like fraternities; they fuzzied his athletes' focus on track and field, he believed. As a fraternity man, Dick had kitchen and dining-room duty responsibilities—and numerous party opportunities. Meanwhile, classes such as physics tested Fosbury like nothing he'd seen at Medford High—he scored a twenty-five on one 100-point test—and often required afternoon labs that cut into track practice at Bell Field. At times, Fosbury was having to show up late and do his workouts virtually alone, sometimes in the dark. He was a time-management bust—how could he pass up a Beaver basketball game, a Theta Chi kegger, or trips home to see Marali?

Sweet, meanwhile, started hanging out at Monroe Street coffee shops and getting involved in anti-war pursuits. The two were aligned politically—Dick, too, was opposed to the war in Vietnam—but Fosbury was already too overcommitted to get involved in anything new; he arrived at school-year's end while running on fumes. His grades were sagging. His high-jumping confidence shot. His future uncertain.

In the summer of 1966, Wagner invited Fosbury to compete on an Oregon junior team in a coed meet against the province of British Columbia, in Vancouver, BC. While watching the girls' high-jump competition—a rarity, since girls' sports were given minimal opportunities in the 1960s—Fosbury was flabbergasted: there was a young Canadian high jumper using a style similar to his. It was the first time he'd ever seen someone else jump backwards over the bar in competition. Her name was Debbie Brill. She was thirteen. When her friends saw Fosbury jump, they rushed up to her.

"Hey, it's amazing—there's someone else who jumps like you," Brill recalled people telling her in her book, *Jump*.

"[It] gave me a tremendous relief and encouragement . . . When he came up to me, I couldn't speak. He just spoke to me, and I sort of felt, Gosh! Wow!"

The meeting surprised Fosbury, too. In a world that saw Brill and Fosbury as different, the two were bonded, if even for a few hours, by their sameness. When they left to go their separate ways, neither foresaw a day when they would blend in like everyone else—not because the two of them would conform to the world, but because the world would conform to them.

Chapter 11

Patience is bitter, but its fruit is sweet.

—Jean-Jacques Rousseau

ON A CRISP fall afternoon in early October 1966, Oregon State's new hot-shot high jumper, freshman John Radetich of California, took one look at Fosbury's backward style and laughed.

"Seriously?" he said to nobody in particular. "Now, *that* is goofy." He thought it was a joke.

Radetich had jumped higher as a high school senior, 6'9¾", than either Fosbury or Kelly had gone heading into their sophomore years—a mark equal to the OSU school record. "I'm planning on being No. 1 by the end of the year," he said without hesitation.

When you're nineteen, you don't dare show fear, particularly to a teammate. Fosbury didn't. But, inside, he stewed. Everyone was impressed with this newcomer, even Sweet. "Radetich was cooler than the rest of us," said Sweet. "He was a California kid. He wore sunglasses."

Fosbury was more concerned about Radetich's jumping ability. Radetich had "hops"—springy legs, not a Fosbury trait. "John was a much better physical jumper than Fosbury," said Chuck McNeil, an Oregon State assistant coach. "If I was predicting Olympic gold, I would have bet on Radetich right then and there."

Wagner liked him, too. "John was definitely the stronger of the two," he said.

Fosbury was duly motivated. For the first time, he committed to tougher workouts. Until Radetich arrived, Fosbury had been as laid back as his new style; his idea of a good workout was a three-on-three basketball game at nearby Gill Coliseum. "I hated to run," he said. On weekends, he'd hitchhike back to Medford to see Marali, having learned that it was way easier to get rides if he wore his new OSU letterman's jacket.

Assistant Coach John Chaplin, a transplant from the University of Washington, introduced Fosbury to plyometric training. "I've seen jumpers improve three inches overnight with this stuff," he told Dick, who bought in. A bony 6'4" and 175 pounds, Fosbury started lifting weights and running stairs at Gill Coliseum or Parker Stadium, sometimes hopping up one foot at a time.

He rarely saw Radetich and Kelly, who, in Dick's eyes, had a peculiar habit during spring practices: they high-jumped. The two might take two dozen jumps in practice. Joe Faust, the 1960 Olympian, sometimes jumped 100 times a session. But Fosbury rarely jumped anytime but in a meet. Because jumping in competition, for him, was highly dependent on him being emotionally primed—and, with nothing on the line, impossible to replicate in practice—he thought jumping in practice developed bad habits.

IN JANUARY 1967, at Cape Kennedy in Florida, a cabin fire during a launch rehearsal for Apollo 1 killed three astronauts: Virgil "Gus" Grissom, Edward White, and Roger Chaffee. NASA called a halt to further missions for nearly two years while it investigated what had gone wrong and made sure it wouldn't happen again. Uncertainty shrouded the man-on-the-moon plans.

MEANWHILE, FOSBURY'S PLIGHT went from bad to worse. In January 1967, rain greeted Dick almost every morning he awoke in the Theta Chi house. As a freshman, he could laugh about the nearly daily drizzle; "what do you call three straight days of rain in Oregon?" someone joked. "A weekend." But he wasn't laughing much anymore. Marali had sent him a "Dear John" letter soon after Christmas recommending that they "just be friends." "I was shattered," he later said.

So he struggled with the loss of Marali, often with a beer in his hand. He struggled to get anywhere with the straddle. And after his poor grades got him kicked out of the Theta Chi house, he struggled to adjust to living in a dorm, McNary Hall. All this came on top of a conflict between an afternoon engineering lab and track practice, which forced Dick to do late workouts.

As an athlete at OSU, Fosbury had become something of an independent contractor. That clashed with Wagner's old-school values suggesting everybody do the same workout at the same time. Some athletes admired Berny. Some saw him as a father figure. But he had an irascible side. He could be a taskmaster. Once, during cross-country practice, Sweet returned from a workout at Avery Park with bloody feet. "Keep running," said Wagner. As the '60s deepened, such tough, "old-school coaches" were being questioned for the first time, sometimes by the very athletes they coached.

Jack Scott, a grad student at University of California-Berkeley, wrote a piece for *Track & Field News*, complete with quotes from French philosopher Albert Camus, arguing that athletes should be able to use their own training methods instead of acquiescing to tradition-bound coaches. Wagner couldn't let that dog lie. He fired off a retort that *T&F News* published, along with similar sentiments from other coaches. If an athlete wants to compete at a particular school, he wrote, "certain obligations go with this privilege . . . he must take on the responsibility of striving for success in the way that the coach deems best. This might mean doing some things which he doesn't particularly agree with."

Wagner's response and similar sentiments from other coaches unleashed a backlash of dissent from those who agreed with Scott that athletes were being exploited. "The ill-conceived comments of . . . Wagner . . . cannot go unanswered," wrote Dr. Sidney Gendin, a philosophy professor at Stony Brook University in Long Island, New York, who went on to lecture Wagner about long-overdue rights for athletes.

Meanwhile, Fosbury showed no more signs of warming up to the straddle. The style experiment got so bizarre that at one point Wagner suggested Fosbury switch takeoff feet, which Dick imagined to be no less difficult, or successful, than moving NASA's launch pad from Cape Kennedy to Idaho.

Late at night, he'd find himself walking across campus with some song about lost love looping in his mind, feeling so depressed he couldn't tell tears from raindrops. Years later, a photo in Fosbury's scrapbook—an odd photo—mirrored Winter Term 1967. It was taken during, or after, a party. He's hunched over a toilet, throwing up.

His father made a rare visit to campus. All Dick remembered about it was the old man reading him the riot act for his slumping grades. "If you don't watch out," he said, "you're going to get yourself drafted."

IN LATE WINTER, Berny asked Dick to come see him. "I'll be blunt," said Wagner. "I don't see you at practice much anymore. And when I do it seems like you're in some sort of fog."

Fosbury's head dropped. Wagner turned up the heat.

"It's a privilege to be on a scholarship, even if it's partial. But, I'll be frank, if things don't improve, we may have to pull yours."

Fosbury leaned forward and placed his face in his hands. Somebody, he figured, had gone to Wagner and said he was slacking. Dick did his best to explain his academic/sports juggling act. Wagner remained unconvinced. But as the two talked more, Dick realized what a huge responsibility Wagner had, trying to keep on top of dozens of athletes. And Wagner, he thought, was getting a touch more understanding of Dick's character—and the challenge of overloaded students. In short, the talk had nudged the two a step closer to one another's worlds.

"Coach," he said, "I'm committed to track, but because of those afternoon labs I sometimes have to work out in the early evenings when nobody's around—but I'm *there*. And I'm into it. I'm working hard. Honest."

Wagner's icy disposition didn't melt, but he warmed up a touch.

"Give me a chance to prove myself in the spring," said Dick.

"OK, the ball's in your court . . . ."

Dick nodded and stood to leave, whereupon Wagner finished his thought. " . . . and time's running out."

WHEN HE STEPPED off the bus in Fresno, California, in late March, Fosbury soaked in the sunshine like the sun-deprived Oregonian he was. ("Oregonians don't tan, they rust.") OSU had arrived for its season-opener with host Fresno State and the University of Nevada-Las Vegas. Sunshine. Palm trees. Short-sleeve weather that didn't elicit goose bumps. Fosbury was stoked. And it showed.

He soared 6'10" the next day to set an OSU record by a quarter-inch. He barely missed on his three attempts at 7'0". Afterward, Wagner didn't use the specific words, but his smile and body language said it all. Dick had somehow redeemed himself in the coach's eyes. "That jump," said Fosbury, "was my salvation with Berny. He wanted some proof, right? I gave him six feet, ten inches worth. Nobody does that in the first meet of the year without having done some work over the winter."

"OK," Wagner told Fosbury. "Forget Plan 'B'. The experiment is over. I'm going to study you, film you, and figure out what you're doing."

A photo by Ralph Thornberry of the *Fresno Bee,* which was sent nationwide via the Associated Press, showed four onlookers—a coach, perhaps, and three athletes?—appearing absolutely flummoxed by Fosbury's style. One had a hand to his mouth, as if in disbelief.

The *San Francisco Chronicle* published the photo later that week, prior to Cal's meet with Oregon State. "Oregon State jumper Bill Fosbury"—the *Grants Pass Courier* and Bowerman weren't the only one who got the name wrong—"literally turns his face on orthodox methods and soars over the bar backwards," read the cutline. A few days later, the *Oakland Tribune* published a photo of Fosbury with the cutline: "OSU's Dick Fosbury won't win prizes for form, but this jump at 6'8" equals Cal meet record." Newspaper writers had a great time naming it. Among the suggestions: "Fosbury Float," "Fosbury Flip," "Feet-First Back Float," and the "Hip Flip."

It wasn't only Fosbury's over-the-bar technique that drew attention. It was his agonizingly long psyche-up sessions before he began his approach. He would often stare at the bar for minutes—once, in a meet with no time limit, four and a half minutes—shaking his fingers, clenching his fists. At OSU's Bell Field, Fosbury started so far away from the bar that he had to run up a small slope that feathered to the edge of the track.

"Fosbury, 20, a sophomore, is the funniest high jumper you ever saw," wrote Georg N. Meyers, sports editor of the *Seattle Times.* "He flies over the bar, feet first, on his back." Meyers's understanding of the mechanics was a touch off—feet first?—but his making fun of the style, instead of trying to understand it, was typical for the times. The technique was new and different, went the conventional thinking; therefore, it couldn't be taken seriously.

Nobody wanted to endorse Fosbury and his style as something that might not only be working for Dick but might also work for other jumpers. Nobody thought Dick was "on to something here." Said Wagner shortly after Dick broke the OSU record: "I wouldn't advise anybody to try Fosbury's method just because he uses it. I just don't know enough about it. Nobody does. Maybe there are more problems with this back-over jump than other techniques. Dick has good fundamentals despite his form. This means his approach, his takeoff [is] solid."

Wagner's phrase alluding to Dick's "good fundamentals *despite his form*" was telling. It underscored an almost universal belief that, to this point at least, Fosbury's style was innately flawed—apparently because the new and unfamiliar must be either dismissed in the name of tradition or laughed at in the name of misunderstanding. The press didn't try to understand Fosbury or his style at a level deeper than garden soil. Newspapers played up the wackiness of the style, not its worth; the edginess, not its efficiency. "Lazy-Dazy—Man, It Was Crazy" read a *San Francisco Examiner* phrase to describe a photo of Fosbury jumping. "World's Laziest High Jumper," wrote the *Los Angeles Herald-Examiner*. "Upside-down and backward to the normal way," wrote *The Oregonian*.

Sweet, who watched Fosbury morph from boy to man, saw Fosbury more clearly than most. "I saw a Jacques Cousteau special on octopi once," he said. "They put a camera on it aboard a ship, slopping and oozing around. Then they filmed it sliding through a gunwale port and into the water. Cameras under water caught this amazingly graceful, stunningly beautiful animal. Dick was like that. Flopping he was grace, beauty, efficacy, strength, but mostly just smoothly perfect, like, of course, that was the way he was going to jump. Like the octopi, he'd reached a homeostasis with his environment."

The press continued to believe Fosbury was a fish out of water. But three meets at the end of the year would finally begin to earn him respect not simply as an oddball innovator, but as a high jumper. In May, Fosbury upped his OSU record an inch to 6'10¾", then claimed his biggest victory to date—the Pac-8 Championships at storied Hayward Field in Eugene—in front of the biggest crowd he'd jumped in front of, 10,500 people. Students in dorms watched from across the street, their legs dangling from open windows. "Fosbury's style," wrote the *Oregon Journal*, "attracts photographers in droves." In Provo, Utah, he finished fifth in the NCAA Championships at 6'10". Steve Brown of Idaho won the competition at 7'1".

Now that he was—in a catch-phrase of the times—"free to be me," Fosbury had become his old self with new confidence. The Wagner experiment had backfired. Going back and forth between the two styles had cluttered a Fosbury mind that could ill-afford confusion. With Dick, jumper and technique, fundamentals and form, were essentially one and the same. The experiment failed largely because it disconnected *inventor* from *invention*, because Wagner's resistance to his style planted the seeds of doubt in Dick. But credit Wagner for not letting his pride preclude ending the experiment. His student had set a school record, won the Pac-8 Championship, and placed in the NCAAs. At the end of Fosbury's sophomore season, the results spoke for themselves. "I decided right then and there I didn't need another triple jumper," said Wagner, in essence waving the white flag in the pair's two-year cold war.

"Good athletes," he said at the time, "always teach a coach something. The really good [athletes] tend to do something different. Everybody can't do things the same way."

As launches go, Fosbury's college experience thus far had been fraught with frustration. As a freshman, he had made three commitments—to a girl back home, to a fraternity, and to a high-jumping process. None had lasted. But as he packed his bags for summer back in Medford, he finally had clearance for takeoff with a jumping style he was confident could work. For the first time since shortly after arriving at OSU, he was looking forward to the future.

Then came a letter that cast a pall on that future. It was from Dan Shepard, a former Grants Pass track athlete—and brother to high-jumper Bob, who had won the meet in which Dick had first tried his new style. Shepard had written the letter from Vietnam, where he was a soldier. He was congratulating Dick on reaching 6'10". "That," he hand-wrote, "is good jumping." A photo and article on Dick had appeared in *Stars and Stripes*, the army newspaper. "So 400,000 troops saw it," wrote Shepard. "I thought you might be interested in it. Good luck in the rest of the season to come."

Two things struck Fosbury as noteworthy about the letter: first, that Shepard—a competitor he'd hardly known—had taken the time to write; it touched him. And, second, that if an average kid like Dan Shepard, a fellow athlete from Southern Oregon, could wind up in Vietnam, then Dick could, too. Fosbury felt a pit in his stomach. Because twenty years old and separated from the draft by only a student deferment requiring a 2.0 GPA, Fosbury knew a secret: between time gobbled up by track and field, dances, Beaver sports, and an occasional date, he was barely clearing the GPA bar at 2.0.

PART III

LIFTOFF

Chapter 12

Follow your bliss and the universe will open doors where there were only walls.

—Joseph Campbell

THE UNITED JET teased passengers with a glimpse of the Golden Gate Bridge before banking into its final approach to San Francisco International Airport. Less than five years before, Dick Fosbury had been sitting on a school bus en route to Grants Pass on the day he spontaneously unveiled the first incarnation of his back-first high-jump style. Now he was jetting to a premiere indoor track and field competition, the Athens Invitational in Oakland. It was late January 1968.

Below, the Haight-Ashbury neighborhood was still hung over from 1967's Summer of Love. The gathering of all things counterculture had galvanized the country's growing anti-establishment spirit in an orgy of peace, love, drugs, sex, music, and whatever else flew in the face of an older generation that watched in horror. Some 100,000 people, mostly free-spirited hippies, had descended on San Francisco for a youthful celebration—one with no real beginning, no real end—that pulsed with the music from the likes of Janis Joplin, Jefferson Airplane, the Byrds, and the Grateful Dead.

Fosbury, meanwhile, had experienced the summer of gloves; he worked in the planer mill, getting rough-sawn lumber ready to ship. In the fall, back in Corvallis, he had earned spending money by helping run the first-down marker at Oregon State football games, including the Beavers' 3–0 upset over top-ranked USC at rainy Parker Stadium as O.J. Simpson bogged down in the mud and California Governor Ronald Reagan watched glumly from the press box.

Fosbury's blue-collar image clashed with that of his psychedelic brethren, suggesting a man behind the times. This, after all, was 1968, a year when change was afoot. Skirts were up. Hair was down. Conformity out. Drugs in. What nobody knew? Fosbury was already forging a quiet nonconformity all his own.

"There had never been a year like 1968," wrote Mark Kurlansky, in his book *1968: The Year That Rocked the World*, "and it is unlikely there will ever be one again." America was in the throes of revolution. Civil rights. Women's rights. Vietnam. Around the world, by year's end, unrest would roil in Czechoslovakia, Poland, France, and Mexico, the latter of which would host the Olympic Games in October.

Fosbury walked through a San Francisco airport where it wasn't unusual for home-from-Vietnam soldiers to be cursed. People had seen the evening-news footage of women and children fleeing villages torched by US soldiers—and quick to blame the many for the misdeeds of the few. The war was being fought, unfairly, by young men, dispro-portionately black, who were made vulnerable to the draft by poverty and lack of education—and by students who couldn't keep their grades up. The November 1967 morning after Oregon State's 3–0 victory over USC, OSU lineman Bob Jeremiah was on a bus to boot camp; because of slipping grades, he'd been drafted. He soon would be in Vietnam, from which he would return but with his spirits shaken and his right eye missing.

Largely because of the Tet Offensive, more Americans would die in Vietnam (3,326) in the first two months of 1968 than Medford High had students when Fosbury attended school (2,500). For the first time, Americans began realizing the hopelessness of Vietnam; "What the hell's going on?" said an off-camera Walter Cronkite of CBS after reading reports from Saigon. "I thought we were winning the war."

Meanwhile, black athletes began seriously considering civil-rights activist Harry Edwards's Thanksgiving Day 1967 call to boycott the 1968 Olympics in Mexico City. "Let Whitey," he said, "run his own Olympics." A pro-segregation governor, Alabama's George Wallace, was poised to launch a presidential bid that would garner more popular votes than any third-party candidate in American history. And a man who, in 1964, had run as "the peace president," Lyndon Johnson, upped monthly draft quotas to nearly 50,000. Young men from high-status families were conveniently "overlooked." Some "draft dodgers" left for Canada. For others, the possibilities of being forced to Vietnam against their wills became a very real possibility; by 1969, draftees would account for more than half the army's battle deaths. In college or not, young men in America were anxiously looking over their shoulders, Dick Fosbury among them.

As a student, Fosbury had a draft deferment, specifically a II-S: "Registrant deferred because of activity in study." The fine print defined that as a student achieving at least a 2.0 GPA or higher. Between track and field and parties, Dick was struggling with that. A 1.7 GPA fall term of his sophomore year dropped his overall GPA below 2.25, which meant if he wasn't in the fire he could feel the flames. In December, at the command of the Selective Service System, he'd taken the bus to Portland to take a physical. When a doctor asked about his medical history, Dick told him about the back injury he'd sustained while working a chain saw all day long on a county youth project. He was told to see his Medford doctor and return with records and X-rays.

The possibility of being drafted haunted Fosbury. In fact, the only place he found peace was high-jumping. That was simple. That allowed him a certain "say" in the matter instead of being at the whim of someone else—the draft board. That was therapeutic. The catch-22 was that high-jumping, because of the time involved, was the very thing that might keep him from making grades and avoiding the draft. The winter's indoor meets would require Dick's most extensive season of travel yet, with competitions in San Francisco, Oakland, Seattle, Los Angeles, New York, and Kentucky. He was worried. In January 1968, lots of Americans were worried.

"From the outset of the year," wrote Kurlansky, "the United States seemed to be run by fear."

NOBODY AT THE Athens Invitational was expecting much from Dick Fosbury. Though they had heard of this new style of his, he wasn't show-ing up on the radar of those starting to wonder who would represent the

US in the Olympics in Mexico City come October. In January, he was the twenty-third ranked jumper in America. When *Track & Field News* polled athletes and its staff about who would be the top six high jumpers vying for the three Olympic spots, nobody mentioned Dick. He'd been invited to the prestigious meet minimally because of his accomplishments and largely because of his style. The kid, figured organizers, could sell a few tickets.

He entered the Oakland Coliseum like a wide-eyed youth with nothing to lose. He wasn't nervous. He wasn't afraid. And he wasn't intimidated by the more experienced and accomplished field, which included two of the best jumpers in the world, Yugoslavian Dragan Anđelković and Ed Caruthers, an American who'd won the previous year's Pan Am Games and had been ranked No. 1 in the world.

Caruthers watched Fosbury take a couple of practice jumps and shook his head. *What a goof ball.* "Looking at him going over backwards with that novelty style," he later said, "I never thought he was going to be someone I'd ever have to worry about."

As some 6,000 fans settled into their seats, the ten high jumpers began their warmups, each finding a rhythm, a zone, and each with a style all his own. High jumpers tended to be the most detached members of any track and field team—young men full of spirit, superstition, and psychological quirks. Valeriy Brumel, slowly recovering from his motorcycle accident in the Soviet Union, would never watch his competition jump. One LA jumper, between attempts, walked in circles, always to the left. Joe Faust, a man of deep faith, would imagine the bar to be a crucifix and see himself ascending over it into the arms of a loving God, then descend, with gratitude, for grace.

Fosbury's "cycle of repair" between jumps was decidedly loose. He could cheer on teammates who were running, check out cute girls in the stands, or sometimes even close his eyes a bit and meditate if the competition were long. Like other field-event athletes, high jumpers trained years for short bursts of efforts where perfection was demanded. A soccer player might be constantly moving for ninety minutes. By contrast, if a high jumper took ten jumps—fairly average for a competition—he would be involved in actual athletic motion for only about twenty-five to thirty seconds.

The bar started at 6'6", which Fosbury made easily, then went to 6'8", which he made on his second attempt. At 6'10", seven jumpers were left. Fosbury cleared the height on his first try. Then, for more than an hour, he watched one of the most stunning streaks of ineptness to taint a competition at this level: one jumper after another failed. Six jumpers. Eighteen straight misses, including three each from the seasoned Anđelković and Caruthers, at a modest height. In surprisingly simple fashion, Fosbury had won his first open high-jump title. But his victory would prove to be a false summit; moments later, he climbed an even higher peak.

On his second attempt at 7'0", Fosbury arched backward over the bar to become the first person in history to clear the magical 7'0" barrier—high-jumping's equivalent of the four-minute mile—while using a style other than the straddle or Western roll. By a gaping four inches, he had out-jumped the veteran field. It was the equivalent of winning a mile race by twelve seconds. Fosbury was the lead story on a sprinkling of Saturday morning sports pages, including the *Oakland Tribune*'s. "The fans love it," wrote Blaine Newnham. "The coaches hate it."

When the first of *Track & Field News*' two February issues featured a full-page photo of Fosbury on the cover winning in Oakland, it was as if Dick had emerged as the feel-good flip side to American angst. If San Francisco's Summer of Love was a breakout party for the country's counterculture, Oakland was the same for Fosbury. Here was a guy climbing into high-jumping's upper echelon by incorporating the same do-your-own-thing spirit that was driving much of young people in the 1960s. "Orthodoxy flees in wild confusion," wrote Arthur Daley of the *New York Times* of Fosbury's style.

Regardless of the 1960s issue—Vietnam, race, women's rights, the environment—the defiance always began with a refusal to keep doing something the way it had always been done. Fosbury's style was a distant echo of such thinking. Just as the decade's music scene braided the pounding intensity of Iron Butterfly and Creedence Clearwater Revival with the more sanguine sounds of the Beach Boys and Lovin' Spoonful, so did the '60s invite cultural innovation and imagination of all types. It was only coincidental that TV's *Laugh-In* premiered the week Fosbury won in Oakland, but for a country that was wound as tightly as it had been since the Cuban Missile Crisis—if not World War II—lighter touches emerged as small but significant leavening. Pete Townshend, of the Who, decried how serious rock music had gotten, calling it "an electric cornucopia." Said Townshend: "There's no bloody youth in music today."

Fosbury was just that: Youth in music. Poetry in motion. Whimsy in flight. The press deepened its interest in him and his offbeat technique. "Whataya call that style of yours?" asked a reporter after Fosbury's Athens win. Fosbury had gotten the same question the week before in San Francisco and had told reporters the "back layout." Most, he noticed, all but yawned. So he changed his tune.

"Listen, back home they call it the Fosbury Flop, so you can go with that." Sportswriters loved it. It was short, memorable, informative, and, of course, alliterative. The term had been unofficially floating around since Dick's high school days, courtesy of a *Medford Mail Tribune* photo caption—"Fosbury Flops Over the Bar." Now, Fosbury himself had made it official.

The parallels between Fosbury's spirit of imagination and what had blossomed at Haight-Ashbury in the Summer of 1967 were deliciously similar. A college roommate, Tom Greerty, called Fosbury "a true revolutionary." Radetich, no longer smirking at his teammate, marveled at the "mischievous streak" that fueled Fosbury's jumps, a subtle touch of bravado that defied conventional thinking.

Never mind that Fosbury's motives had always leaned more toward desperation than defiance. "I never tried to be a nonconformist," he told *Sports Illustrated.* Intentional or not, in the safe and secure world of status quo, Fosbury had defied authority with a winsome smile on his face. Maybe that's what scared some people about the Flop. As Newnham had written, coaches hated his new style. Was it because it was the kid's invention and, thus, snubbed a coaching establishment that could take no credit for it? Because Fosbury symbolized a new generation of athlete just beginning to show defiance for the athletic establishment whose boys would run through a brick wall for Old Coach? Or simply because the "we've-never-done-it-that-way-before" mentality was more deeply entrenched in America's establishment than some might have thought?

"Things were splitting apart in the country," said Newnham, nearly half a century later. "Authority was being questioned, and to some coaches, Dick's style was doing just that. They looked at Fosbury's Flop and said: 'What the hell's wrong with the old way?'"

They didn't want the style to succeed, so they rationalized it couldn't. Informed that another jumper at OSU, Jeff Kolberg, had reached 6'4" with Fosbury's style, Al Moss of the *Los Angeles Times* wrote: "One coach dismisses it with: 'Remember, 6'4" isn't 7'2". When the second man clears seven feet that way, then come back and we'll talk about it.'"

The biggest doubters were foreign coaches. "They were fanatics about it," said Fosbury. "They thought it was a fluke. Impossible." Some opined that Fosbury would be a one-hit wonder, that he'd reached his limit—a comment that, ironically, would come after Fosbury had gone a few inches higher than when the last coach said the same thing.

"Fosbury was suddenly this 'disruptor,'" said Miller, the *Oregon Stater* editor. "Here's this style born out of desperation by what, back then, would have been the equivalent of the guy who, decades later, founded Uber. Guys like this are bad at taking orders. He's big and gangly and kind of awkward. And he's the definition of a disruptor. He's a pioneer. He's brave. He just keeps hanging in there and look what happens: success comes out of sadness and loss and failure."

The new realization: an athlete originally dismissed as a "man-behind-the-times" might actually be a man *ahead* of his times. The kid who, in 1963, challenged the status quo long before it was cool to do so, now graced the cover of *Track & Field News'* 20th anniversary issue, the first of its two February 1968 editions. In a classic photo that hinted at a changing of the guards, a handful of Oakland high jumpers whom Fosbury had defeated—including Caruthers, Anđelković, and Gary Hines—are watching Fosbury on his successful 7'0" jump. Their expressions drip with a combination of resentment, resistance, and refusal to believe. Three have their arms folded, their expressions and body language suggesting Fosbury were some interloper not particularly welcome in their town with that silly new style of his.

"It was like in *Butch Cassidy and the Sundance Kid,* when they say, 'Who *was* that guy?'" said Radetich.

Fosbury and his easygoing nature didn't begrudge his detractors a thing. Their doubt only motivated him to jump higher. What empowers revolutionaries isn't comfort and ease. It's resistance. It's push-back. It's others saying "we won't allow you to change the world that we like just as it is."

"Everyone has set an 'ultimate' for me because of my style," Fosbury told Newnham on that night in Oakland. "But I've always surpassed them. When people doubt you, that's when it gets you going inside."

Top-flight jumpers remained suspicious of the Flop, even if a few gave it a shot themselves in practice. *T&F News* reported that the Soviets' Valentin Gavrilov managed only 4'10."

"It still seems like a pie-and-cheese nightmare, but Dick Fosbury, the belly-up high jumper from Oregon State, soared high enough here to have won a bronze medal in the 1964 Olympic Games," wrote the *Seattle Times'* Meyers the following week when he cleared a personal-best 7'1" to win the Seattle Invitational Indoor. In front of 10,800 fans, he beat Gavrilov, one of the world's best, by three inches. "Any biophysicist will tell you it is impossible to levitate a human body seven feet, one inch by lying on the back in the air . . . . Soviet guests in Seattle's Invitational meet just shook their heads in disbelief."

Debbie Brill, who was pioneering a similar high-jump technique in the obscurity of British Columbia, believed the incubation of the two jumpers' styles was clearly rooted in the soils of the free-thinking youth of the times. In her book, *Jump,* she argued that Eastern European countries were "deeply into the science of sport, with heavily regimented coaching. I don't think individual instinct flourishes in that kind of atmosphere." She and Fosbury, on the other hand, shared a certain free-spiritedness that was all about feel, instincts, and spontaneity. "What Dick Fosbury and I did, it would have happened anyway eventually, but it could never have come from somebody who had lots of coaching."

She wrote that her style was "a natural extension of what my body was telling me to do. It was physical intuition; it wasn't anything taught." And so it was with Fosbury, who let the "spirit of survival" lead. His decision to flop hadn't been made by a team of sports scientists after analyzing rolls of 8mm film, but in mid-air—by Dick himself—at a time when he desperately wanted to stay on the team.

Now, IN THE dance of the Fosbury Flop, it was hard to tell who was leading, innovator or innovation. But as 1968 deepened, both were finding success. On the winter indoor circuit, Fosbury raised his top mark to 7'1¼", consistently jumping 7'0". Competing in LA, Kentucky, and New York—often two meets a weekend—he lost only twice, grew in confidence, and gained notoriety.

But in the week before the New York meet, a more serious side of the '60s grabbed the headlines. Edwards, a San Jose State sociology professor who had called for an Olympic boycott three months earlier, was now demanding that black athletes skip the New York Athletic Club indoor in February. And did so with a veiled threat. "Any black athlete who does cross this picket line could find himself in trouble," he said, "and I, or any member of this committee, would not be responsible for anything that happens."

Only six weeks into the new year, a line had been drawn in the sand by a small but vocal group of black American athletes. Their demands? First, remove Avery Brundage as president of the International Olympic Committee. Eighty at the time, Brundage had pushed to keep the 1936 Games in Berlin at a time when some Americans wanted to boycott because of the country's white-supremacist ways. He was a Chicago millionaire who belonged to a country club that didn't allow blacks or Jews; called Jesse Owens "boy"; and had seemingly no empathy for the concerns of black athletes, which, in 1968, hardly made him unique.

Beyond getting rid of Brundage, the would-be boycotters wanted to disinvite South Africa and Rhodesia from the 1968 Olympics because of their apartheid policies; hire more black coaches; restore Muhammad Ali's heavyweight boxing title that had been stripped when he resisted the draft; and, of course, boycott the NYAC.

As 1968 unraveled, a twenty-year-old, wide-eyed, white kid—from an Oregon town that had some skeletons in its race-relations closet—would learn some lessons, even if he might not have realized he was in school.

Chapter 13

*Rather than run and jump for medals, we are standing up for human-
ity. Won't you join us?*

—*Protester's sign at the boycott of the NYAC Invitational meet,
February 1968*

IF A SINGLE athletic event mirrored the seriousness of 1960s revolt
with the relative sanguinity of sports, it was the 100th annual NYAC
Invitational at Madison Square Garden. Here was ABC-TV's *Wide
World of Sports* concentrating its cameras on Fosbury's "Flop," using a
new technology called "instant replay" to show viewers not once, not
twice, but three times, the young man's backward style as he cleared
7'0". And *there* was Edwards's boycott, a reminder that in a world
straining from unprecedented pressure to change, not even sports were
safe from the upheaval.

The NYAC meet wasn't chosen randomly for the stand. It was
chosen because New York was the center of media attention—lots of
bang for the boycott buck—and because the NYAC itself was off-limits
to blacks and Jews. Why should black athletes, reasoned Edwards, help
make a success of a meet for a host organization whose only entry as a
black man could be as a waiter or bus boy? An announcement by the
IOC's Brundage the day before the event only added fuel to the NYAC
boycott's fire: South Africa, which had been banned from the Olympics
since 1963 because of its apartheid policies, had been voted back in by
the IOC to compete in Mexico City come October. The news was stunning. All the more reason for black athletes to boycott the NYAC event,
figured Edwards.

Among the dozens of black athletes, only eleven crossed the picket line to compete that night. High jumper John Thomas and sprinter Jim Hines planned to compete but backed out at the last minute after saying they'd been threatened with violence if they did. In solidarity, New York schools pulled out of the high school portion of the meet. The Soviet Union's seven-man team refused to compete. So did a few other white athletes, to show their support.

OSU's three athletes, including Fosbury, never seriously considered backing out. "The boys went because they wanted to compete," Berny Wagner told reporters. "Everyone was given a choice before we left on not going. But we did take precautions."

Wagner came to Fosbury, half-miler John Lilly, and pole vaulter Dennis Phillips the day before the Friday meet. "There's talk of possible violence on the picket lines outside the Garden. Athletes are protesting. We'll be given an escort to and from the hotel, and we'll enter the Garden through a back way."

"The boycott was more of a distraction than anything else," remembered Fosbury, "because we had never heard about what the issues were. We were completely naïve. We were so green that when we rode in from the airport to the hotel, the cab driver charged each of us the fare on the meter. We'd never been in a taxi and the guy had three suckers from Oregon to fatten his wallet. Being so young, we were just focused on our events, not on any peripheral issues."

Despite hundreds of protesters, the OSU contingent had no difficulty getting into the arena and competed well. Their naiveté buffered them from harsher realities. So did their skin color. All three were white.

"I'm scared, man," said Texas-El Paso long jumper Bob Beamon, who is black, in the locker room before the meet.

Kelly Myrick, a black teammate of Beamon's, was asked if he was going to go loosen up. "I'm not going to warm up out there," he said. "Might be a Lee Harvey Oswald up there."

Someone phoned the New York police shortly before the meet was to start to report that three bombs would explode in the building at 9 pm. Some minor scuffles took place in the area where about 500 picketers were set up. But no serious violence was reported before, during, or after the meet, in which Fosbury won at 7'0" after a jump-off with

Ed Hanks of Brigham Young, the reigning NCAA outdoor champ. And no bombs exploded.

The boycott angered Wagner. "It's getting so you can't even talk about track without getting onto a controversial subject these days," he later told the Oregon Sportswriters and Sportscasters in Portland. "The worst thing about it is that the accomplishments of many fine athletes are being overlooked in favor of controversial topics in the press. In many international meets, the wire services are assigning political writers instead of sportswriters to cover them—and that's a bad situation."

With the exception of the Harvard crew, which backed a boycott, and a few others, Wagner's reaction was the predominant response among whites. California Governor Ronald Reagan, whose state would be hosting the Olympic Trials in the summer, agreed. "I disapprove greatly of what he [Edwards] is trying to accomplish," he said.

OSU had only a handful of black athletes on its track team at the time, including world-class sprinter Willie Turner; Ernie Joe Smith, the brother of San Jose State's Tommie Smith, who was a "disciple" of Harry Edwards; and hurdler Don Parish.

"I haven't talked to a Negro athlete who really wants to boycott the Olympics," said Wagner. "And that goes for Tommie Smith. Don't get me wrong; I'm in favor of the civil rights movement, but I don't feel this is the way to improve the situation."

Wagner had not accurately described Tommie Smith's feelings about the boycott. "I am not willing to sacrifice the basic dignity of my people to participate in the Games," Smith told *Track & Field News*. "I am quite willing not only to give up participating in the Games but my life as well if necessary to open a door by which the oppression and injustice suffered by black people in the US might be alleviated."

On the other hand, some black athletes saw competing as the better way to strengthen their cause for equality. "Our participating in the Olympics has given the young Negro kids something to look up to," said Caruthers, the high jumper.

The US had threatened a boycott in a previous Olympics, 1936, but that was an NAACP-led effort against the host country, Germany, because of Adolf Hitler's obvious racist policies against blacks and Jews. The irony was that, at the time, the US wouldn't hold Olympic Trials in the Deep South because southern states banned blacks from participating in events with whites.

Now, thirty-two years later, racism still ran deep in America—and not just in the Deep South. Beyond Edwards's incessant efforts to stir the pot, other factors intensified the possibility of a boycott, including the publishing of a *Sports Illustrated* series called "The Black Athlete—A Shameful Story" and the IOC's decision to allow South Africa back into the Games.

Nation after nation—mostly African and Asia countries, and, notably, *not* the US—said they would boycott the Games if South Africa were allowed to compete. For years, Brundage had contended that racial segregation was not a question for sports, but for politics. However, the mass threat to boycott gave him little choice: the IOC reversed itself and reinstated the ban on South Africa.

Amid the swirl of emotion, Fosbury caught little of the wind. In the 1960s, when 10 percent of America was black, only 1 percent of Oregon was. And the bulk of that population was concentrated in Portland. Fosbury doesn't recall competing against a single black athlete in the Southern Oregon Conference during high school. A Portland team might have a few black players. "But that experience lasted only an hour or two, and then it was going back home to our white culture."

Sports drew only a sprinkling of black players to Oregon State. In the mid-1960s, the football team might have half a dozen black players on it, the track team about that or a few more. The basketball team didn't give a scholarship to a black athlete until 1966 (Charlie White). OSU's international programs drew some people of color. But for the most part, Corvallis, with just under 30,000 people in 1968, was like lots of small cities in the Northwest at the time: thoroughly white and, thus, removed from any *overt* racial strife.

"Going to Oregon State was really the first introduction I had to a mix of races, in class, around campus, with teachers—and yet it was still a white majority," said Fosbury. "It felt normal. No confrontations."

But the incendiary 1960s weren't over.

THE LETTER LOOKED ominous—and was. In 1968, no young man wanted to find mail with a "Selective Service" return address. But coming home from practice in the winter of 1968, Fosbury saw it at his College Inn apartment as he sifted through mail that usually included nothing but record-club offers. ("Five free albums!!!!!") Fosbury was to report to military headquarters in Portland—again—February 23 so Selective Service could take its own X-rays of his back. "If you fail to report for examination as directed," said the letter, "you may be declared delinquent and ordered to report for induction into the Armed Forces. You will also be subject to fine and imprisonment . . . ."

"No!" Fosbury screamed.

Two repercussions shrouded him in instant gloom: the possibility of getting drafted and the certainty that he was going to miss the AAU Indoor Track and Field Championships in Oakland, where Dick would have had a chance to compete against the strongest field he'd ever faced. But the military wasn't budging. He missed the meet to have his back x-rayed in Portland.

If fretting about the draft though, he was flying high with the Flop. In February, Fosbury set a personal best 7'1¼" at the Mason-Dixon Games in Kentucky. In March, he won the NCAA Indoor Track and Field Championships in Detroit with a 7'0" jump that tied the meet record. It marked the sixth time of the year he'd gone that high or higher. One paper called Fosbury "the biggest sensation of the indoor track season."

Not only was Fosbury in the groove during competition, but his teammates and coaches were pushing him during workouts like never before. In the AAU meet Dick had missed, fellow junior Steve Kelly had gone 7'0". Radetich, now a sophomore, was nipping at their heels at 6'10". OSU was poised to become the first college with three seven-foot high jumpers at the same time. Wagner worked with campus grounds crew to extend Fosbury's high-jump runway, building a hard-packed berm so Dick could begin his long run-up on level ground instead of up a slight grade.

He entered the spring outdoor season bristling with confidence— and agonizing with fear. "I did *not* want to go to Vietnam," he said.

On the high-jumping front, the press peppered him and Wagner with questions about the style. How did he invent it? Why does it work?

Will others start using it? Their answers became as rote as Oregon's rain come winter.

"Dick exposes less of himself to the bar than any other jumper," Wagner was fond of pointing out. But despite watching hundreds of Fosbury's jumps live and on film, he still couldn't understand how Dick converted so much speed into upward momentum. The approach wasn't unlike a basketball player's run-up for a reverse layup or dunk.

"From a physics standpoint, it's very economical," Fosbury would say. "Every coach I've had has tried to change me, but I've always gone back to my way."

"Fearless Fosbury Comes to Town" read a headline in the *Los Angeles Herald-Examiner* before an Oregon State-UCLA dual meet in April 1968. "A year ago you could count the number of people on one hand who knew Dick Fosbury was a high jumper," wrote Steve Brand. "Fosbury, if not the world's best high jumper (some venture to say once he gets his famous 'Fosbury Flop' down pat, he will be among the best), is by far the most publicized."

All sorts of urban legends began sprouting about how Fosbury had invented the style. One suggested that his backyard was so small he had to use the scissors, which became the Flop. Another proposed that he stumbled while straddling and accidentally fell over the bar backward. If both were wrong, per se, they were right in the sense that the invention was unplanned and haphazard.

"I was," said Fosbury, "an accidental inventor—a pretty average athlete who happened to be in the right place at the right time." But if the Flop was thus rooted in a sort of "if-it-feels-good-do-it" morass, it now was at least being looked at as good science.

Wagner was realizing that the Flop he'd tried to get Fosbury to discard had three advantages over the straddle: more speed in the approach and, thus, at liftoff ("Dick goes to the bar harder than anyone else high jumping," said the coach); a more efficient, and lower, center of gravity (keeping most of the body below the bar with the arching); and the ease of learning (months instead of years).

IF FOSBURY'S DRAFT fears coursed deep within him, the nation's angst played out for all to see. On April 4, 1968, tragedy struck in Memphis:

Martin Luther King Jr., the man trying to lead blacks to the equal-rights promised land, was assassinated by a white gunman. His death triggered the worst race riots America had ever seen and sent a portion of America into deep mourning. One-hundred thousand people, including new presidential candidate Bobby Kennedy, joined the post-funeral, three-mile procession that ended with the singing of "We Shall Overcome." But it also magnified anti-black spite. Georgia Governor Lester Maddox refused King a state funeral, considering him to be an "enemy of the country." Maddox stationed sixty-four riot-helmeted state troopers at the steps of the state capitol in Atlanta to protect state property.

King's death only deepened the resolve of those wanting to boycott the Olympics—and other meets as well. Black America's strongest voice had been silenced, went the thinking; others needed to step up. When Oregon State went to LA for a dual meet with UCLA, Ernie Smith and Don Parish, two black members of the team, were confronted during a Friday workout and encouraged to not compete at the meet. Both ran anyway. And, along with Fosbury (6'10"), both won—Smith the 100-yard dash and Parish the 120-yard high hurdles.

As Barry McGuire's "Eve of Destruction" pounded on car radios, waves of anti-war and anti-discrimination protests washed across hundreds of college campuses in April and May. At Columbia University in New York, protesters not only took over buildings but took a handful of administrators hostage.

By now, the median age of a soldier in Vietnam had dipped to nineteen, the lowest in American history. Among Fosbury and his friends in Corvallis, dodging the draft had joined sports, girls, and the nuances of various beers as small-talk fodder. Getting married didn't seem like a practical option, so they talked about fall-back plans: ingesting great quantities of drugs and alcohol—for some, not that much of a lifestyle departure—prior to one's medical examination to appear as if suffering from addiction; feigning homosexuality; or moving to Canada. Most, like Fosbury, just trusted the roll of the dice.

Forty miles south, in Eugene, Oregon, distance runner Kenny Moore had graduated and lost his student deferment. But his former coach, Bowerman, went to the Selective Service folks on his behalf, convincing the board that it could have Moore later, but for now, "his country would be better served by having him represent it in the 1968 Olympics." The board agreed.

Fosbury, whose father and grandfather had both been in the Marine Corps, never considered going to Wagner in hopes that Dick's athletic prowess might get him off the draft hook. Instead, as instructed, Fosbury again reported to Portland in May for yet another physical exam, this time by a back specialist. He was told he'd be notified by mail of the board's final decision.

Since Dick's initial letter from the Selective Service System in December, this had now gone on for nearly half a year. It didn't help Fosbury's impending sense of doom when he heard of the April 28 plane crash that killed five members, and the coach, of the Lamar Tech track and field team returning from the Drake Relays. Traditionally, college students deemed themselves immortal, especially with a few beers under their belts. For Fosbury, that blind faith was being shaken.

The future was incessantly on his mind, though seldom regarding high-jumping. Wagner, meanwhile, was just the opposite. For the first time, he and other coaches began wondering just how far this style could take Fosbury. The sports world had seen plenty of modifications in styles, track and field's most notable example being Parry O'Brien. In 1951, the US shot-putter started rotating 180 degrees across the circle. But Fosbury's technique diverged far more from the norm than that. "If you'd asked me six months ago if I thought this was a revolutionary technique, I would have answered 'no,'" Wagner told the *Christian Science Monitor* in spring 1968. "But now I'm beginning to think it might be, because it seems very easy to pick up."

THE EARLIEST DISCIPLES of The Flop were young boys. In Medford, in an alley near East Main Street, kids built their own high-jump setup, complete with sawdust, and dubbed it the "Fosbury High Jump Pit." In Corvallis, dozens of kids would watch their hero at Bell Field on Saturday, then return Sunday and scale the fence for "Hop and Flop" sessions, at times bringing along a dowel-rod bar so they could Flop on the same foam pit their hero had.

"The Flop was magic, and Dick was the magician," said John Woodman, a Corvallis resident who turned fourteen in the winter of 1968. "We loved the guy. We all started copying his style."

Track was big in Corvallis, and it was an Olympic year. Woodman and a group of friends held their own neighborhood Olympics, running laps around the blocks and tossing barbell weights for the shot-put and discus. "Then you'd go to Bell Field to Flop," said Woodman. "That was the final event, the *piece de resistance*."

"Dick actually taught me to high jump," said Harold Reynolds, a Corvallis eight-year-old at the time whose family—one of the few black families in town—lived half a block from Bell Field. "We were always hanging out there and Foz was more than happy to show us the secret: push your butt to the sky." Reynolds Flopped 6'0" in eighth grade before deciding to concentrate on baseball. Ultimately, he became an All-Star second baseman with the Seattle Mariners and then an analyst for MLB Network and Fox Sports. "I always felt having Foz teach you to Flop," said Reynolds, "was like having the Pope teach you to pray."

One Corvallis mother came back from running an errand to find her "sick" thirteen-year-old son trying to repair a bed whose slats had snapped while he was using it as a landing for Flop jumps. A drummer in the school band, he'd use two drum stands to raise a wooden molding—his "bar"—from the stash belonging to his father, the boat builder.

But these Fosbury imitators didn't just exist in Corvallis. And they weren't just in Oregon, or even just in the United States. In New Zealand, a seventeen-year-old boy broke the Christchurch under-seventeen record with a jump of 6'6½" using the Fosbury Flop.

AFTER A LACKLUSTER spring—par for Dick's course with not much on the line—Fosbury rebounded, in May, to win the Pac-8 title in Berkeley at 7'0". Life was good, if "good" still had an asterisk next to it because of his unknown draft status. It had been four and a half years since Defense Secretary Robert McNamara had told JFK in a cabinet meeting, "We need a way to get out of Vietnam." Now, the war was escalating; in April 1968, more American troops died in Vietnam—520—than during any other month to that point. John Kennedy, less than two months after the advice from McNamara, had been assassinated. And now his brother, Bobby, was a latecomer to the Democratic primaries in the race for president.

Senator Robert Kennedy, forty-two, was idealistic and passionate about ending the war in Vietnam, healing racial strife, and curbing poverty. He had grown up considerably since the death of his brother; once chastised by a group of blacks for arrogantly thinking his brother's administration had done wonders for the cause of civil rights, RFK listened, humbled himself, and visited poverty-stricken swaths of Mississippi and New York. The trips gave him a whole new perspective on race.

Though he campaigned twice in Oregon for the May primaries, he and the state's voters never clicked. He appealed most to states with deep troubles; Oregonians, he said, were too content, though not with his appearance. In May, a sign at Portland State College read "Cut your hair, then we'll vote!"

On Kennedy's May 27 visit to Medford, he had Freckles the family dog on hand to lighten the mood as he spoke on the steps of the Medford City Hall to about 1,500 supporters. But it was too little too late. The next day Kennedy lost in the Oregon primary to Eugene McCarthy by six percentage points, marking the first time in twenty-eight elections that a Kennedy had lost.

Bobby jokingly blamed Freckles for the loss, saying he would "take a new look at my organization and may send my dog Freckles home." Then, with a smile on his face, it was on to California, where he hoped—and many political strategists expected—the campaign would find redemption. It did. Followed, four hours later, by tragedy. On June 5, Kennedy won the California primary; afterward, in front of the unblinking eyes of press cameras at the Ambassador Hotel in Los Angeles, he was shot.

As Kennedy lay wounded, a busboy, Juan Romero, cradled the senator's head and placed a rosary in his hand.

"Is everybody OK?" Kennedy asked.

"Yes, everybody's OK," said Romero.

Kennedy then turned away from Romero and said, "Everything's going to be OK."

Twenty-six hours later Bobby Kennedy was pronounced dead.

Chapter 14

It is generally the man who doesn't know any better who does the things that can't be done. You see the blamed fool doesn't know that it can't be done, so he goes ahead and does it.

— *Charles Austin Bates*

LONG BEFORE THE 1960 Olympic Games in Rome, John Thomas, a Boston University sophomore, had taken a felt pen and circled September 1, 1960, on his calendar in his Myles Standish dorm room. That would be the day the high-jump finals would take place. Thomas, eighteen, had been the first person to clear 7'0" in an indoor meet. But that wasn't enough. He wanted to win an Olympic gold medal.

Dick Fosbury in early 1968? "Uh, I didn't even realize that it was an Olympic year."

His national-level success had come fast and furious. That, combined with Dick's laid-back, live-for-the-moment nature meant the only dates he was circling on the calendar were draft-board appointments. In some ways, Fosbury felt like an outsider in the high-jumping world; the idea of him competing in the Olympics seemed no more practical to him than walking in space, which Gemini IV astronaut Ed White had done June 3, 1965, the same day Fosbury graduated from Medford High.

At the start of 1968, an inventory of the international high-jumping scene showed forty-five men on the planet who had cleared 7'0" or better. Forty-four used some variation of the straddle method. Only one did not. Therein lay an overlooked challenge Fosbury faced that nobody else did: at a convention of company men, he was self-employed.

Coaches of straddlers spoke a common language. They compared notes on a technique that, beyond minor differences, was the same for all. They shared a common history. They pored over film footage of Brumel, Thomas, and Otis Burrell in search of secrets to success. Meanwhile, Fosbury was alone in a wilderness of his own choosing—but alone nevertheless. True, Wagner had bought into Dick and the Flop; he did what he could to help. But, essentially, Dick was driving a vehicle with no owner's manual. Though Wagner had a few reels of film of Fosbury jumping, that's all he had: no background working with other jumpers who'd used the style, no books, no film, and nobody else with even a touch of context for whatever it was this kid was doing.

As a student, how can you learn when you literally invented the subject—and know more about it than anyone? How can you contrast yourself to the prototype when you *are* the prototype? How can you reach for the heavens when nobody of your ilk has ever been there? By mid-1968, other than a sprinkling of younger kids trying the Flop, there was nobody near Fosbury's level who knew what it felt like to fling himself over the bar backwards, much less be qualified to share insight that might help Fosbury jump higher. Every inch was an inch he'd need to find on his own.

By now, Fosbury understood he was on a solo journey. Wagner had taught Dick to be an athlete, to train, to work harder, but neither he, nor any other coach, could point to a blueprint and say "Here, modify your jump like this to improve." Fosbury *was* the blueprint. He was, in essence, Robin Lee Graham, who, in the summer of 1965, at the age of sixteen, set off to sail alone around the world. *National Geographic* chronicled much of his trip. If there was another knot or two of speed to be gained by adjusting the boat's sails just right, it was the sailor who had to figure it out. And if a storm de-masted the boat, nobody else was going to be around to help him find the safety of a port.

All of which was fine with Fosbury because he'd never known any other way to sail. When it came to even minor course changes, his answers came from the inside, not the outside. His job was to listen to the teacher—his own body. "Fosbury had this kinesthetic model, this blueprint in his mind," said sports psychologist and author Steven Ungerleider, "and even before he got to the pit, it was locked in, built into his muscle memory. And he had this curiosity about what might make him better. That's what took him to the next level. He was a great student—of himself."

In that respect, Fosbury was a little like the Wright Brothers and other such pioneers—visionaries who dream up, design, build, hone, and test their own inventions. Unlike for Orville and Wilbur however, Fosbury's Kitty Hawk was not a fixed place. Instead, he was involved in high-jump competitions spread across America. And when Fosbury took his show on the road, the unorthodox style caught the imagination of people in the same way the airplane barnstormers of the 1920s and '30s did with their aerial circuses.

"The difference," said John Mills, one of the Corvallis boys who watched Fosbury's career blossom at OSU, "is that Fosbury was a one-man circus."

"When you first see Fosbury high jump, particularly at heights approximating 7'0", you are filled with a feeling of disbelief," wrote staff writer Shav Glick of the *Los Angeles Times*. "It just can't be."

Here and there, people began wondering if the Fosbury-as-oddity image might someday shift. They began wondering if the emerging narrative wasn't about his being left out because he couldn't relate to the forty-four straddlers but about the straddlers being left out because they couldn't relate to him. Slowly, some started wondering if the Flop might not be more than a here-and-gone fad. "Fosbury is consistent and he's a crowd pleaser," said USC Coach Vern Wolfe. "I see merit in his technique . . . kids all over are mimicking him—and with good results. He may have something real revolutionary . . . maybe it's easier going over the bar backwards."

Such possibilities brought to mind the story of the mother whose little boy marched in the parade with dozens of well-tuned, experienced bands.

"How did you like the parade?" she was later asked.

"Oh, it was wonderful. But I couldn't help but notice that when it came to marching correctly, only one person kept in step—my little boy. The others were all off."

WHEN PIONEERS DARE to shoot for the sky, people's expectations soar as well. Inventors constantly work against an archenemy, "the unknown," the challenge of going where nobody has gone before. But the public is far too interested in results to appreciate what a painstaking process it might be—and far too interested in what the inventor is going to do next to appreciate where he or she has been. Which isn't to suggest that when the five people who watched the Wright Brothers' first plane take to the sky in 1903, they weren't appreciative of the first-ever feat. But once the craft was airborne their natural encouragement was: *Higher! Higher! Higher!*

In the same spirit, as Fosbury prepared for the NCAA championships in Berkeley June 13 to 15, NASA engineers were feverishly preparing to make good on the late President Kennedy's challenge to place a man on the moon by decade's end. "There were a lot of unknowns in the early days of spaceflight," said former astronaut Scott Carpenter, who completed an orbital mission in May 1962, three months after John Glenn. There were also a lot of high expectations. "We were considered guilty of being unable to fly in space and required to prove our innocence, counter to the American custom."

Similarly, if Fosbury had proven he could fly, he was, thus far, considered guilty of being unable to fly "in space." Wins in Oakland, Seattle, and New York were noteworthy. A couple of conference championships looked good. But "space" for athletes such as Fosbury meant only one thing: the Olympic Games. Nothing else validated track and field athletes so assuredly.

If the Cold War had climaxed in the Cuban Missile Crisis in 1962, the US and the Soviet Union had spent much of the decade locked in the race for space, specifically in an attempt to place a man on the moon. The international rivalry also spilled over to track and field. US-Soviet dual meets were legendary showdowns, though, as of late, marked by good sportsmanship. In 1962, during what the *San Francisco Examiner* called "the greatest track meet of all time," Soviet high jumper Valeriy Brumel upped his world record to 7'5". As the bar quivered— he'd brushed it—and Brumel raised his arms in triumph, some 80,000 fans erupted into a standing ovation that lasted more than five minutes. "I was filled with inexpressible joy," he said.

After his 1965 motorcycle accident, Brumel had courageously tried to return to high-jumping at a world level, but the injuries proved insurmountable. He would not be making the Soviet team for Mexico City. The Olympic high-jump competition, *Track & Field News* reported, was considered to be wide open, though another US-Soviet faceoff was likely. Brumel's heir apparent, Valentin Gavrilov, had first seen the Flop in Seattle back in January when Dick had beaten him, 7'1" to 6'10". Gavrilov only shook his head about the style. "It is impossible," he said. "It cannot be done."

FOSBURY LOVED THE setting of the 1968 NCAA Outdoor Track and Field Championships. Berkeley's Edwards Stadium at the University of California was backdropped by the beautiful Berkeley Hills. And he loved big meets like this one; the more adrenaline coursing through his veins, the higher he jumped.

The meet featured the strongest group of college jumpers ever assembled, all of whom knew that more was on the line than an individual title and points for their school in the team competition: the top six placers in each category would qualify for the Olympic Trials. Fosbury greeted some of the competition, among them Cal's Clarence Johnson and Stanford's Peter Boyce, an Australian.

By now, the official's rules explanations were the equivalent of flight attendants offering their obligatory safety talk. In Berkeley, on this sun-splashed day, it was the usual: Any ties would be settled by a "count back" on the *fewest misses at the last height cleared*. In this respect, missing a height would be like bad debt—the more recent it was, the more trouble the jumper would be in, but once he proved himself responsible—cleared a height—the bank would forgive the earlier miscues. The exception? If jumpers were still tied after comparing *fewest misses at the last height cleared*, the next tiebreaker would be *fewest misses overall*—so distant history would come back into play. If, after those two comparisons, competitors were still tied, a "jump-off" would be held to determine the top six finishers.

Fosbury had finished fifth the previous year in the NCAA meet—and was coming off wins in the NCAA Indoor Championships and the Pac-8 championships—so he wasn't expected to have much trouble qualifying for the Trials. Like a seasoned pianist, he went up the scale flawlessly: 6'8", 6'10", 7'0", and 7'1". The bar went to 7'2¼", which would be a new personal best and break the meet record of 7'2" set in 1961 by Thomas, the former Boston University student. Fosbury cleared it to win the competition.

Dick's day was efficiency personified: Five jumps. Five makes. One national individual championship. And a spot in the late-June Olympic Trials in Los Angeles. His 7'2¼" was the fourth-best jump in US history and eleventh-best in the world. Whether it was also a victory for the counterculture generation, some saw it as such. "How the crowd savored it," wrote the *San Francisco Examiner*, "when Oregon State's Dick Fosbury made the conservatives swallow hard by using his colorful 'Fosbury Flop' to win . . . ."

Afterward, Fosbury ran into Sue Lowery, a Medford High classmate who was living in the Bay Area and had come to see Dick jump. As often happens in such cases, the two were comparing notes of the whereabouts of classmates. Suddenly, her sunny disposition darkened.

"Did you hear about Fred?" she asked.

"Graten? No, what?"

She looked away, then back. "Died," she said, "in Vietnam."

"No way," said Fosbury. "When? How?"

"April. Helicopter crash."

Dick stared off in the distance for a moment. Later, on the team's trip back to Corvallis, the thought of being the NCAA champion would settle in Dick's mind with warm satisfaction when news of Graten scared it off like a vulture coming for its prey. Fosbury's GPA had not only dipped below 2.0, but he'd recently learned he'd flunked out of OSU's engineering program. That gnawed at Dick for a number of reasons: it was a sign of failure that, frankly, embarrassed him. It doomed his chances of becoming something he really wanted to be—a civil engineer. And his student deferment was gone. There was no longer anyplace to hide from the draft.

Unless he were to be passed up because of his back, Fosbury realized he might be the next Fred Graten. As the 6 o'clock news was reminding Americans each night, seventy men were dying each day in Vietnam. If Graten, reasoned Fosbury, why not me?

The letter arrived a few days later at his College Inn mailbox. "Statement of Acceptability," it said across the top. "Fosbury, Richard Douglas."

Below, two statements followed tiny boxes, whichever one was checked certain to affect his life for better or worse. "The qualifications of the registrant have been considered in accordance with the current regulations governing acceptance of selective service registration and he was on this date:

"1. Found fully acceptable for induction into the armed forces."

"2. Found not acceptable for induction under current standards."

The second box was checked. Dick sunk into the couch in relief; for six months, he'd felt as if a shadow had been following him everywhere he went. Now it was gone.

The document listed no reason for his rejection. Perhaps his compressed vertebrae was, indeed, the result of that day with the chain saw he spent on the youth work crew. To think otherwise was to believe that the Fosbury Flop, which had required Dick to repeatedly land on his back on sawdust or wood chips, had not only saved him from his boyhood blues, but perhaps from going to war.

Chapter 15

Bill Bowerman was designed . . . to process. The defining act of his life was preparation, not completion.

—Barbara Bowerman

WHEN CONFRONTED WITH the challenge of preparing track and field athletes to compete at 7,350 feet in Mexico City, the US Olympic Committee didn't know what to expect—nor, initially, what to do. Since World War II, the Summer Olympic Games had always been conducted at essentially sea-level cities: London, 1948; Helsinki, 1952; Melbourne, 1956; Rome, 1960; and Tokyo, 1964. Now athletes would be expected to perform well at mile-and-a-half altitudes, a particularly daunting prospect for distance runners who need more oxygen than, say, high jumpers.

"Some will die at Mexico City," warned the headline above a column by British journalist Chris Brasher.

To prepare for a venue that would have 25 percent less oxygen than at sea level, the Soviets planned to train in the mountains. The French had an opulent facility 6,070 feet atop the Pyrenees. What could the US do to prepare for an Olympics venue like no other? When the USOC met to discuss preparations for Mexico City, the conversation quickly turned to altitude and, soon thereafter, to a man who, most agreed, would be perfect for coordinating such training: University of Oregon coach Bill Bowerman, the former Medford High student, athlete, and coach.

Bowerman's influence already had Eugene on its way to becoming known as "Track Town USA." He had been the catalyst for the early-'60s jogging craze in the US. He had led Oregon to NCAA track and field championships in 1964, 1965, and 1967, and had coached nearly a dozen Olympic athletes. What's more, pointed out some committee members, hadn't Bill been part of that 10th Mountain Division in World War II? *Hell, he has to know a thing or two about operating at altitude, right?*

There was little time or money to test, decide on, and implement whatever plan was chosen. But, to the surprise of nobody, the adventurous Bowerman accepted the committee's challenge to prepare America's men's track and field team for Mexico City.

Though of two far-different generations, Bowerman and Fosbury had much in common besides Medford roots. Like Fosbury, Bowerman had lost a brother. Bill's twin, at age two, had been killed in a gruesome elevator accident. Like Fosbury, Bowerman's parents later divorced. And like Fosbury, Bowerman was a track and field innovator, forever trying to develop a lighter racing shoe, a new kind of track surface, or a covered long-jump area beneath the Hayward Field stands.

Though serious about producing great track and field men—and highly respected—he was, in a sense, track and field's "nutty professor." Wade Bell, a half-miler for Oregon at the time, remembers first meeting Bowerman on the Oregon track. The coach was standing beside a cement mixer full of rubber asphalt being used to resurface a long-jump runway. "He had holes burned in his overalls and his boots were smoking," remembered Bell in Moore's *Bowerman and the Men of Oregon*. When the two shook hands, Bell winced; his hand, thanks to Bowerman's, was covered with hot tar.

Bowerman wasted no time when it came to preparation for Mexico City. "First thing he did was buttonhole a geology professor at Oregon," said Bell. "He wanted to know everything there was to know about Mexico City: altitude, climate, pollen—you name it. Preferably, by tomorrow morning. Then he started looking for training sites."

After considering a handful, Bowerman favored South Lake Tahoe, California, right on the Nevada line. A purist, he didn't like that, at 6,329 feet, it was still about a thousand feet below Mexico City, but when he was taken into the High Sierras and shown the partially forested parking lot of a small, defunct ski area, his eyes widened. In the end, Bowerman recommended—and quickly got the committee's green light for—holding a six-week training camp capped by a Trials at a place called Echo Summit. It was almost the only flat spot in the area, a shelf chiseled into the mountains just off Highway 50, about ten miles west of South Lake Tahoe, in the El Dorado National Forest.

Beyond the highway, which snaked its way from Tahoe to Sacramento, wilderness dominated the landscape, frequented mainly by bear, deer, and intrepid hikers testing themselves on the soon-to-be-opened Pacific Crest Trail, which wound 2,650 miles from Mexico to Canada—and was but a javelin heave from the track. At 7,377 feet, the track would be twenty-seven feet higher than Mexico City's.

The South Lake Tahoe site was the perfect marriage of an Olympic Trials needing a place and a place needing something like the Olympic Trials. Having only incorporated in 1965, South Lake Tahoe (pop. 22,500) was looking for ways to promote its recreational opportunities—and the legal gambling offered just across the border, in Stateline, Nevada. A casino, Harrah's Tahoe, chipped in some financial support. That, along with revenue from a five-cent motel tax, would allow Tahoe officials to pay $260,000 for track- and accompanying field-event setups at Echo Summit. Housing and feeding nearly 200 athletes for six weeks—if only in trailers, cabins, and two-bit motels—was a tab to be picked up by the USOC, on whose door corporations, in 1968, weren't knocking to make seven-digit donations. From where, some wondered, was the money going to come?

That wasn't Bowerman's responsibility. His task, as he saw it, was to replicate the same altitude and conditions of Mexico City. To that end, he planned to mirror the Mexico City event schedule—right down to qualifying heats and flights for the high-altitude Trials. Instead of a weekend meet as in the past, the US would stretch the Trials over eight days, just like the Games themselves.

"Bowerman was a competitive son of a gun, and it bothered him that our track teams hadn't done better in Tokyo in '64," said Bell. Never mind that the US had won twenty-two medals, ten of them gold; Bowerman still remembered some distance runners woefully out of shape because, after making the team in a two-tiered trials, coaches hadn't held athletes accountable for pre-Olympics workouts. Tahoe,

Bowerman figured, would fix that—and because it was ostensibly "voluntary," it skirted any violation of IOC regulations.

Beyond his competitiveness—he constantly analyzed everything that might come between an athlete and victory—Bowerman believed strongly in camaraderie. At Oregon, his teams worked together, ate together, socialized together, and, in some cases, lived together. He believed in a team ethic, which would certainly be fostered by the young men gathering for six weeks at Echo Summit. Shortly before the high-altitude camp was to open, Barbara Bowerman accompanied her husband to the Sierra site.

"I wondered if he knew how much responsibility he had assumed," she told Moore in *Bowerman and the Men of Oregon*. "He had huge expectations and many doubts from the Olympic Committee, not to mention other critics."

"It was a huge undertaking," said Bell. The effort was like setting up a temporary base camp for a military operation in a remote spot with few amenities. "It wasn't like we were going to a hotel in the city. We were going to the mountains and putting in our own temporary facility to do it."

Along with choosing a site, Bowerman had gone to great lengths to make sure the track itself and the field-event setups were top-notch, similar to what the athletes would find at Mexico City. As at the Olympic site, the high-jump and pole-vault pits would be the gold standard—Don Gordon's Port-a-Pits. But one small difference separated the two track and field venues: in Mexico City's 80,000-seat stadium, more than a hundred towering Ponderosa pines would not reach skyward from inside the oval, nor would the high-jump pit and long-jump runway be flanked by granite boulders the size of Volkswagen bugs. Echo Summit was not a track and field facility back-dropped by a forest. This was a facility *within* a forest, a merger so seamless that one could hardly tell where one began and the other ended.

Los Angeles, from June 29 to 30, was designated as the first of a two-tiered Trial; Echo Summit's Trials would follow September 6 to 16. With the sites chosen, all the USOC needed to do now was select a team. But how hard could that be?

Chapter 16

Like all valuable commodities, truth is often counterfeited.

—*James Cardinal Gibbons*

DICK FOSBURY'S STYLE, naturally, lent itself to humor. "Fosbury goes over the bar like a guy pushed out of a 30-story window or like a reluctant parachutist out of a plane's hatch," wrote Jim Murray of the *Los Angeles Times*. "The crowds were laughing so hard they didn't notice he won." But after his NCAA championships and his qualifying for the Olympic Trials, more people were considering the Flop with renewed seriousness. In particular, astute track and field followers began wondering something for the first time: maybe it wasn't only about The Flop. Maybe it was about the kid using it.

The same jumper who'd just set an NCAA meet record at 7'2¼" had, earlier in the outdoor season, failed to reach 7'0" in four straight dual meets. In a rare home meet, he'd lost to Cal's Clarence Johnson, a non-placer in the NCAA meet. In short, he'd had a very so-so spring. But the bigger the meet, the better he performed. On the national stage, during the winter indoor season, Fosbury had cleared 7'0" five times—more than anyone else in the world at the time—and won all but two events. Then, after his spring slump, he'd successfully defended his Pac-8 title by going 7'0" to beat, on fewer misses, the same Johnson who'd defeated him in Corvallis, before capping the outdoor season with the NCAA championship.

It was becoming a Fosbury trait: finding a way to win when he *had to*, even if it was by the slimmest of margins. If he broke a record—or, as in Oakland, when he first cleared 7'0"—he rarely would go higher.

At times, he wouldn't even make an attempt. The pessimist would use such evidence to suggest Fosbury was a just-get-by guy, the optimist to suggest he was a jumper who, when big chips were on the table, found a way to win.

Still, only eight months earlier Fosbury had been ranked, among the world's high jumpers, in a twelve-way tie for 50th. How had he gotten here, to this place where some thought he could represent the US in the Olympics Games in Mexico City come October?

It wasn't necessarily his pedigree. His father was a solid half-miler and end on his high school football team, though no star. True, Fosbury was tall at 6'4", but didn't have the exceptional "hops" of, say, teammate Radetich.

It wasn't necessarily his athleticism. "Poor ol' Dick, he'd hate me for saying this, but it doesn't require an awful lot of ability," said Wagner of the Flop. "And I had a discus thrower who had a better jump-reach than him." The Soviets' Brumel once won a bet by touching a basketball hoop with his foot—five times in a row. Fosbury once *lost* a bet by failing to clear a stuffed chair in OSU's Theta Chi fraternity—and broke his hand in the process.

It wasn't necessarily some Soviet-centric work ethic. Though Fosbury worked harder than many gave him credit for, neither was he a glutton for daily punishment. "He was not a hard trainer," said McNeil, the OSU assistant coach at the time.

As the June 29 to 30 Olympic Trials in LA approached, the irony was that for all the attention Fosbury's newfangled style got—the visible stuff—what was getting him to the top was the invisible stuff: the mind, the will, the competitive spirit. Fosbury's newfound greatness was like a ventriloquism act. The magic wasn't about the real guy *or* the dummy, but about their collective effect to make the impossible, *possible*.

"What made Fosbury different from so many other athletes, even really good athletes, was his ability to really concentrate and mentally imagine what he wanted to do," said McNeil. "He had the ability to focus all his energy into each jump. Radetich was a much better physical jumper than Fosbury, but Foz had the ability to put everything he had—*everything*—into those jumps."

Athletes, of course, have exploited the mental side of their pursuits since the original Olympic Games were first held in 776 BC. But Fosbury was literally taking it to new heights in his lengthy psyche-up before each jump. "I used to watch him rocking back and forth and think: *What the hell is he thinking about?*" said Sweet. "Then I'd think back to how he was doing the same thing at Medford High, standing out there in our lane of the track, and when we ran by it was like we weren't even there. Like his single-mindedness was so strong he didn't even notice. He could disassociate as if in a Zen moment."

Ungerleider, who has studied more than one thousand athletes over a forty-year period, said Fosbury was a man ahead of his times. "Ninety-five percent of his success was his mental preparation," he said. "Remember, in those days no coach was saying, 'Go visualize yourself succeeding.' You'll find similarities in one-tenth of one percent of athletes at that 'locked-in' level, but Dick had a curiosity that took him to the next level."

He did not dream of greatness, nor prepare for it. He wasn't Ernie Shelton, making a mark seven feet up on his bedroom wall, nor John Thomas, circling the day of the Olympic high-jump event ten months in advance. "I don't think he was ever thinking, *Someday I could win a gold medal*," said Sweet. "Never. He always stayed in that one little moment."

To the crowd, Fosbury's clenched fists and rocking made him look like a frightened five-year-old before his first roller-coaster ride. But that was only the outward manifestation of inward preparation that, though not as concisely labeled back then, contained three parts.

First, the *corrective*. Fosbury would think: *What, if anything, needs fixing from my previous jump?* Often, for example, it was a reminder not to drift into the bar and, instead, to jump vertically, not horizontally.

Second, the *connective*. Once he'd determined what needed to be fixed on this coming jump, he would connect that action to the particular part of the body responsible for making that happen, to *feel* it. To think that thought—*more pronounced arch,* for example—would help the body rehearse, or memorize, what it needed to do.

And, finally, the *disconnective*. In the final few seconds before the jump, he wanted nothing more on his mind regarding the past. All of his energy needed to feed his *now*. "I never started forward on my approach," he said, "until I was absolutely convinced I was going over that bar."

The rocking was to Fosbury's high jump what a waggle is to a golfer's swing—gently short-swinging the club over and behind the ball before letting 'er rip. If he might have looked tense, *doing something physical* relaxed his body for the internal preparation, as if he were mentally pulling back the rubber strip of a slingshot for a release of focused power.

Early on, Fosbury had learned to ride positive and negative vibes like the wind. If the crowd was behind him and he was jumping well, he channeled that stimuli into jump-high energy. If people were laughing at him or expressing doubt about his abilities, he did the same thing. Brill, the Canadian jumper who had developed her own backward style, struggled with the latter—at least early on in her career. Once, in a huge meet, the laughter that emanated from the crowd drained her of every ounce of confidence she'd had. She could hardly jump.

The only thing that drained Fosbury was when nothing much was on the line. He abhorred jumping in practice. And it wasn't uncommon for him to lose a dual meet. That's because quietly, over the years, he'd developed another element to his "game": an intense competitiveness that belied his low-key, almost shy, nature. Honed in his years competing against Steve Davis, his competitive spirit was never something he expressed outwardly. It was never haughty, revenge-oriented, or rude. But make no mistake: Fosbury loved to win—and great competition in Kelly and Radetich at OSU only furthered the iron-sharpening-iron experience he had with Davis in high school.

He was a self-admitted "nervous" jumper. "Watching the guy rock back and forth, he could drive some people nuts," said Caruthers, who was just the opposite. But like a hydro dam can turn river water into electricity, Fosbury could turn nervous energy into height.

Where was such energy rooted? In a place, Medford, where young men were raised by competitive coaches in a competitive system surrounded by a competitive community? In a will that he forged himself after losing a brother? Regardless of where it began, by the summer of 1968 some were intrigued about where it all might lead.

With the Mexico City Games only four months away, there was talk that this could be the finest men's track and field team the US had ever entered in the Olympics—if, of course, a boycott by black athletes didn't dilute the squad. And if Mexico itself, teetering on violence as students rallied against what they saw as government oppression, didn't explode before, or during, the October Games, and the event be canceled.

Whether the US could end the Soviets' high-jump domination was another matter. Thomas, who had won silver in Tokyo, had retired. Six-foot-seven-inch John Rambo, who had won bronze in Tokyo, was having a sub-par 1968. The US's best bet looked to be Caruthers, who had finished eighth in Tokyo in 1964 and was ranked No. 1 in the world in *T&F News*' January 1968 rankings. But Fosbury, with a best of 7'2¼", was within a quarter-inch of Caruthers's best.

"Fosbury, of course, has emerged as a strong candidate to make the United States Olympic team," wrote the *Christian Science Monitor*'s Cliff Gewecke. "If he does, the 'Fosbury Flop' might extend worldwide. And who's to stop a world revolution?"

THE CHALLENGE OF choosing the 1968 men's US Olympic track and field team was fraught with obstacles from the beginning. Black athletes were ratcheting up their boycott rhetoric; 400-meter runner Lee Evans warned sprint coach Stan Wright, who was black but opposed the boycott, *not* to come to the Los Angeles Trials because he'd learned Wright's name was on a "hit list." Athletes here and there were starting to question coaches as Jack Scott had championed in his *T&F News* essay. And the US, because of concerns about its distance runners having to run in the thin air of Mexico City, was placing a track and field facility 7,377 feet up in the Sierra Nevada, with plans to have 200 athletes train there for six weeks—despite having little money.

In the end, though, none of these fouled the process. What *did* was the USOC's unwillingness to be decisive in how the team was to be chosen, unwillingness to stick to its original plan, and unwillingness to be up front with the athletes it served.

It's clear that the committee decided to hold two meets to choose America's 1968 Olympic track and field team: one in Los Angeles June 29 to 30 and one at Echo Summit, above South Lake Tahoe, September

6 to 16. It's less clear, in hindsight, what the purpose of each meet was. (Marathoners and walkers were to be chosen at their own trials in Alamosa, Colorado.)

Athletes were led to believe that, as with the New York-LA Trials of 1964, the winners from the first Trial in LA and the second- and third-place finishers from the second Trial in Tahoe would earn spots on the team. "The Olympic Committee had stated that winners in LA would be on the team," said Bill Clark, a twenty-four-year-old Marine who was running the 10,000 meters. "It was cut-and-dried." The LA meet was called the "Olympic *Trials.*" The first two words inside the program were "Final Trials." And fans in LA were to be charged $6 a day, the committee knowing it needed a good turnout to help subsidize costs for the high-altitude camp. Nobody, of course, would pay a dime to watch what was essentially a workout, thus the win-and-you're-in carrot.

However, after Saturday's first day of competition—Fosbury was to jump Sunday—Hilmer Lodge, chairman of the USOC's track and field committee, backed off the winners-go edict. In emphasizing the importance of the athletes being altitude-ready for Mexico City, he told the *Los Angeles Times*: "Even the winner here [in LA] will not necessarily go to Mexico City. The Olympic Committee will meet Sunday night and determine the number of athletes in each event to invite to the high-altitude training."

Dick Fosbury did not read the Sunday *Los Angeles Times.* That afternoon, he arrived at Memorial Coliseum with a single thought in mind: *win and you're in. Track & Field News* had dubbed him the favorite, and he was anxious to make them look smart.

At Memorial Coliseum, tension over a possible black Olympic boycott hung in the air like smog for the two-day meet. Pro-boycott signs bobbed from the stands. In the 200-meter race, a squabble broke out after some people's perception that Tommie Smith had unfairly drawn the less-than-optimal outside lane.

Fosbury reminded himself to stay focused. The competition—by far the toughest Dick had ever faced—involved twenty-three other jumpers, eleven of whom had gone 7'0" or higher: twelve fellow collegiate jumpers, including teammate Radetich; nine jumpers affiliated with track and field clubs; one military representative, 7'0" foot-jumper

Lew Hoyt, of the Marines; and a seventeen-year-old Compton High phenomenon, Reynaldo Brown, who had just finished his junior year of high school only a few miles away. Brown had already cleared 7'¾", far higher than the 6'3½" Dick had managed at the same age.

As sprint coach Wright walked around the Coliseum with what appeared to be two body guards, six jumpers had cleared 7'0", including Fosbury. "The bar goes to seven feet, one inch," said the official.

When it was his turn, Fosbury readied himself at his mark, then focused on the bar, beyond which a blue Don Gordon Port-a-Pit awaited. Fosbury began his typical rocking motion, shaking his fingers, eyes fixed on the bar. A murmur swept through the crowd and got louder as more of the roughly 25,654 fans started locking into his lengthy preparation. Fosbury heard it and channeled it into mental energy. *Win and you're in.* The rocking got faster, the crowd louder. Fosbury readied to bolt for the—

"Foul!"

Fosbury wilted in disbelief. *What?*

"Time violation," said a judge as he walked out onto the apron. "Over the two-minute limit."

In his entire career, Fosbury had never been called for a time violation. The crowd booed its displeasure. Dick stood there, disbelieving. How could he have gone his entire career without a foul and get one in the most important competition of his life? Suddenly, his margin of error had melted by a third. Two misses and his Olympic hopes might die.

The five other jumpers all tried their first attempt; none was successful.

"Fosbury up," said the judge.

Dick took his mark, exhaled, locked in. *Think ahead, not behind.* This jump would be for the judge. *Prove yourself.* Up. Over. He rocked, then, *boom*, raced for the bar. Gather. Plant. Jump. Arch. *Over!*

"The crowd went wild with joy," said *T&F News.* Fosbury was "one of the most popular athletes on the field." It was too early to celebrate, but when the five others all failed twice more, Dick looked skyward in satisfaction, two words coming to mind: *Mexico City.*

He did a few interviews, was officially invited to the Echo Summit camp to begin in two weeks, and headed for the airport pumped to his core. Meanwhile, back at the Coliseum, Lodge again appeared at a hastily called—and awkward—press conference. And again back-pedaled on the win-and-you're-in setup.

"The winner of each event at Los Angeles will be considered as having made the team—provided he can demonstrate his excellence at high-altitude training to the satisfaction of the committee," Lodge said.

The timing of this announcement was interesting, to say the least. Though Lodge had, indeed, told the *Times* Saturday night about no guarantees for winners, it wasn't until the day's events were over—until the USOC had pocketed ticket and concession money from 25,654 fans—that he had dispensed the news: what had been billed as part one of the two-part Olympic Trials had really been no part at all.

The *Oregon Journal's* Carl Cluff called the meet nothing but a "shakedown" for South Lake Tahoe. "I felt hoodwinked," said Clark, who won the 10,000 meters in LA but later heard it might not be a guarantee of going to Mexico City. "You grow up dreaming of being an Olympian and then meet the criteria to do so, only to be told you're not on the team."

After crossing the finish line in exhaustion after twenty-five laps, he exalted in the idea that all his years of long-distance training had finally paid off; he was going to represent his country in the Olympics. He says he was told, point blank, that winners were going to Mexico City. "Then that became: *you're not on the team unless you show an ability to compete at altitude.*" What exactly did that nebulous phrase mean? Nobody was saying.

"[The meet] served only to eliminate some athletes from the Echo Summit meeting and was a poorly organized affair," wrote Richard Hymans in *The History of the U.S. Olympic Trials.* "The crowd [was] dissatisfied after conflicting announcements were made as to whether winners were automatic Olympic qualifiers (they weren't), and the possibility of an Olympic boycott by black athletes led to shouting matches between athletes, officials, and the press."

Hymans said the USOC published no guidelines prior to the two-day meet. During the meet, an announcer stated that "All winners

Shortly before tragedy struck, the Fosbury family during a break at a 1961 square-dance
event: l to r, Greg, Helen, Gail, Dick, and Doug.
(Dick Fosbury collection)

Dick in eighth grade at age fourteen, complete with a
little butch-wax in the hair.
(Dick Fosbury collection)

(Left) Don Gordon's foam pits, here tested by diving champ Joe Gerlach, emerged, serendipitously, just as Fosbury came out with his Flop.

(Courtesy, JoAnne Gordon)

(Above) When Dick cleared 6'3½" in Grants Pass as a junior in 1964, he not only won for the first time but set a school record.

(Medford Mail Tribune)

Dick's second-place finish in state Class A-1 meet at OSU's Bell Field in Corvallis in 1965 got fans' full attention. Few looked away when he jumped.

(The Register-Guard)

Though OSU Coach Berny Wagner was slow to warm up to the Flop, Dick won him over in the spring of his sophomore year—shortly after Wagner threatened to pull Dick's scholarship.
(OSU Special Collections and Archives Research Center, Corvallis)

What rocketed Fosbury to stardom wasn't only the Flop technique, but an intensity as Dick mentally locked in to success—as in this meet at OSU's Bell Field.
(OSU Special Collections and Archives Research Center, Corvallis)

A February 1968 *Track & Field News* cover introduced Fosbury and his 7-foot Flop to the world, much to the chagrin of Ed Caruthers (left) and a few other high jumpers he beat in Oakland in January 1968.
(Courtesy, Track & Field News*)*

In August 1968, Dick's mother, Helen, visited the high-altitude training camp at Echo Summit, joining her son and steeplechaser Mike Manley.
(Dick Fosbury collection)

A swim to Fannette Island in Lake Tahoe's Emerald Bay nearly ended Dick's Olympic quest prematurely.
(Bob Welch)

Surrounded by grass, trees, and boulders, the high-jump setup at Echo Summit almost had the feel of a high-mountain golf course.
(Courtesy Wade Bell)

On a Don Gordon Port-a-Pit bookended by towering pines, Fosbury was down to his final jump to make the Olympic Team at Echo Summit.

(Associated Press)

When the historic high-jump competition at Echo Summit ended, ABC's Jim McKay interviewed the three who won spots to the Olympics: (left to right) Reynaldo Brown, Dick Fosbury, and Ed Caruthers. Behind them: the canvas training tent.

(Courtesy, Track & Field News)

(Left) Fosbury's last-jump clearance of 7'4¼" in Mexico City left him beaming, even if, technically, he hadn't secured the gold medal yet.
(Associated Press)

(Above) Flanked by silver medalist Caruthers, left, and bronze medalist Gavrilov of the Soviet Union, Fosbury thrust a fist in the air while on the Olympic podium after receiving his gold medal.
(Associated Press)

In Mexico City, when US Olympic sprinters Tommie Smith, center, and John Carlos lifted gloved hands skyward in racial protest, Fosbury hadn't reacted with any particular emotion. Only later would he realize their courage had helped him find his more noble self—and make a stand of his own. Australian silver medalist Peter Norman is at left.
(Associated Press)

In Medford, the city threw a ticker-tape parade for their hometown hero.

(Associated Press)

Fosbury Appears In Support Of Stand Of Black Students

In February 1969, when nearly all OSU athletes supported football coach Dee Andros in a race-related controversy, Fosbury raised eyebrows when he stood in support of black athlete Fred Milton.

(Medford Mail Tribune)

On September 16, 2017, exactly forty-nine years since winning an Olympic berth, Fosbury returned to Echo Summit and, with help from a photo on a laptop, found the spot he'd started his high-jump approach.

(Bob Welch)

would make the Olympic team . . . ." However, shortly thereafter he added a hastily prepared amendment that each winner would go ". . . provided he demonstrated his competitive excellence in the finals to the satisfaction of the track and field committee . . ." and, after another pause, yet another amendment: ". . . and if he demonstrates his ability to perform at altitude."

Fiery Wade Bell of Oregon had barely taken his spikes off after winning the 800 meters when he caught wind of the USOC's new caveat. "I don't like the idea that even though I won in LA, I didn't clinch a position on the team," he told reporters.

Almost five decades later, he was sticking to his story. "We didn't select a team, or even part of a team, in LA. We sold tickets to make money."

Lodge himself had publicly declared the financial need for the meet. "Without this meet we would have been strapped for funds," he told the *Fresno Bee* in early July. Based on ticket prices and not counting concession sales, the two-day meet brought in about $300,000, or $2.25 million in 2018 dollars.

About ten athletes in each event were invited to Tahoe. Some believed the huge number had less to do with making sure guys could perform well at high altitude than with making sure the US had enough competitive white athletes should the black athletes boycott. At any rate, Fosbury, asleep on a plane headed back to Oregon, had heard nothing of the caveat suggesting winners either weren't, or might not be, locks. Once home, he busied himself in seeing family and friends, packed for Echo Summit, and worked out, all the time convinced that he was an Olympian.

Fosbury did not read *The Oregonian* story that said, "All the Los Angeles confrontation provided was a showpiece. It was literally a workout. But the 50,000-plus fans put a piece of change in the USOC coffers and it's going to take a bundle to finance the Tahoe production. What the committee really needed was charity . . . and was too proud to ask."

Fosbury did not read the questions from 5,000-meter winner Tracy Smith, Dick's OSU teammate, who asked, "What is the use of finishing first when sixth will get you in the same place? What if I finish fourth in September?" Nor did he read the *Philadelphia Inquirer* in which columnist Frank Dolson pressed Lodge about exactly that.

"What if a man wins here in Los Angeles and finished fourth or fifth in Lake Tahoe?"

"I can't answer that question," said Lodge. "I would say anything is possible."

The latter would prove to be truer than anything else he or the committee had said. Anything was possible—and Echo Summit, unfortunately, would prove it.

Chapter 17

*. . . It was the season of Light, it was the season of Darkness, it was the
spring of hope, it was the winter of despair, we had everything before us,
we had nothing before us . . . .*

—*Charles Dickens,* A Tale of Two Cities

IN THE DARKNESS of the drive, Steppenwolf's "Born to Be Wild"
pounded from the radio as Dick Fosbury guided his blue-and-white
Chevy II south on Interstate 5, out of Oregon and into California. It
was early evening hours on July 14, 1968, and life was good—good,
that is, if you could forget about, or at least temporarily disconnect
from, the haunting photo of Bobby Kennedy lying near death on a
hotel pantry floor; the Memphis police officer taking a nightstick to a
young black man as if chopping wood; and the wounded US soldier in
Vietnam with his arms wrapped around the necks of two buddies as a
fellow soldier raises his arms to the heavens, either to guide in an evacu-
ation helicopter or to cry out to God.

Author William Manchester called 1968 "the year everything went
wrong." Assassinations. War. Bitter protests. Racial tensions. All happened, all served up on the nightly news, now often in living color. And
yet, for Fosbury, 1968 was the year everything was going right. He'd
found out a few weeks before, in mid-June, that he wasn't going to
be drafted, apparently—and ironically—because of an unsound back.
He'd emerged as one of the top high jumpers in the world. And he'd
placed first at the Trials in Los Angeles and was looking forward to the
Olympics. It wasn't an insensitivity to the pain of others that led Dick
to appreciate the good fortune of his own. Simply put, he felt blessed.

"Dick Fosbury," wrote *Track & Field News'* Jon Hendershott in the July issue, "has turned high jumping upside down."

Fosbury was headed to South Lake Tahoe, California, for six weeks of high-altitude training capped by an Olympic Trials that would be nothing but a workout for him. Two hundred athletes would be arriving from all over the country, each having finished in the top ten in Los Angeles—or been granted a waiver because of injury or some other reason.

Fosbury knew little about this training camp that the USOC had placed in the High Sierra: only that it was chosen largely because its elevation, 7,377 feet, replicated that of Mexico City. And that a Tartan track—and field-event setups—had been plopped down in the middle of some forest. And that it was only twenty minutes from Stateline, Nevada, where gambling casinos beckoned. Fosbury might have looked sixteen, but Dick would be more than happy to provide a driver's license that showed that, as of March 6, he was, indeed, twenty-one.

WHEN FOSBURY ARRIVED and first saw the Echo Summit track, a smile morphed into laughter. *Oh. My. Gosh.* It was even cooler than the cover photo on the July issue of *Track & Field News* suggested. More than a hundred ponderosa pines reached skyward from inside the oval. Field-event runways and aprons gave way to fresh-mowed grass and boulders made of granite.

Inside the oval, Don Gordon's Port-a-Pits, brand new, awaited high jumpers (red) and pole-vaulters (blue). Javelin throwers would launch their spears from deep down a hallway of evergreens. Tree trunks on the inside of the track were so close to the first lane that runners could almost reach out and touch them. "Echo Summit," said Fosbury, "was a magical place, a fantasy."

Like his Flop style, it was an extension of the imagination, an innovative leap into something that had never been done before, an example of what can happen when one isn't tethered by "we've-never-done-it-this-way" thinking. "It was sort of like Mt. Olympus," said decathlete Bill Toomey. "You could imagine Zeus looking down on that track, telling the gods and goddesses, 'This is the way I imagined it.'"

Nobody had used chain saws and bulldozers to level a forest and put in a track. Instead, Bowerman had taken what the land and the US Forest Service offered—a tiny ski operation's tree-studded parking lot—and wrapped a track around it: six lanes wide, eight lanes down the homestretch, with, of course, the extension for sprinters and hurdlers. Bowerman and the USOC had worked closely to honor the US Forest Service's edict that the track—later to be donated to a South Lake Tahoe intermediate school—do little to alter the ecosystem. The maker of the Tartan track, 3M, had even developed a releasing agent that made for a simple setup and takedown procedure.

Distance runners weren't thrilled that, beyond the track, the only flat spots to run were ten miles down at South Lake Tahoe, often on a golf course. Beyond that, the men had few complaints.

"It was perfect," said Radetich. "Simply perfect. So quiet that, instead of cars and stuff, you could only hear your heartbeat."

Most of the athletes stayed in a cluster of trailers—the "athletes' village"—about four miles down the highway. Meals were offered three times a day at a dining facility adjacent to the trailers. Any pertinent news might be thumb-tacked to the door of the motel's dining room-turned-cafeteria. Married athletes and their families were provided hotel and motel rooms in Tahoe, about fifteen minutes down from Echo Summit. Shuttle busses moved athletes around.

Fosbury checked in, found his trailer, and met up with his roommate and teammate, Radetich. In the days to come, the two would join the other nine jumpers for workouts, sometimes even doing some light running with non-jumpers. "I've never forgotten doing strides with Fosbury at Echo Summit," said Roscoe Divine, a 1,500-meter runner from Oregon, which, of course, was Oregon State's archrival. "Great guy."

Sprinter Tommie Smith had been intrigued by Fosbury since hearing of him and found him to be a light-hearted, upbeat presence at Echo Summit. "Honest, generous, fun. That was Dick. Always laughing."

Among other things, Fosbury was confident enough to compete with the best jumpers in the world but humble enough to take a job at a South Lake Tahoe burger joint to make money. A number of athletes worked part-time while training at altitude. Sprinter John Carlos worked in a casino. Radetich drove a shuttle bus. Bell, who held the American record in the half-mile, worked as a (laid-back) security guard at the front gate in the afternoon, simultaneously helping babysit discus-thrower Jay Silvester's children. His pay for the latter? A quart of ice cream.

Distance runners went for runs on the Pacific Crest Trail, sometimes climbing to 9,000 feet. Decathletes Russ Hodge and Jeff Bannister ran intervals straight up the ski mountain that rose from the track's south end. A motorized golf cart zipped around the track and field layout, where a young man with a cutting-edge "video camera" captured athletes not on film, but on "tape," so they could quickly examine, and learn from, their techniques. From time to time, athletes left for one of a handful of developmental meets held mainly on the West Coast.

Beyond their workouts on the track or in the weight room, athletes found an array of entertainment. They golfed. They swam. They fished. With antennas adjusted just right, they watched on a little TV as CBS previewed a new investigative journalism show called *60 Minutes*. Republican presidential nominee Richard Nixon was scheduled to be a guest on *Rowan & Martin's Laugh-In* September 16, the last day of the Echo Summit Trials.

At night, card games enlivened trailers and cabins here and there. Evening music wafted from eight-track tape players, with black athletes sometimes introducing white athletes to true soul music. Occasionally, the athletes got a taste of some live music. Thanks to ex-Oregon State javelin thrower Gary Stenlund, who had a VW camper and a hankering for fun and frosties, Fosbury saw The Chambers Brothers play their just-released hit "Time Has Come Today"—all eleven minutes of it— in a South Lake Tahoe club.

Despite all this, by far the most common entertainment was venturing to nearby Stateline, Nevada, for nights in the casinos. Harrah's would regularly comp athletes' dinner and shows, which, of course, got them in front of the slots. Soon, a scheme was hatched in the Echo Summit dining room for athletes to pool their money in hopes of striking it rich at a roulette or blackjack table. It didn't work. The salt in the wound: they missed the shuttle and had to hitchhike back up the mountain to Echo Summit.

Spirits were high. The men had it all: a surreal training facility, sunshine, casinos, a $2 per-diem for incidentals, and three square meals—that is, once Bowerman realized the best shot-putters in the world were getting a meager 800 calories a day and rectified the situation in a hurry.

What they also had was each other, which was one of the prime reasons Bowerman wanted the athletes clustered: to build a sense of camaraderie. That said, there were many reasons to suggest such camaraderie would *not* come to fruition. In the LA Olympic Trials two weeks earlier, black male athletes had split 13-13 on whether to boycott the Games; to maintain unity, they decided to compete and let individuals decide what, if anything, they would do to make a statement. So that was a lingering distraction. There were others: the unspoken reality that the guy lifting weights or playing blackjack next to an athlete might be a guy he needed to beat in the trials to fulfill his Olympic dream. And there was escalating banter about whether the USOC's "prove-fitness" method was really the best way to choose a team.

Like jaybirds waiting for camper-crumbs, the press flitted around Echo Summit's woods in search of stories, its home base a press room fashioned from inside the old ski lodge. Reporters were anxious to hear about protest possibilities, but few seemed interested in trying to understand, at a deeper level, the social prejudice that had triggered boycott talk in the first place. For example, the realization that as sprinter Mel Pender's military unit had stopped in Athens, Georgia, to eat, the whites went to the front door and the blacks through the "Colored Only" side door. Or that Tommie Smith, in San Jose, got turned down for housing so often near campus that he ran an experiment; right after the landlord of a "For Rent" apartment turned him down, the same landlord would gladly rent to a white friend who inquired on Tommie's behalf. Or that although the US had been competing around the world in track and field for more than half a century, it hadn't been until 1966 that a black man was allowed to head up a team—sprint coach Stan Wright.

Pender had a double hurt in his heart as he trained at Echo Summit: that of a black man and of a soldier who'd fought in—and would soon be returning to—Vietnam. Only back a few weeks, he'd already endured the verbal slaps as a "baby killer." "I can't begin to tell you how much that hurt," he wrote in his book, *Expression of Hope*. "In the jungles of Vietnam, we were soldiers (both black and white) who fought and died together as one. My heart ached for every soldier who was injured or killed." And yet as much as he wanted change in America, he thought, as did plenty of his black teammates, that, instead of boycotting, the cause was better served by letting their results in Mexico City do the talking. But neither did he simply let it go when Brundage, the IOC president, threatened, as he had three months earlier, that "If those *boys* act up, I'm going to send them home." Pender and other black athletes gathered with Wright, who called Brundage on the spot. "These athletes," Wright told Brundage, "are not *boys*, they are men. And you aren't to call them that again—*ever*."

In retrospect, the wonder of Echo Summit wasn't that there was tension in the thin air, it was that *despite* the tension, athletes generally got along well with each other. What Bowerman hoped Echo Summit would do, it did: bonded the team. Bowerman himself forged a friendship with 400-meter ace Lee Evans that would last the rest of his life. After Washington State distance runner Gerry Lindgren begged for the chance, Fosbury taught him to Flop; Lindgren managed 5'0", not bad considering Gerry was only 5'6". Divine, an Oregon distance runner, became a regular at cabin card games organized by Carlos. When Fosbury's mother stopped at Echo Summit for a visit, the boyish-looking Dick posed for a photo with her and just-home-from-Vietnam soldier Mike Manley, a Marine who ran the steeplechase. Smiling broadly, as usual, Dick looked like a Boy Scout on his first day of summer camp.

"I grew up on the East Coast, and I didn't know places like that existed in the United States," said 400-meter runner Larry James of Echo Summit. "To this day, I can taste the air. In the morning it was like a fresh glass of spring water."

Given the potential for conflict, it was almost as if the serenity of Echo Summit bound the men in a spirit of oneness; as if conflict would have been sacrilegious in this tranquil setting; as if the athletes owed something not only to each other, but to this place that had drawn them together and whispered peace in a country at war. "It all made the team a lot closer," said Carlos. "It was such a serene atmosphere. Everyone just fell in love with the place and the situation. The team bonded."

It was a bond that would soon be tested.

FROM SOME VIEWPOINTS, Fannette Island looked like a giant Hershey's Kiss rising 150 feet high out of Lake Tahoe's Emerald Bay—with trees, of course. Photographers loved it. Sightseers loved it. But the El Dorado County Sheriff's search and rescue team hated it. Their divers spent far too much time dragging drowning victims out of the crystal-clear waters surrounding it, often teenagers with a few beers under their belts who couldn't resist the challenge—or the dare.

The nearest nub of shore on Tahoe's west edge was about a thousand feet away—three football fields. It made an out-and-back swim seem far enough to justify bragging rights but near enough to accomplish. What the kids underestimated, rescue divers were forever telling reporters, wasn't the distance. It was the coldness of the water. This wasn't the bathwater of some Midwest reservoir. This was the highest lake of its size (191 square miles) in America—elevation 6,225 feet—and, at nearly a mile down, second only to Oregon's Crater Lake as America's deepest. It was fed by creeks and streams that pounded down from the snow-packed spine of the Sierra Nevada, whose peaks reached beyond 10,000 feet to the lake's western shore.

On the August afternoon that Radetich talked Fosbury into swimming to Fannette Island, Lake Tahoe's temperature was in the low 60s. Radetich and some others had made it to the island and back a few days before. But, then, he also had completed his senior lifesaving training; Fosbury, on the other hand, was only a so-so swimmer.

"God, it's cold," said Dick as they began wading out. But after Radetich dove forward, so did Dick. He surfaced, whooped, then, alongside John, started swimming toward the island, wondering if he was still going to have a pair of testicles at the end of this frigid swim.

Halfway to the island, a shiver shuddered through Fosbury's body.

"C-c-c-cold," Dick said, breathing heavily. "Real c-c-c-old."

John dog-paddled to a turn. "You OK?"

Dick was gassed. Freezing. And suddenly afraid.

"I dunno, Rat—n-n-not sure I can make it." His heart pounded, his breaths coming quick and frantic.

John started swimming toward Dick, whose arms started flailing as if he were a wounded pelican. He coughed. He spit out water. He started to sink, then splashed frantically to stay afloat.

"Hang on, Foz," said John, coming alongside him. "Relax. Grab my shoulders and hang on. I'll swim you to shore."

Radetich's frame was roughly the size of Dick's, though he was stronger. Dick grabbed hold for the slow tow to the island. Once there, both collapsed on the beach, shivering, exhausted. "I honestly don't think I could have made it on my own," Fosbury said decades later. "It's a day I'll never forget, the day my journey to be an Olympian almost ended."

IN THE SUMMER of 1968, the whole world was seemingly flailing in the icy waters of dissent. In France, millions of workers barricaded themselves inside factories and offices to protest sagging wages. In Prague, Czechoslovakia, Soviet tanks clanked down city streets to quell the "Prague Spring" quest for freedom. In Chicago, police used night sticks and tear gas to subdue anti-war demonstrators in a bloody clash back-dropped by the Democratic National Convention, where Hubert Humphrey was nominated to face Nixon in November. "Shoot to kill," Chicago Mayor Richard Daley said to his police officers. "The whole world is watching, the whole world is watching!" chanted protesters.

In Oregon, Governor Tom McCall lashed out at leaders who were, in essence, "leaving our boys" in Vietnam hanging out to dry. McCall himself had a son en route. "I suffer every night," he said, "over Vietnam." In Mexico City, college students escalated their quiet revolution against what they saw as a repressive government.

"Sixty-eight had been a weird nervous-breakdown of a year," wrote Peter Jennings and Todd Brewster in *The Century*. For now, Echo Summit beckoned as a world apart. In August, *Track & Field News* featured a cover photo of a lone athlete, Kansan Jim Ryun, running amid the trees, a setting as tranquil as the rest of the world was not.

WHEN THE TRIALS were over, Bill Bowerman didn't want the new team scattering back to their homes as had happened in 1964. That would diffuse the energy that the Echo Summit experience would create. Instead, he wanted the athletes to head straight to Denver to be outfitted for their opening-and-closing-ceremony garb and then fly to Mexico City, where cloistered in the Olympic Village, they could continue to hone their physical conditioning and their newfound camaraderie before the October 13–20 track and field events.

Thus, in early September, shortly before the high-altitude Trials were to begin, Fosbury drove back to his mother's house in Medford. He dropped off his nonessentials, left his car, then flew back to Reno/South Lake Tahoe; this way, he would be ready to leave for Mexico City with his teammates once the Trials were over. After his trip home—and a more vibrant good-luck hug from his rejuvenated mother than he got from her as a high schooler—he arrived back at Echo Summit.

Fosbury wouldn't be jumping in the Trials for a week. He planned to do some light workouts each day and watch his friends compete, at times with Wagner, who was to have arrived. Before heading up to the track, Dick stopped by the dining room for a quick bite. That's when he saw the note tacked to the front door. As he read it, his eyes squinted, then widened. *What the hell?* While he'd been gone, it seems, there'd been a change in plans. The USOC had decided that the winners in LA no longer had guaranteed spots on the Olympic team; instead, the top three placers from each event at the Echo Summit Trials would represent the US.

Dick felt as if he'd been gut-shot. *Was this someone's idea of a prank? Could the coaches really do this—change the rules in the middle of the game? Why hadn't anyone told him about this?*

He headed into the woods in a daze, his eyes misting with tears. Did Fosbury have the confidence that he could win a spot on the Olympic team? Of course. He'd beaten everyone else in LA at 7'1" and knew he could do it again. But what if he had an off day—or some out-of-nowhere jumper got hot? What if he tweaked an ankle? Or got food poisoning the night before the finals? He shouldn't have to prove himself again. Rules were rules, promises were promises. Or so he'd thought.

Now he had a sinking feeling that he might not be going to Mexico City as an Olympian after all.

He soon tracked down Wagner, who had, indeed, arrived.

"So what happened?" Fosbury asked.

"Who knows? Maybe the committee got cowed by a bunch of whiny athletes who didn't win in LA like you—or by some coaches whose guys didn't win, and wanted a second chance for them. You're just going to have to prove it again in the pit. But you can do it. I know that. You know that."

Fosbury's forte as a high-jumper had always been his mental focus, his ability to all but *will* himself over a bar. Now, his mental game had been shattered into a thousand pieces like glass. Instead of a gradual psyching up for a world competition in Mexico City in October, he would need to urgently revamp his mental approach for competition in a week. Everything was suddenly out of whack. Everything that had been so perfect was now imperfect. Everything that was so certain was now uncertain.

Though it seemed incredulous that Fosbury could have gone more than a month without realizing he didn't actually have the guaranteed spot he thought he did, he insists, nearly half a century later, that such was the case. "I believed what I had been told," he said. "I had made the team in the LA Trials."

Chapter 18

All great innovations are built on rejections.

—Louise Nevelson

SINK OR SWIM. Dick Fosbury's South Lake Tahoe experience had now been imbued with a new, if unwelcome, theme. After his brush with death in Emerald Bay, he now faced a do-or-die challenge in the high jump trials: finish in the top three in the Trials or go home, perhaps work a few swing shifts at the mill, and return to winter term classes at Oregon State in January. The new edict was a high-stakes version of basketball's game of H-O-R-S-E, where the winner only wins if he can "prove it"—once again make the shot used to originally vanquish the opponent.

Fair? Sure, if all participants agree, at the start, that those are the rules. Not so fair if the rules are changed mid-game, as many believe happened at Echo Summit. Distance runners Wade Bell, Dave Patrick, Bill Clark, Roscoe Divine, among other athletes at Echo Summit, believed the USOC was unfair in how it selected the 1968 team.

"The entire selection process was misleading," said *Sports Illustrated*. "The system should have been established early and adhered to. Then no one would have had grounds to complain that the officials had in effect reneged on an earlier promise."

The USOC may have erred out of negligence, lack of leadership, lack of communication skills, or plain lack of courage. But as Payton Jordan, head coach of the US track and field team would admit decades later, the USOC *did* err. "I'm sure the USOC meant well," said Hymans, "but they weren't a very efficient organization."

The most powerful track and field coalition in the world had just changed horses in the middle of the stream—and notified some of its athletes with a thumb-tacked note on a dining room door. If it hadn't been such jolting news to Fosbury and others who thought they'd earned spots on the team in LA, it would have almost been funny, the sports version of an astronaut stepping out of his module on the moon to find a small sign: "Sorry, no vacancy."

In this case, however, nobody was laughing. When the fiasco was over, it proved to have been comprised of two parts: first, the afore-mentioned waffling by the USOC, during and after the LA Trials in late June, on its win-and-you're-in promise. And, second, the athletes at Echo Summit, in early September, convincing the USOC to more drastically change those already-altered qualifying rules.

In LA, when the USOC backed off its promise to first-placers, it was as if it had placed eighteen athletes—the winners of each event—on a giant victory podium, the floor of which had eighteen trap doors. However it chose to define the nebulous "prove-fitness-at-altitude" edict, the USOC was prepared to pull the trap-door lever for any winner who didn't do so. *Whoosh!* The LA winner would be gone.

Immediately after the LA "trials," the winners who'd heard of the USOC's last-minute caveat—Fosbury an obvious exception—grumbled about what they saw as a broken promise. However, seeing little recourse, they resigned themselves to training hard and "proving their fitness" at altitude.

It was the non-winners who started grumbling at Echo Summit—and, given all the fuzziness about how the team was going to be chosen—proposed a solution that was as black-and-white as it was self-serving: throw out the results from LA and take the top three in each event from the high-altitude Trials. In other words, pull the trap-door levers for all eighteen winners—*whoosh!*—and start with an empty winners podium, knowing that, in each event, there was now one more available spot for themselves, the guys who hadn't won in LA.

Which athlete or athletes at Echo Summit started promoting the start-over-from-scratch movement isn't clear. Nor is it clear whether coaches or the USOC were complicit in helping promote the movement in the way a powerful country might, for political leverage, help back an insurrection in some third-world country. One school of thought suggests that in the weeks after training began, it appeared that some athletes, a few LA winners among them, weren't responding well to the altitude. "At Tahoe, as they say, the cream was rising to the top," said long jumper Ralph Boston, "and that led to some antagonistic attitudes."

"Specifically, the distance winners at the sea-level LA Trials might not be able to place in the top six at altitude, let alone the top three," wrote Moore in *Bowerman and the Men of Oregon*. (Moore had already earned a spot on the Olympic team in the marathon trials but hoped to make it in the 10,000 meters as well. After missing the LA Trials because of illness, he was among a handful of athletes who, for various reasons, were given waivers to compete at the final trials at Echo Summit.)

It's debatable whether the non-LA winners were motivated by: (a) seeing others respond poorly to altitude; (b) wanting to replace the USOC's subjective, and nebulous, "prove-fitness" system; (c) wanting to increase their chances of making the team; or (d) a combination of the above. What's *not* debatable is that: (a) the non-LA-winners' idea would benefit them at the expense of the LA winners and (b) because of the numerical imbalance of the two, those non-winners had a 9:1 advantage over the winners if they could bring the issue to a vote. Of the 180 athletes shooting for fifty-four spots on the Olympic Team—three in each event—only eighteen had won in LA, leaving 162 inclined to believe a "redo" trials with eighteen more available spots made sense for them, personally.

Over a beer in Tahoe or on a trail run in the High Sierras or a late-night card game, a quiet consensus built among the athletes: *You want to represent the US at altitude in Mexico City? Prove it at altitude. Allow no wiggle room for the USOC to subjectively choose the team. Top three from each event in the Tahoe trials make the team, period.*

Whether athlete-instigated or coaches/USOC-instigated, Lodge and Bowerman—with Fosbury still in Oregon—chaired a meeting in the dining hall shortly before the start of the September Trials. The purpose was to either listen to concerns of athletes or have athletes listen to *their* concerns; like defining where fresh water meets salt water at the mouth of a coastal river, defining which group instigated the gathering is murky.

Some, including Dave Patrick, suggested it started with Bowerman, who had two 1,500-meter runners—Roscoe Divine and Dave Wilborn—who hadn't won in LA. He told the Montgomery County (Maryland) *Gazette* that Bowerman called the meeting and proposed throwing out the LA results. He then reportedly recommended it be put up to a vote.

Clark, among others, remembers it differently. He thinks the athletes themselves raised the idea of letting the Tahoe results decide which three would go in each event. "The athletes were unhappy," he said. "There was a lot of grumbling. So the USOC figured the democratic thing was to put it to a vote."

Even if head coach Payton Jordan had wanted to defend those who had won in LA., he was not at Echo Summit at the time and, thus, couldn't.

"I don't think Bowerman acquiesced," said Clark. "If anything, he was fighting for us to be on the team. It was the committee's decision to put it to a vote." As Lodge, Bowerman, and the athletes met that night in what Moore called "a terrible meeting . . . a grave assembly of athletes," it was the Oregon coach who tried to stave off a "reshuffle-the-deck" decision in favor of the committee's "show-fitness" plan, according to Clark, to honor the athletes' winning efforts in LA.

Steeplechase winner George Young and 5,000-meter winner Tracy Smith argued that changing the rules was unfair to them, the breaking of a promise that they were "in" unless they proved themselves unworthy at altitude. Triple-jump winner Art Walker and 100-meter winner Jim Hines said as much, too. But passionate dissent drowned them out. Clark didn't even enter the discussion. "I could see it was hopeless," he said. Most non-winners were adamant that their top-three-at-Tahoe plan was the way to go.

Ultimately, it was an unlikely athlete whose words brought the rising hub-bub to a halt: Villanova's Patrick, one of Fosbury's favorite athletes at the camp. To this point, most of the LA winners had stayed quiet, caught in a damned-if-I-do-damned-if-I-don't position: speak up for themselves and fellow LA winners, and risk being snubbed by a

9:1 ratio of teammates; *not* speak up and, in essence, throw their hard-earned LA victories—Patrick had to run two qualifying heats before winning the 1,500 finals—into the sacrificial fire.

Tall, muscular, and blond, Patrick commanded immediate attention as he stood. The room came to a hush. "If I can't make the top three here," he said. "I don't deserve to go."

The vote was decisive. "Guess what?" steeplechaser George Young later said. "They voted 9–1 against me." Nobody any longer had a spot on the team, including Dick Fosbury. With nearly half a century's perspective, he still believed it to be an unfair decision, even if he understood what drove it: the times. The '60s. The spirit of questioning authority. "Those were the days of 'power to the people,'" he said.

From college campuses to the streets of Selma, Alabama, people were rising up, questioning authority, seeking justice, demanding rights. One of the legacies of Echo Summit was that, amid such strife, the training camp was one of the few places where the people's voices—regardless of whether one agreed with those voices—were not only heard but listened to and acted upon. "Democracy can be messy," said Fosbury. "'We the people' won."

To give athletes this kind of say was as unprecedented as it was unexpected. *Sports Illustrated* called the Echo Summit revision "an experiment in democracy" stemming from "reasons still not clear." The strongest theory was that the times themselves had become a silent force, like the cold that could gradually freeze a High Sierra lake.

"The upheaval of young people in the country emboldened the athletes," said Jon Hendershott, the former *T&F News* writer. "They stood up for what they thought was right and, even though it hurt a few people, they thought this was right. And they had their rights. I don't blame them. Things had gotten too nebulous. They wanted it definite: top three go."

T&F News writers Cordner Nelson and Dick Drake put it like this at the time: "The 1968 athletes were more vocal in questioning and, indeed, challenging policies, principles, and methods prescribed by USOC hierarchy." The inspiration for it, Nelson and Drake wrote, may well have been the black-boycott movement, out of which the Olympic Project for Human Rights developed.

After the meeting, Lodge issued a statement that, according to *T&F News*, "should have been issued more than two months ago. It said, in effect, that the first 'Final Trials' were meaningless, little more than a fund-raising gimmick, and that a man who won in Los Angeles would have to win again—or at least finish in the top three—here." The media shrugged when hearing word of the about-face. Wrote the Associated Press, deep down in a general story about the Trials: "The U.S. Olympic Committee . . . confirmed Monday that the first three finishers in each event will be chosen for the team." That would be Monday—as in the first day of the non-decathlon portion of the Trials.

With four years to decide how to choose a team, it needn't have come down to this. "The format by which the United States Olympic Committee selected the team in 1968," wrote Bob Burns for the *Chicago Tribune*, "was confusing at best, duplicitous at worst."

In the end, the USOC and the non-LA victors emerged as winners. The committee got what it wanted: money from an LA meet and a team that had to prove itself at altitude and, thus, was likely stronger than what it otherwise might have been. The non-LA winners got what they wanted: an objective "top-three-go" format that, as a side benefit, increased their chances of being among the qualifiers.

What was sacrificed in the process was the integrity of the USOC— it broke a promise—and the guarantee of eighteen winners who were suddenly told: *Prove it.*

Chapter 19

The mountains are calling and I must go.

— John Muir

WITH THE POP of a starter's pistol amid the pines of Echo Summit, the non-decathlon portion of the Final Olympic Trials began Monday, September 9. (The decathlon had been contested the previous Friday and Saturday, with Bill Toomey winning.) To the claps and cheers of a smattering of a few hundred fans, five sprinters bolted out of their blocks and down a tree-lined corridor as part of a 100-meter qualifying heat.

"It was like a fantasy land, really," said Dave Kayfes, whose job at the Echo Summit trials was to grab athletes after their events so they could meet with the press. "It was a back-to-nature lab for selecting a superior team at a most troubled time, all in the beauty of the high Sierras. It's still like a foggy dream to me."

Interrupted, on occasion, by real-world reality: "Carlos," a reporter would yell, "any chance you'll change your mind and boycott the Olympics?" Sprinter Larry Questad called home to tell his folks he'd made the team—by .01 seconds—in the 200 meters. "Congratulations," said his mother. "Oh, I've got news for you, too. You've been drafted."

The trials would be contested like no other track and field competition ever held in America: a mile and a half above sea level amid a seemingly endless forest of trees, some wider at their base than a shot-putter. Occasionally, the wind whipped up, but usually skies were UCLA-blue and temperatures warm but not hot. Kayfes doesn't remember seeing, hearing, or feeling a single mosquito.

For fans, it was a mixed bag. Echo Summit was a breathtaking setting, almost like watching cross-country or golf, splashes of the athletes' different-colored uniforms contrasted against nature's earth tones. Spectators could get close enough to the shot-put event south of the track to feel the thud of the sixteen-pound ball of steel. But because of trees covering more than half of the infield, runners were obscured for good portions of races of 200 meters and longer.

Bleacher tickets ran $4. For $2, fans could sit on the rocky hill slope, but it was BYOB (Bring Your Own Blanket). Average attendance was about 2,500 a day—a tenth of what the "trials" in LA drew. But beyond locals, those fans who came to Echo Summit tended to be diehards: families and friends of the competitors, and hardcore track and field fans not deterred by—in fact, perhaps *inspired* by—the Trials' middle-of-nowhere locale. A few makeshift grandstands had been erected along homestretch for a few hundred fans and beyond the track's south end. Beyond that, spectators stood or sat alongside the outside of the track, as if watching a junior high meet.

In the area inside the track, Bowerman had managed to tuck among the evergreens all field-event setups but the shot put. Once, sprinter Tommie Smith looked up and saw pole vaulter Bob Seagren hurtling toward the earth. "I thought he'd fallen out of a tree." Ralph Boston marveled at the long-jump layout. "You came out of the forest down this strip of track and into the long-jump pit. I've shown photos of it to athletes of this current generation, and they couldn't believe it."

On the track's inside, the first turn offered only a sprinkling of trees—and an army-green tent used as a "training room"—but the second featured a bona fide forest; as such, watching races was the equivalent of neighborhood kids racing around the outside of a house: would the leader heading into the backyard be the leader returning to the front?

"It just added to the mystery," said Rich Clarkson, a *Topeka News* photographer who shot the event for *Sports Illustrated*—and whose photos of "Kansas schoolboy" phenomenon Jim Ryun had been featured on *SI*'s covers.

Beyond the trees, granite rocks and boulders contributed to the wilderness feel. "It was great," said Radetich. "First time I've ever figured out where to start my run-up by measuring paces from a big rock." Towering trees made high-jump and pole-vault bars seem low by contrast. Except for tree-created shadows, ABC, which was televising the event for Saturday's *Wide World of Sports,* loved the aesthetics; so did still photographers.

"It was fun looking for ways you could involve trees and athletes in the same frame," said Clarkson. "The more challenging part was getting my film to New York in a hurry."

ABC, Clarkson learned, was having an intern drive its 16mm film to the Reno/South Lake Tahoe Airport each evening so editing could begin for Saturday's *Wide World of Sports.* From there, the film was flown to LA, then to New York. "I arranged for the same intern to take my film each day, maybe ten to twenty rolls," said Clarkson. "He was a twenty-one-year-old Yale kid." The name of that "kid" was Dick Ebersol, who someday would become president of NBC Sports, produce a handful of Olympic Games, and, in 1996, be named by *Sport* magazine as "the most powerful man in sports."

In the 1960s, track and field was revered among sports in America. The 1962 US-Soviet dual meet in Palo Alto, California, drew 155,000 fans in two days; more than 5,000 showed up simply to watch the Soviets practice. *Wide World of Sports* consistently featured meets; track stars were regulars on *Sports Illustrated* covers. When Jim Ryun, just nineteen at the time, broke the world record in the mile in 1966, CBS's Walter Cronkite broke into his regular news to announce the late-breaking story from Berkeley, California.

In South Lake Tahoe, the press corps worked hard and played hard. *Sports Illustrated,* with what Clarkson calls "an unlimited expense account," wined and dined athletes it interviewed. The daily rhythm had already begun: trees and track by day, drinks and blackjack by night. "It was the most bizarre yet fun event I've ever worked at or watched," said Kayfes. "It was exhilarating—from the smell of fresh pine in the morning to the dry mountain heat in the afternoon to lobster and steak dinners in Tahoe that night, each tab stamped with 'Do Not Pay.'"

Among those watching the meet on this opening day was Geoff Hollister, a former Oregon runner in a Blue Ribbon Sports tracksuit with a shoe bag slung over his shoulder and a brand-new pair of Cortez running shoes on his feet. Hollister was selling them from the back of his car, BRS daring to toe the line with the two mainstays of running shoes, Puma and Adidas. On-site reps from the two German companies snubbed Hollister and the upstart company he represented; Puma and Adidas, not BRS, were the companies with full-page ads in *Track & Field News* and the growing bottom lines. They owned these athletes. But after BRS would pay a Portland State student $35 to create a logo she called a "swoosh"—and the company changed its name to the head-scratching "Nike"—Hollister would have the last laugh.

That was Echo Summit, a literal backwoods track and field competition that was about to become a launching pad for dreams. But it would also prove to be a graveyard for dreams.

"Go, Willie!" Fosbury yelled as Willie Turner, an Oregon State teammate with a heavily taped leg, pounded past him to make the 100-meter semifinal round. "Go, OSU!"

His race over, Turner slowed, turned, and flashed a smile Fosbury's way. By nightfall, he would be en route to the airport for a return flight to Yakima, Washington. His Olympic dreams would die with the aggravation of a hamstring injury in a semifinal heat. If there was a reminder that roughly three out of four athletes would leave Echo Summit without tickets to Mexico City, it was the presence of an on-site travel agent, courtesy of the USOC. Winners stayed. Losers left. Harsh as it might have seemed, that was the purpose of this event: unlike LA, to decide who was worthy and who was not.

Timing was everything. Had Turner's hamstring held up for only two more races, he might well have been an Olympian; the year before, he'd briefly shared the world record for 100 meters. Instead, the injury relegated him to Yakima instead of Mexico City. Conversely, only two days before the Trials' start, Seagren had popped something in his back so seriously that he was hauled away in an ambulance. And yet less than a week later, he pole-vaulted 17'9" for a new world record. Had Seagren's injury happened a day or two later, he probably would *not* have been an Olympian.

"At this level, you need two things to succeed," said Divine, the Oregon 1,500-meter runner. "You gotta be good. And you gotta be lucky."

Fosbury knew he was good. But after the reversal on who qualified for Mexico City, he wasn't so sure about being lucky. "I was nervous all week," he later said, in anticipation of his having to prove himself Sunday and Monday. "It was a challenge getting in training time with the trials going on. I had suddenly realized I was going to have to uncork a peak performance. All in all, I was just feeling a lot of uncertainty."

Since winning in LA at 7'1", he had not jumped higher than 6'10" in a few low-key development meets in Oregon and California. "I've got to get out of this rut," he told the *Oregon Journal* in late August.

Part of it, he admitted, was sheer weariness. Until 1968, spring was essentially the only season he jumped competitively. But in January he'd embarked on a six-meet indoor season, competed outdoors in the spring, and now was in the midst of essentially a third season. "I've been competing since January without a break," he told the *Journal.* "I'm mentally and physically tired."

By the time Fosbury would jump in Sunday's qualifying round, Echo Summit had already left its imprint on track and field history. No US trials had ever produced as many world records: four, though Carlos's 19.7 in the 200 meters was never ratified because of his brush spikes. Already, sportswriters and other track and field aficionados were debating the question over drinks each night in Lake Tahoe: could whatever team the US comes up with be the best Olympic track and field team ever?

IN THE HIGH jump, a handful of athletes would be challenging Fosbury for one of the three spots, foremost among them Edward Julius Caruthers, Jr. "Big Ed," as Fosbury called him, was a tall, broad-shouldered veteran of the 1964 Olympic team as a kid fresh out of high school. He was African American, strong, and serious. At twenty-three, he was only two years older than Fosbury but looked nearly ten years older. At 6'4½", he was only slightly taller than Dick but, at 205 pounds, twenty pounds heavier. He had played wide receiver and safety for the University of Arizona football team and aspired to play in the

NFL. He was power to Fosbury's finesse, strength to Dick's speed, and, at least in his own mind—and with tongue only slightly in cheek—athlete to Fosbury's "novelty."

"I played football and basketball," he would say later. "Fosbury couldn't make a basketball team or football team. He couldn't straddle. He was just this hippie kid with a novelty style." Caruthers exuded a sort of mature, blue-collar seriousness; Fosbury smiled easily and soared on the wings of youthful whimsy, as if high jumping to him were simply fun. For Caruthers, it was a quest, his eighth-place finish in Tokyo in 1964 having steeled him to the goal of winning a gold medal four years later in Mexico City. And he was clearly on track. In January 1968, *Track & Field News* ranked him as the top high jumper in the world.

Yet Fosbury had the edge on Caruthers in 1968 competition, starting in January in Oakland. Caruthers was among those jumpers on the cover of the February 1968 (first of two issues) *Track & Field News*, standing in the background with looks of resentment on their faces. Now, eight months later, Caruthers no longer wanted to be the out-of-focus guy in a photo of a jumper he called the "hippie kid."

Other competition lurked: among veteran jumpers, Otis Burrell had been runner-up at the recent AAU championships (7'¾") and had won that meet the previous three years. John Rambo, 6'7" tall, was a bronze-medal winner at Tokyo in 1964 and, though not having a stellar year, had finished third in LA at 7'0". Among the upstarts, Ed Hanks of Brigham Young, though only 5'9" tall, had defeated Dick in the 1967 NCAA outdoor meet that he won and had recently won the AAU outdoor title. And then there were a couple of jumpers—"unknowns"—few people had seen in action: Reynaldo Brown and John Hartfield.

Brown, 6'4" and 195 pounds, was a Compton (California) High senior; in fact, if the seventeen-year-old were to earn one of the three spots, he would become one of the youngest US Olympic track and field athletes in history. He had a best of 7'¾", and like Caruthers, he'd shown his athletic prowess in another sport—basketball. *Track & Field News* named him its High School Athlete of the Year. The concern about Brown, of course, was his lack of experience at this level. *T&F News*, in its predictions, gave him nothing more than an "also competing" tag.

Hartfield, twenty-two, was a Texas Southern University grad whom *T&F News* had ranked seventh in the world in January 1968. He had a best of 7'0" this season but had managed only 6'10"—and ninth place—in the LA Trials. At least one Olympic Trials coach believed in him: Stan Wright, Hartfield's father-in-law. John, figured Wright, had made two great decisions in life—attending Wright's alma mater, Texas Southern, and marrying his daughter, Toni. Indeed, John's stars seemed to be lining up: husband, father-to-be (his wife Toni, on hand for the trials, was five months pregnant), and soon, he hoped, a member of the US Olympic team.

That night, as the saw-toothed Sierras merged with the creeping darkness, Fosbury wondered if he would make a team he already thought he had back in June. At twenty-one, it seemed light years—not five years—since he'd first began experimenting with the Flop as a high school sophomore in Medford. But in another sense, it seemed like only yesterday. He was still that sixteen-year-old kid who had no illusions of gold-medal grandeur. Still the kid living for the moment. Still the kid who just wanted to be on the team.

PART IV

SPACE

Chapter 20

Temper us in fire, and we grow stronger. When we suffer, we survive.

—Cassandra Clare, City of Heavenly Fire

MICROPHONE IN HAND, ABC's Jim McKay welcomed the television audience to *Wide World of Sports,* on which a segment of the South Lake Tahoe trials, along with the Gold Cup Power Boat Race from Detroit, would air the following Saturday at 5 pm. The "thrill of victory and the agony of defeat" line that would become the show's introductory calling card was about to poignantly play out in one of the final events of the trials—the high jump.

Fosbury's sister, Gail, perched herself on the small bleachers across from the track for a stellar doubleheader: at 2:30 pm, the high-jump final featuring her older brother and, after that, the 1,500-meter final as Ryun tried to redeem himself after faltering in the 800 meters.

A gentle breeze tickled the boughs of pines that flanked the high-jump pit like bookends. Jumpers would make their approaches—partly on grass, partly on the all-weather surface—by running toward the center of the track's infield. Beyond the pit: the landing area for the now-completed javelin, discus, and hammer events. Behind the jumpers: fans ringing the track, sitting in the small stands, and perched on the ski slope.

"As far-flung as you might have imagined the Echo Summit setting to be, it was *more* far-flung," the *Oakland Tribune*'s Newnham said. "I remember watching Fosbury Flop and his fellow competitors sitting on huge rocks, watching him. It was so serene—and yet just below the surface was all the politics of the 1960s."

THERE WAS NOTHING serene about Fosbury as the competition began. High jumpers, more than some athletes, rely heavily on mojo. Bravado. Confidence that nothing can stop them from getting over that bar. Fosbury, at the onset of the high-jump finals, was still searching for that zone. He was uptight.

The previous day's qualifying flight had been predictable: ten jumpers cleared 6'9" to make Monday's finals: Fosbury, Caruthers, Radetich, Rambo, Burrell, Hanks, Brown, Hartfield, Stan Curry, and Mike Bowers. All but one jumper, Fosbury, employed the traditional straddle method. Now, as the shadows lengthened during the finals, the field had been whittled to four, the biggest surprise being the "no-height" ouster of Burrell, who passed at the opening height of 6'10" and missed all three at 6'11". His Mexico City dreams were dead on arrival.

When Fosbury cleared 7'0" and three others—Caruthers, Brown, and Hartfield—did the same, the competition became a high-pressure game of odd man out. Four jumpers were left. Three would make the team. One would be given the rarely satisfying role of "alternate."

"The bar goes to seven feet, one inch," said an official. "Caruthers up. Brown on deck. Fosbury in the hole."

All four jumpers made it on their first attempts. The competition took on the feel of musical chairs. The only question was: when the music stopped, who was going to be left standing?

"The bar," said the official, "goes to seven feet, two inches."

The height was unfamiliar territory for Brown and Hartfield—and only rarely visited by Caruthers (7'2½") and Fosbury (7'2 ¼"). On his first attempt at 7'2", Caruthers missed. So did Brown. Fosbury was next. Dick had not missed a significant jump in a major meet since the previous winter's indoor season; he was at his best in the big ones, and none was bigger than a meet with the Olympics on the line. The crowd quieted, eyes riveted to the young man in black satin shorts with the black interlocking "OSU" staircasing down his orange singlet.

Fosbury toed his mark in white Adidas shoes accented by black stripes and black socks. He eyed the bar, clenched and unclenched his fists, then started his customary rocking back and forth. A dozen times. Two dozen. Three. Then: *three, two, one.* With powerful strides,

Fosbury angled toward the pit from the left, planted his right foot, leapt, arched, cleared with his hips—and felt the sickening scrape of the bar on his heels. The crowd groaned. The bar fell.

Nothing was more frustrating than losing a jump because of a trailing foot; later, Fosbury would blame himself for a "lazy" jump. But as was his style, Fosbury capped the negative thought with a positive one: *the two other jumpers who've jumped have missed. I'm fine.* Hartfield had already gone an inch higher than he had all year; the chances of him going higher were slight.

In a light blue jersey and red pants, Hartfield went to his mark. Representing the Houston Striders Track Club, he was the thinnest and shortest of the four, a wiry 6'1", but, at least outwardly, the most amped. Clearly he wanted this. Having finished only ninth in LA, he was already living on borrowed time at Echo Summit. But his early success seemed to have energized him—that and perhaps having his wife, Toni, on hand, along with her father, Stan. The two stood on the infield, amid the trees. Toni loved the setting. "It was simply beautiful up there. And we were having so much fun."

As was his routine, John Hartfield stared down at the ground for agonizingly long moments, then began his approach. He leapt, kicked high, twisted, and cleared the bar with elegant grace. A cheer shattered the silence. Hartfield had gone 7'2", another personal best and his fourth straight jump without a miss. He pumped a fist in the air, then pointed across the way, to where Toni and Stan were. He could almost hear the mariachi bands of Mexico City. Toni waved a single warning finger at him as if to say: *It's not over yet, baby.* "I don't know how many times I had to remind him not to start celebrating too early," she said later.

With that single leap, the momentum shifted decidedly; it was now advantage Hartfield, the out-of-nowhere kid. What had been a four-way battle for three spots now appeared to be a three-way battle for two. And Hartfield appeared to be the odd man *in*. In fact, if Caruthers, Brown, and Fosbury each missed two more times, Hartfield would be flying to Mexico City first class, as the Olympic Trials winner. If so, his triumph would go down as one of the biggest upsets in high-jumping history. And the Fosbury Flop—its innovator left home—would go down as just that: a flop.

If Fosbury got aced out, nobody was going to rationalize that he had been the victim of a cruel reversal by the USOC on who would make the team; with some exceptions, the press, frankly, hadn't made much of a fuss about the committee's turnabout. Neither were most track and field fans likely to come to his defense.

Now, as late afternoon shadows from trees grew longer, Caruthers prepped for his second attempt. With his slow approach, he ran, gathered himself, jumped, and twisted over 7'2". The crowd erupted. With two jumpers having cleared the height, the competition's ever-changing nuances now suggested a two-way battle for the final spot: Brown versus Fosbury.

Had he not been high jumping on this day for a chance to go to the Olympics, Rey Brown would have just gotten out of school back at Compton High, where he was a senior. He was clearly enjoying his moment in the sun. At seventeen, he was too young to overthink things, fear failure, or consider broader perspectives—for example, that if he made this jump he might become the youngest member of the 1968 men's US Olympic track and field team.

Brown's inexperience, *Track & Field News* had opined before the meet, was likely to be his downfall. And yet, sometimes neophytes, with no expectations to weigh them down, are like the javelins thrown from deep within the Echo Summit trees: they come out of nowhere. In 1964, Caruthers was a case in point: only nineteen and with minimal big-meet experience, he had won the AAU championships in New Jersey, then defeated 1960 Olympian John Thomas in the Olympic Trials Finals in LA to make the team. Four years later in this Echo Summit drama, was Brown playing Caruthers's 1964 role?

With a deer-like bounce, Brown sprinted, jumped, and rolled over the bar. Another roar from the crowd. Brown raised his arms in triumph; *This was way cooler than Algebra II!*

With the crowd now approaching what the *Fresno Bee* estimated as 600 people, all focused on this one event, three men were over the bar at 7'2". Dick Fosbury was not among them. Caruthers, Brown, and Hartfield could, if not totally relax, at least enjoy the role of being the proverbial "leaders in the clubhouse." Two more Fosbury misses and all three were in. From her seat in the bleachers, Gail Fosbury rocked slightly forward and backward, an unconscious facsimile of Dick's jump preparation, a nervous exhortation for her big-brother-the-rebel to fly high.

But on this, his second attempt at 7'2", he did not fly high—at least not high enough. The bar, slightly brushed by his butt, followed him into the pit. Fosbury bounced out and shook his head in disgust. The crowd groaned. "Fosbury," wrote *T&F News,* "was now virtually certain to lose." He was the only one of the three who hadn't made 7'2"—and even if he did, would still be in fourth place based on more misses. The tiebreaker's "countback rule" was, per usual, fewest misses on the last height made: Fosbury had two, Caruthers and Brown one each; Hartfield, the leader, none.

In essence, Fosbury was flailing in the waters of Emerald Bay— and Rat, encouraging him from atop a boulder not far from the Port-a-Pit—couldn't save him this time. Fosbury had to save himself. From the stands, Gail took a deep breath. But on the infield, even the ever-cautious Toni Hartfield was buying in to what looked like an obvious outcome. The thought not only crossed her mind but settled in as if to say: *We're going to Mexico City!*

A tenseness settled over the crowd. By now, fans were so engrossed in the intense competition that the idea of someone having to lose seemed diabolically unfair. They loved Caruthers, who had battled back from the disappointment in Tokyo. They loved Brown, the happy-go-lucky high school kid. They loved Hartfield, having the day of his life as his father-in-law and pregnant wife cheered him on. And, of course, they loved Fosbury and his radical style; for these spectators, it was like being at Kitty Hawk watching the Wright Brothers try to fly.

But why did someone have to lose?

Others, paid to be more objective, weren't as emotionally involved. Seeing Fosbury's second miss and sensing the almost insurmountable hole he'd dug for himself, a few reporters on tight deadlines peeled back their notebooks to the blank pages near the end and began scribbling stories that they would soon phone in to their papers. Their "ledes" may well have read like this:

SOUTH LAKE TAHOE—John Hartfield, a soon-to-be father who had managed only a ninth place in the Los Angeles Trials, and Reynaldo Brown, a 17-year Compton High senior who was "skipping school," shocked the American high-jump world Monday when they earned spots along with veteran Ed Caruthers on the US Olympic track and field team that will compete in Mexico City next month.

Missing on his bid for the Olympics was "Fosbury Flop" inventor Dick . . .

"Fosbury, down to his last jump at 7'2"," whispered ABC's McKay into his microphone, "or he won't go to Mexico City."

Fosbury toed his mark. Exhaled. Shook the fingers. Started the rocking, anxious rocking, confident rocking.

"Look at that determination," whispered McKay.

A blue jay squawked in the distance; Fosbury didn't hear it. Cigarette smoke from the crowd hung in the still air; Fosbury didn't smell it. He was mentally locked in. *Okay, take off straight up, not into the bar. Keep your hips up high. Stay away from the bar; it's poison. And kick those heels up and over, all clear. All good. Now, you know you're gonna make it. Make it. All clear. Three, two, one . . .* He bolted for the bar like a man on a mission and lunged for the sky with every ounce of energy in him.

"Fosbury," *T&F News* later wrote, "made one of the greatest clutch performances ever—clearing the bar by almost two inches."

"He did it!" said McKay, "and is he a happy guy!" Fosbury bolted upward while still in the pit, right arm stretched to the sky, face beaming. A cheer thundered through the forest. The response wasn't just about Dick, it was about a sense that this was becoming a competition for the ages. Most didn't know the particulars, but a few of the track and field nuts—the guys with stop watches in their jean pockets and shelves of black-and-white *T&F News* copies back home—did. They realized they were watching history.

For the first time in more than a century of high jumping around the world, four competitors had all cleared 7'2" in the same meet. "The great jumping," wrote *T&F News*, "was the result of ideal conditions: thin air, a spring Tartan takeoff, a good background, warm weather, fierce competition . . . ." But the event wasn't over—not by a long shot.

FOSBURY'S REACTION TO clearing a height only ¼" short of his best ever was split: unbridled joy transitioning quickly to unequivocal resolve.

Despite his make, he was still last of the four, based on the nagging misses. All the jumpers had now cleared 7'2", but Fosbury had one more miss than Caruthers and Brown and two more than Hartfield; indeed, Dick was dragging those two misses at 7'2" through the competition like a ball and chain. Meanwhile, Brown and Hartfield were jumping out of their minds and "Big Ed" was his usual steady self. Dick needed to dig deeper. To make this team—the team he thought he'd already made back in June—he needed to get to a height he'd never been to before.

"The bar," said the official, "goes to seven feet, three inches. First, Mr. Caruthers, followed by Mr. Brown. Mr. Fosbury in the hole."

Like heavyweight boxers looking for a knockout punch, Caruthers and Brown soared over 7'3" in quick succession as the crowd roared approval; among Americans, only Thomas had ever reached such a height (7'3⅜"). Now, Fosbury's only realistic hope was to find a way over 7'3" to join them—and hope the ante was too high for Hartfield. Fosbury had only attempted 7'3" one other time, unsuccessfully, at the NCAA meet in June.

By now, the competition was nearly ninety minutes old. On the track, Ryun, Patrick, and the other 1,500-meter runners were loosening up for the trials' final running event. The sun in the southwest sky was low above Mokelumne Peak and shadows would soon give way to mid-September dusk. Other athletes perched on rocks. A teenager and his pal had climbed high into a pine for a bird's-eye view. The setting was golf-tournament quiet, only whispers breaking the silence of the High Sierra like ripples on a glass-smooth lake.

Clarkson, the *Sports Illustrated* photographer, quietly positioned himself at an angle extending straight from the bar itself so he could get the jump and the jumper's reaction. Newnham, the *Oakland Tribune* reporter, penciled notes of the scene. "I'd never seen the Flop," he remembered. "It was fascinating. This big, tall, angular kid who didn't look like an athlete—and folks watching while perched on boulders."

Fosbury toed his mark. Exhaled. Shook his hands. Started the rocking. *Correction: Reach for the sky, not the bar; go "up," not "forward." Head up, not in . . . Connection: Feel the power, the lift, from the right leg as you climb into the air. Disconnection: Now is the time. Your time. You're going to make this, right now. OK, here we go: three, two, one . . .*

Later, OSU coach Berny Wagner would say it was the finest jump Dick Fosbury had ever made. Like an artist in italic motion, Fosbury leapt, leaned backward, arched, and, until landing on the Port-a-Pit a second later, felt nothing but the glorious nothingness of Echo Summit air. In unison, the reaction burst forth: Dick's smile of relief, two arms thrust in the air while motor-drive cameras whirred, and hundreds of fans—Gail among them—clapped and cheered for the inventor of the Fosbury Flop. No event all week had mesmerized the crowd for so long as this one.

"I saw it," a German reporter said, "but I don't believe it."

Dick had joined Caruthers and Brown as co-owner of 1968's highest leaps in the world. What's more, 7'3" was the new collegiate record and, of course, a new Oregon State school record. Wagner, Dick's coach, approached an official to request a measurement, not uncommon when records are on the line. Meanwhile, like a match-play golf event where the first golfer to go sinks his putt, there was a sense among the crowd that the event was over, so climactic seemed Fosbury's jump. But it wasn't. Hartfield had yet to "putt." He was not only very much alive but in a position to effectively eliminate Fosbury with a single successful jump.

It had come down to a game of Russian roulette. If Hartfield had just one more bullet in his chamber—if he made this next jump—it was almost certainly over for Dick; he'd drop to fourth place based on more misses. In such a case, his only chance would be to make 7'4"—essentially half a foot higher than he'd jumped at the start of 1968—and hope one of the others couldn't, an unlikely proposition.

On the other hand, if Hartfield missed on his first attempt, *he* would sink to fourth place because even if he cleared on his second or third attempts, the other three would still have fewer misses at their most recent height made. With a miss here, the only way Hartfield could finish among the top three would be to clear 7'3" on his second or third attempt, then win the battle at 7'4", improbable at best.

Hartfield headed for his mark. Meanwhile, Dick got a quick pat on the back from a beaming Berny Wagner. "Way to go, baby!" he whispered. "The officials are gonna give you a measure for the record book." Dick smiled. It felt good to make Wagner proud. Radetich hopped off his rock and offered a quick handshake. Dick nodded at other athletes who were giving him thumbs-ups and air claps.

Meanwhile, with late-afternoon shadows shading the ski hill behind him, Hartfield faced the bar. He exhaled. Steeled his focus. Loped to the bar. And jumped. The crowd groaned. He'd missed. With that single failure, his first of the day, Hartfield had suddenly dropped to last place. The other three had cleared the same height on their first attempts. Now, his lone hope was to make 7'3" on one of his last two attempts and somehow get over 7'4".

Jump two. Hartfield returned to his mark, faced the bar, and tried to compose himself. As was his routine, he looked down to find his mental "zone." Just as he did so, the two track officials—apparently not anticipating him already in the "go" position—quietly took a tape and stool to the center of the bar. They were going to measure to confirm the height for Dick's probable records, a procedure that should have been done before Hartfield's first attempt.

Meanwhile, Hartfield locked into his psyche routine. Eyes down, mind lost in preparation, waiting for just the right moment. On the stool so he could be eye-level with the bar, one official looked closely at the vertical tape and whispered "seven-three on the nose" to the other official. A few fans fidgeted. *Didn't the officials realize Hartfield was almost ready for takeoff? And didn't Hartfield realize the runway wasn't clear?*

Finished with their task, the two officials headed to the side of the pit, but the one carrying the stool lagged behind. Hartfield glanced up and sprang toward the bar. Suddenly, he lurched to a halt, seeing the official out front. He glared at the official in disbelief, then spread his arms, palms up, as if pleading for respect. "Hey, man, get out of there! I got to jump. I don't care about no foolish record." He turned and walked away, shaking his head.

Verne Boatner, sports editor of the *Arizona Republic,* quickly scribbled Hartfield's comments on his note pad. Nearby, long-jumper Ralph Boston shook his head. "That wasn't a smart thing to do," he later said. "The officials totally disrupted John's rhythm."

Hartfield kept walking away from the pit, facing the fans who ringed the outside of the track. A few minutes later, after failing to regain his mental focus, he missed. Now he readied for his final attempt at 7'3". Make it and the bar would go to 7'4" with all four jumpers still alive. Miss it and his Olympic dream would die; he, not the guy who had trailed all afternoon, Fosbury, would be the odd man out.

All was quiet. Stan put his arm around Toni's shoulder in encouragement. Gail pursed her lips. Fosbury awaited his fate.

Hartfield looked up, then began his approach. Fosbury froze in anticipation.

Hartfield gathered himself for the jump. Fosbury's heart pounded.

Hartfield kicked up a straight leg and curled over the bar. Fosbury winced.

Hartfield nudged the bar off with a trailing leg. Fosbury exhaled.

In the split-second it took for the bar to fall, Dick Fosbury became an Olympian. The crowd groaned in empathy for Hartfield. Fosbury wilted in relief, bending over, hands over his face, eyes wet with tears. He'd made it. *Mom! Gotta call Mom!* This was no time for tumult and shouting, particularly with Hartfield nearby, but Fosbury quietly reveled in his success. In his surviving. In his future. No high-jump competition had drained him as much.

Meanwhile, like a wounded animal, Hartfield instinctively bolted for the woods—"tears in his eyes," remembered Boston—and, minutes later, only looked back when he heard the footsteps. They belonged to his wife, Toni, of course, going to comfort him. "We'd gone from being so high to so low just like *that*," she later said.

Her father, Stan, drew his hands to his face in anguish, feeling his son-in-law's—and daughter's—pain. The moment was the high-altitude version of the 1956 Trials when Ernie Shelton, who'd marked his bedroom wall to inspire him to be the first jumper over 7'0", took a double-hit at LA's Memorial Coliseum: Charles Dumas cleared 7'0"—for the first time in history—and Shelton missed making the team, a photo in *Life* magazine capturing his agonized exit through a Coliseum tunnel.

At Echo Summit, the crowd, out of reverence for Hartfield, momentarily held its applause, then filled the thin air with wild approval—"Way to go, Foz!"—and not only for Dick, but for the three men who would represent the US in the Olympics. They cheered for the experience of watching an unprecedented performance of four athletes in a storybook place, in a time, 1968, when America was aching for something triumphant. And they cheered for Hartfield, who had kept reaching, and finding, more and more and more—until there was no "more" to find.

He had put together the finest high-jumping day of his life but he was one make, or one Fosbury miss, away. After struggling earlier, Dick's two-miss clearance of 7'2" and first-jump make of 7'3" had been a one-two jab for which the Texan had no answer. Across the track, Gail whooped and hollered, the revelry accompanied by a singular thought: *My brother's going to win the Olympics. I just know it.*

A few minutes after the high jump concluded, Ryun roared back from last place on the final lap to win the 1,500 meters. Dave Patrick, who'd won in LA and had the fastest time of the two Tahoe preliminary heats, finished fourth, one spot from making the team.

Fosbury and his two new teammates, Caruthers and Brown, each took an unsuccessful shot at 7'4"—it would have been a new American record—and then congratulated each other for making the team, posed for photos, and answered reporters' questions. The three qualifiers were a diverse mix: Two black, one white. Two straddlers, one Flopper. A veteran, Caruthers; a newcomer, Fosbury; and a babe in the literal woods, Brown. But now, they were one as American teammates.

Nearby, in a ski lodge's press room, Bruce Ferris of the *Fresno Bee* typed " . . . the US track and field squad concluded its week-long meet at this high altitude camp with one of the most dramatic high-jump duels in history . . . ." US Olympic Coach Payton Jordan went a step further, saying it was one of the most dramatic track and field events he'd ever witnessed, period.

Dick went to the pay phone. "Mom," he said. "I did it. I'm going to the Olympics!"

With the trials now over, the fifty-four men who would represent America in the Games had been decided. But for every athlete who'd raised a fist in joy there were three or four who had not. Of the "agony of defeat," there was much, among the most poignant Hartfield's near miss. "I watched him run into the woods," remembered Fosbury, "and didn't see him again for twenty years." Earlier, Billy Mills, the Native American who'd won gold in the 10,000 meters in 1964, beseeched the committee to grant him a waiver to run the 5,000-meter event after stomach cramps felled him in the 10,000. *Sorry,* replied the USOC track committee; *rules are rules.* Well, unless they get changed in midstream as they had a week ago.

Nobody had learned that more painfully than Dave Patrick and Bill Clark. They were both winners in LA. But at the eleventh-hour meeting called to question the qualifying system, it had been Patrick's statement that broke the political log jam: if he couldn't prove myself at altitude, he'd told his fellow athletes, he didn't deserve to go to Mexico City. In his silence, Clark said as much. And, in the end, only two of the eighteen winners in LA failed to earn a ticket to the Games: Patrick and Clark, the latter who wilted at altitude, running nearly three minutes slower than he had in LA (29:11.0 to 32:05.6).

Patrick was inconsolable. Forty feet from the finish line in the 1,500 meters, he realized he was going to finish fourth, one spot out. He'd thrown his arms in the air and started sobbing, according to the *Fresno Bee.* Later, as his father tried to console him, Patrick said: "Why? Why did I have to pick today to run a bad race?" In the days to come, his coach at Villanova, Jim "Jumbo" Elliott, would make a well-publicized protest, demanding Patrick be included on the team, but to no avail. The same USOC that had listened to "the people" wasn't listening to the coach, Elliott.

Patrick's misfortune could have just as easily been that of Fosbury, who had quietly stewed all week about such possibilities and who was one miss away from not making the team. Instead, the committee's on-site travel agent wasn't booking him on a flight home to Medford but to Denver, where the US team would gather, be outfitted, go through an orientation, and leave for Mexico City.

That night, Fosbury celebrated (a lot), slept (a little), and soon was on a plane to Denver. As he dozed, it was as if, for the first time since his 7'0" jump in Oakland nearly eight months before, he'd relaxed. By now, seven years since Greg's death, six weeks since the near-drowning at Lake Tahoe, and a day after securing a spot on the team with the jump of a lifetime, Dick Fosbury was more than an Olympian. He was a survivor, the reminder imbued forever in what decathlete Bill Toomey called the "sacred ground of Echo Summit."

Chapter 21

To be great, one does not have to be mad, but definitely it helps.

—*Percy Cerutty*

AS OCTOBER ARRIVED, more political tension charged an Olympic prelude than at any other time since Berlin in 1936. It had been thirty-two years since Adolf Hitler dared showcase the splendors of his country, its well-camouflaged racist and militaristic ways hidden beneath a cloak of propaganda that, despite an insistence by the NAACP that the US boycott the Games, effectively worked. Now, twelve days before the opening ceremonies would welcome 5,500 athletes from 112 countries, pent-up anger among university students in Mexico City roiled like late-summer thunderstorms. Since July, students—up to 50,000—had taken to the streets to defy a repressive government. Since July, the police had pushed back.

On October 2, lightning struck. In the Plaza de las Tres Culturas, amid the Aztec ruins of the Tlatelolco section of Mexico City, two police helicopters and one army helicopter hovered over a throng of some 5,000 students. Flares streaked through the darkness. Shots rang out. Amid the whir of chopper blades, screams pierced the night. People ran for cover. More shots. More chaos. In the end, some 300 to 400 protesters lay dead and more than a thousand people were arrested. In Mexico, it would become known as La Noche Triste (the Sad Night). It was an ominous prelude to the 1968 Olympic Games.

Fosbury and the US men's track and field team arrived Sunday, October 6, four days after the massacre and a week before the opening ceremonies. Dick had only vaguely heard of the tragedy, living, as it were, in something of an Olympic Games bubble: aware of a weary world but momentarily safe from it.

On Friday, October 11, Apollo 7 launched from Cape Kennedy, the first US mission into space since the fire had killed a three-man crew in 1967. Walter Schirra was in command of this three-man crew whose eleven-day mission involved 163 orbits of earth.

On that same day, Fosbury was thirsty for adventure, too. When former OSU teammate Gary Stenlund—a javelin thrower—informed Dick that he'd had a friend drive his 1965 VW camper to Mexico City, Dick's ears perked up. Stenlund recommended a quick road trip, and Dick was all in. They took in some sites, tested some beer, picked up some American women who had swum on the 1964 Olympic team, and ultimately wound up thirty miles from the village at the Pyramid of the Moon in the ancient city of Teotihuacan. The Olympic torch was soon to pass through on its way to its final destination at the stadium. Tens of thousands had gathered for the festivities, replete with music, drinking, and costumed dancers.

"Hey, gringos," a local intoned, "come have tortilla soup with us!"

Dick was infatuated with the whole scene. So enchanted was he by the people, the pyramid—and, of course, the cute swimmers—that he, along with the others, decided to stay all night at the nearly 2,000-year-old stone structure. Heading back to Mexico City the next day, he and Stenlund underestimated the heavy traffic. They missed the opening ceremony entirely.

Had Fosbury gone mad? No, but Rich Roberts, in a column for the *Long Beach Independent Press-Telegram,* called him "slightly flaky." In terms of cultural significance, Fosbury contended that celebrating the opening of the game "with the Mexican people" enriched the experience in a way that 500 Americans dressing as one probably did not.

In another eight days, Fosbury would shoot for the moon. For now, with the trip behind him, he settled into the more mundane routine of waiting. Meanwhile, in Dick's hometown of Medford, the *Mail Tribune* announced that the deadline for signing the telegram wishing their favorite son good luck in the Olympics was Saturday, October 12. People could add their names at the Ice Cream Palace, Lamport's

Sporting Goods, Robinson Brothers, and Drew's Manstore. "Fosbury jumped 7 feet 3 inches to qualify for the US track and field team," wrote the *Medford Mail Tribune*, "and it is felt that he just might bring back a medal—perhaps the gold one."

In Mexico City, reporters, fans—even competitors and coaches—wanted to see Fosbury jump in practice. But that had never been his mode of operation, nor was he about to change it for the Games. He loved jumping in front of people at meets, affording fans the opportunity to enjoy the feats of Fosbury and Dick to enjoy the fans. But making meaningless jumps in front of a throng seemed too much like animal-in-the-zoo stuff to him.

After the track and field competition started Sunday, October 13, and with his prelims set for six days later, he worked out daily. But jumping? Only after prodding from Wagner did he do so—and only one session. He went 6'11". What made the day memorable for Fosbury was a rainstorm forcing the jumpers to huddle under traps, and Dick finding himself next to the Soviet star, Valentin Gavrilov. The two couldn't have been more different, in one sense Cold War enemies. They represented two countries that had nearly come to nuclear blows six years before. They couldn't speak much of each other's language. And given the Soviets' heavily regimented approach to jumping, the two were decidedly different. Gavrilov was like the drum majorette in a precision marching band, Fosbury a rock star sliding onto the stage on his knees, electric-guitar wailing. Though the Cold War had thawed considerably in the 1960s, in part because each country had messes of their own that required attention they might have otherwise given each other, the press still played on the international rivalry—though not as intensely as the propaganda war of the 1960 Games in Rome.

"What I found," said Dick, "was how much the two of us had in common." They talked—awkwardly—of human rights. Of the Mexico students' protests. Of the Flop and straddle. "It was," Fosbury later said, "an experience I'll never forget. It opened my eyes to a larger world—to the value of what I'd later call Olympism."

Gavrilov, for Fosbury, had become both friend and foe, the former built on the same kind of spirit that had carried the day six years earlier when, after a dual meet in Palo Alto, American and Soviet athletes dispensed with the planned protocol for a post-meet flag ceremony. When Soviet javelin thrower Viktor Tsybulenko met American high jumper John Thomas in the middle of the field, the two flag bearers spontaneously hugged, and the other athletes followed suit, then walked arm-in-arm around the stadium, blowing kisses to the crowd in unrehearsed international unity.

High-jump qualifying would be on a Saturday, October 19, with the finals on Sunday, October 20, the closing day of track and field competition. Other than the last of the marathoners, the high jump would be the last event of the day. The waiting game continued. The pressure started to build. "Pressure at the trials doesn't compare to this," Fosbury told Leo Davis of *The Oregonian*.

He worried about his mental state, so critical to his jumping well. Some jumpers were methodical in their approach, as if powered by repeatable, mechanical scripts that they had honed in practice. Fosbury was different. He was powered by his mind—and by a style about which the world was still scratching its collective head. Like the launch of a spacecraft, Fosbury's rocketing into the sky was the culmination of myriad parts creating optimum energy: a big meet, intense competition, the right frame of mind, every fiber of his body attuned to the moment, undiluted confidence, the crowd itself, even the doubters—all was fodder for the mental fuel Fosbury relied on. But only days before the biggest meet of his life, Dick was sensing doubt. The *Oregon Journal* labeled it "depression." Dick called it uncertainty. "Frankly, I don't know," he told Davis.

His living conditions weren't helping. Fosbury was, for privacy's sake, sleeping in the laundry room of an Olympic Village apartment that he was sharing with "about 112" other US athletes. "I can't say I really like it." Boredom was gnawing at him. "There isn't anything to do at the village—except what recreation you can create for yourself." (Like what he didn't tell Davis—how he and Stenlund had spent a few afternoons at Hotel Del Angel's penthouse bar, hobnobbing with the likes of ABC's Howard Cosell and Jim McKay.)

Each day, to millions of viewers, McKay and Cosell narrated the televised story of American triumph, trials, and, it turned out, tension. At *Estadio Olímpico*, the US track team was in the midst of winning more gold medals than any men's track and field team in history. The never-aging Al Oerter captured his fourth straight discus gold medal, Jim Hines won the 100-meter dash with a world record, and Bob Seagren took the pole vault. None matched Bob Beamon's otherworldly 29'2½" in the long jump, breaking the previous world record by 1.74 *feet.*

The most painful story may have been that of Oregon's Wade Bell, the favorite in the 800 meters who, slammed by Montezuma's revenge, never made it past the first heat. He'd lost seven pounds since arriving and, as Kenny Moore wrote in *Bowerman and the Men of Oregon,* "walked the streets of Mexico until dawn, trying to reconcile himself to the fact that microbes on a random piece of bacon had so destroyed his world."

As feared, Mexico City's altitude took its toll on US distance runners; despite two months of high-altitude training, the US won only three of eighteen medals in the six distance events, none gold.

Then came one of the defining moments of the 1968 Olympics—indeed, of the entire decade. On Wednesday, Tommie Smith and John Carlos placed first and third, respectively, in the 200-meter dash. On the awards stand, the two black athletes raised single, black-gloved fists—and wore Olympic Project for Human Rights badges—during the playing of "The Star-Spangled Banner." Boos rained down from the stands, though the in-stadium response was muted compared to that of television viewers because, in the days before giant video screens, many fans didn't understand what had happened. Those at home, watching close-up shots and hearing ABC's commentary, certainly did: while runner-up Peter Norman of Australia displayed an OPHR badge to show his solidarity, the two had done more than call attention to racial discrimination but had defied Brundage, the IOC president.

Brundage reacted quickly, angrily, and forcefully. He ordered the two suspended and banned from the Olympic Village. When the USOC refused, Brundage threatened to boot the entire men's track and field team, which, of course, would have included Fosbury. That threat gave the USOC no choice but to send Smith and Carlos home.

Some rose to the pair's defense; Bowerman called Brundage's reaction "childish, the kind of thing you get from the old aristocracy." Most scolded Smith and Carlos for what they saw as snubbing the sanctity of The Games. *Time* magazine's cover, playing off the "Faster, Higher, Stronger" motto of the Games, countered later in the week with "Angrier, Nastier, Uglier." Smith and Carlos got death threats. Harry Edwards's dog was killed and butchered. Countered Carlos: "Where was the outrage when blacks were being billy-clubbed?"

Few press outlets—*Sports Illustrated* a notable exception—seemed interested in the deeper story: what Smith and Carlos's experiences as black men in America had led them to make a stand that they surely knew would cost them dearly for the remainder of their lives. *Los Angeles Times* columnist Jim Murray mocked the two, opening a column on Fosbury, "If this comes to you garbled, don't blame the transmission. I'm wearing my black glove." It was the type of line written by someone who'd never been refused housing or had to eat at the side door of a diner—nor seemed interested in hearing what that's like for those who had.

On Thursday morning, Fosbury opened the building door to find dozens of reporters wanting to know "whose side he was on." Fosbury fled like a hiker besieged by mosquitoes. He had an event to prepare for; he couldn't afford to get embroiled in politics.

BERNY WAGNER BRISTLED with confidence in Dick. "I think he'll win at 7'4"," he told *T&F News*. Fosbury, meanwhile, remained in a self-described "rut," encased in an emotional fog that only got thicker after a walk through the village on Thursday. He was heading down some rock steps while wearing huarache sandals when he slipped. The edge of a rock sliced the heel of his left (non-jumping) foot like a carpenter's plane on wood. Blood soaked into the sandal. Fosbury limped back to the Olympic Village in search of a trainer and began fretting about the disastrous timing of it all. He'd never missed a meet because of injury. Now, on the eve of his Olympic debut, his fretting soon turned to what he would later call "freaking out."

Forget his mental state. Forget the boredom. Forget the pesky press. Those weren't problems now. The problem was: Could he even jump?

Chapter 22

The ultimate measure of a man is not where he stands in moments of comfort and convenience, but where he stands at times of challenge and controversy.

—Martin Luther King Jr.

FOR DR. DONALD Cooper, the trip to see Fosbury was the first time he'd ever made a house call to a laundry room. Cooper, an Oklahoma sports medicine specialist and the team doctor, put the final touches on dressing a wound that, to Dick, felt as if someone had wrapped a hot coal to his heel.

"How's that?" asked Dr. Cooper with a touch of Midwestern drawl.

"Hurts, but it'll be OK."

It was Friday, the day before the high-jump prelims.

"There's no medical reason you can't jump, Dick, so it all depends on how much of the pain you can put up with," said Cooper. "What do you think?"

Fosbury knew pain. Long-ago pain. "It's the Olympics. I'll be fine."

A timid knock came from the apartment's front door.

"Telegrama para Dick Fosbury," came a voice. One of Dick's "112" roommates opened the door. A Mexican courier timidly walked in. "In here!" said Dick. The courier handed him a large envelope. When he opened it, Fosbury smiled for the first time in days. The telegram included the name of seemingly everybody who lived in Medford, Oregon, beneath an exhortation to go for the gold. Hundreds and hundreds of names from the place he'd grown up. He recognized most of them, including, of course, his father (his mother was here to watch in person), Coach Benson, Coach Spiegelberg, teachers, grocers, police officers, civic leaders, fellow Medford High students, and hundreds of people whose names he didn't recognize but somehow believed in him.

Dick's eyes glistened, which didn't go unnoticed by Dr. Cooper, who smiled.

"No way you can bow out now, kid," said the doctor after gathering his bag and heading out the door. "Good luck, Mr. Fosbury."

FLAGS FROM 112 nations—and armed troops fearing possible rioters at this portion of the University of Mexico campus—ringed *Estadio Olímpico* as Fosbury arrived for the first of what he hoped would be two days of competition. Dick did some light jogging and was pleasantly surprised with the results; he hardly felt the heel pain. He took a few jumps, relieved. He was good to go.

Thirty-nine jumpers, by far more than Fosbury had ever competed against, warmed up for the prelims at two high-jump setups in the stadium, which spread symmetrically in an oval-shaped, and more modern, version of LA's Memorial Coliseum. The Olympic torch blazed from atop the stadium rim. Somewhere in the vast sea of people was his mother, Helen, and his coach Berny Wagner, basking in the mid-70s sunshine and the anticipation of the event to come.

Of all the men's track and field events, said *Track & Field News*, none was more wide open than the high jump. Had Brumel not had the motorcycle accident, that might not have been the case; at twenty-six, he would have been older than most in the field but clearly the odds-on favorite. He had jumped 7'5¾"—on cinders, into a sawdust pit—compared to the 7'3" of the three Americans. But now, the Soviets' quest for a third straight gold medal was wrought with uncertainty.

The Soviets had dominated international high-jumping in the 1960s. Robert Shavlakadze and Brumel had gone one-two in the 1960 Olympics in Rome. Brumel had won in Tokyo in 1964 and had now held the world record for seven years. The last time an American had set the top mark— Thomas at 7'3⅜" in July 1960—Fosbury had been a thirteen-year-old kid in Medford jumping over a wooden bar in his backyard. It had been nearly twelve years since an American had won a gold medal in high jumping; in 1956, in Melbourne, Charles Dumas triumphed at 2.12 meters (6'11½").

In head-to-head competition at the *Los Angeles Times* games in February 1968, the Soviets' Valentin Gavrilov (7'2") had defeated Caruthers (7'1"), Fosbury (7'0"), and Otis Burrell (7'0"). Even so, Gavrilov's Soviet teammate, Valeriy Skvortsov (7'1⅞"), was jumping more consistently than his teammate and was considered by *Track & Field News* to be the more serious threat.

France's Robert Sainte-Rose had Olympic experience and had set a French record at 7'2¼" in August, so he was hot. Giacomo Crosa of Italy and Lawrie Peckham of Australia could be dangerous as well. Still, *T&F News's* Hendershott expected a US-Soviet showdown; Skvortsov was the most consistent Soviet jumper, but Gavrilov had the best mark (7'2⅝"). On the US side of the ledger, the inexperienced Brown, wrote Jon Hendershott, "may be in a little deep," but he thought Caruthers and Fosbury were "definite medal possibilities."

Magazines were split on who they thought would win. *Sport* magazine said Fosbury was America's "best bet." *Sports Illustrated* predicted gold for Caruthers, silver for Gavrilov, and bronze for Skvortsov. Caruthers had steeled his focus on Mexico City as soon as he'd finished eighth in Tokyo four years before, a victim, he said, of wide eyes (he was only nineteen) and too many desserts before the competition. He had researched, and to a large degree followed, the Soviets' stringent training schedules, heavy on weight lifting, all to redeem himself. In his eyes, this was the event he'd been waiting for since 1964.

The top twelve, plus ties, would qualify for Sunday's finals. As expected, Fosbury and Caruthers cruised through the prelims, and Brown slipped into what turned out to be a field of thirteen. That night, Dick slept restlessly in his re-purposed laundry room. These weren't Grants Pass and Ashland jumpers he'd be facing in Sunday's finals. These were the best of the best. As sleep tugged, he shook such thoughts from his mind. *You and the bar; you and the bar.*

As always, Fosbury rose with the sun. The high jump was to start at 2:30 pm (12:30 pm back in Oregon). At mid-morning, he and Wagner took the bus to the practice field next to the stadium. Dick jogged a few laps, did a few short sprints, and uncorked a few pop-ups. No jumping. The loudspeaker soon crackled to life. "*Saltadores de altura, repórtese al funcionario del evento.*" ("High jumpers, report to the event official.") As he walked down the ramp into the tunnel that marathoners would later use to enter the stadium, he was already in the zone. Loose. Confident. Anxious, but not fearful.

Each jumper had his own plan. Fosbury would start at 2.03 meters (6'8") and, until 2.20 meters (7'2⁵⁄₁₆"), jump at even-inch heights and pass at odd-inch heights. He liked that rhythm because it got him in the flow of jumping but didn't overtax him. The Soviets' Gavrilov, on the other hand, would start at the opening height of 2.00 meters (6'6¾") and jump at nearly every height.

But "plans" didn't win gold medals, athletes did. Especially athletes driven to prevail regardless of what obstacles came their way. On June 29, 1956, at the US Olympic Track and Field Trials in Los Angeles's Memorial Coliseum, nineteen-year-old Charles Dumas had shown up without his participant's pass. He pleaded with the folks at the gate. "I'm one of the athletes, I'm a high jumper, let me in!" Sorry. No pass, no entry. His shot to become an Olympian seemed thwarted, until, in his desperation, he realized he had but one choice. He bought a ticket and entered with the spectators. He then became the first human being to high-jump 7'0"—and went on to win a gold medal in Melbourne. *Whatever it takes.*

Soon it came time for Fosbury to begin the biggest competition of his young life. A teal-colored Port-a-Pit welcomed jumpers from a sand-colored Tartan apron, the finest setup Fosbury had ever seen; because of the sprawling apron, for the first time in his career, he wouldn't have to begin on one surface—grass, dirt, or cinders—and transition to another. A standard black-and-white Gill triangular bar framed the pit. Eight officials, two women and six men, stood or sat poker-faced, in burgundy blazers and gray, felt fedoras. Near the track, the heads of photographers popped out of two sunken photo pits like camera-toting groundhogs.

Fosbury wore the standard US uniform—white silk bottoms with red piping and a blue singlet with "USA" stitched bold in red and white across the chest, above his number (272). On his left foot: a blue Adidas spike shoe. On his right: a white Adidas jump shoe, spikes on the heel as well, plus a one-centimeter lift that offered jumpers a slight mechanical advantage, like jumping off a low box. He wished good luck to his teammates—Brown, the high school kid, and Caruthers, the veteran who'd been waiting for this chance for nearly 1,500 days.

Fosbury, on the other hand, arrived as something of an unexpected guest—a jumper who, in a ten-month period, had gone from being ranked in a twelve-way tie for fiftieth in the world to being a gold-medal contender at the Olympics. Two years prior, in the fall of 1966, he'd been fretting about staying on the OSU team, still trying to break 6'0" with the straddle. Two months ago he'd been working at a burger shack in South Lake Tahoe.

The task before him was formidable. "Fosbury," wrote *Track & Field News'* Hendershott, "[is] up against the toughest field ever assembled to do battle for the Olympic title." Fifteen members of the field had cleared 7'0". Virtually all had international experience; other than his just-over-the-border competition in Vancouver, BC, Fosbury had never jumped outside the US.

The stadium, the crowd, the blue sky, the torch—for an athlete, the scene was the essence of inspiration. But weirdly, Dick's epiphany had come weeks before, when the team had bussed from Denver to Colorado Springs for some high-altitude workouts. At one point, the bus stopped along the way, and as he watched his teammates pile off, it dawned on Dick what an amazing collage of humanity this was: guys who were white, black, rich, poor, from different regions, no two alike but all Americans with a quest to excel at this thing called sport. It was a noble undertaking, Fosbury thought, and he was humbled to be part of it. To *belong*.

"You have earned the highest athletic honors your country can bestow upon you," Coach Payton Jordan had written to the 1968 team. Dick did not take that lightly.

In the stadium, the anticipation ended for the start of the competition. Jumpers from around the world began taking their first attempts. Soon the official looked Dick's way. "*Siguiente saltador, Dick Fosbury, Estados Unidos.*"

Fosbury exhaled, took his mark, shook his hands, fixed his gaze on the bar, and slowly began to rock back and forth.

Whatever it takes.

Chapter 23

Time is an illusion, timing is an art.

—*Stefan Emunds*

WHEN DICK FOSBURY curled backward over the bar, "a yowl" erupted from the Mexico City crowd like nothing *Seattle Times* columnist Georg N. Meyers had heard in the stadium all week. Never mind that the bar was set at the ho-hum height of 2.03 meters (6'8"); the reaction for Fosbury was strikingly loud. "From then on," Meyers wrote, "every time the freckle-faced youngster from Medford poised and started at the bar, nothing else in the stadium existed for the fans."

"Only a triple somersault off a flying trapeze with no net below could be more thrilling," scrawled a German reporter, down the press-box row from Meyers, on a notepad. Around the world, viewers seeing the style for the first time did double takes. "I grew up with the roll and the straddle," said Per Anderson, a jumper in the US, "but when I saw Fosbury on TV from Mexico City it absolutely took my breath away. The speed, lightness, and simplicity totally changed the way I looked at high jumping."

With the stadium crowd predominantly Mexican and with Mexico having no competitors in the event, it quickly became apparent who their favorite was: Dick Fosbury. The jumpers were all different sizes, shapes, and skin colors. They represented different countries. They wore an array of uniforms. But only one jumped backward over the bar.

"The Mexicans love style," wrote *The Oregonian*'s Leo Davis. "They adopted Dick immediately."

Fosbury easily cleared 2.09 meters (6'10¼") and 2.14 meters (7'¼"). He passed at 2.16 (7'1"). When the bar went to 2.18 meters (7'1⅞"), only five jumpers were left. Three—Fosbury, Brown, and Gavrilov—had nailed every one of their attempts, while two—Caruthers and Skvortsov—were struggling to keep pace. Caruthers, bothered with the slow pace of the competition, couldn't relax and find the groove. Uncharacteristically, he needed all three of his attempts at 2.14 meters (7'¼"). "I had some scary jumps in there," he remembered. "I was having trouble staying loose and warm because earlier, with the bar starting so low (2.00 meters, 6'6¾"), there'd been so much time between jumps."

Soon came the competition's first surprise: Gavrilov passed at 2.18 meters (7'1⅞"). Such a strategy wasn't unheard of, but was unusual, particularly in a competition in which he'd already made seven straight jumps at every height offered. As Fosbury psyched up for the same height, rocking back and forth, he was so deep into the "zone" that he didn't even notice a virtual parade of officials walking close behind him, almost as if with military precision, each carrying a green lawn chair. No matter. Fosbury cleared the height by at least two inches.

At times, between jumps, Fosbury sat down, closed his eyes, and meditated. At other times, he connected with all that was going on around him. With a glimpse here and a glimpse there, he watched Kip Keino outrace Jim Ryun to victory in the 1,500 meters. He watched fellow Oregonian Margaret Johnson Bailes, a seventeen-year-old sprinter from Eugene, run a leg on the US women's 400-meter relay team that won gold. And he watched Lee Evans lean into the first turn on the final leg of the 4x400 relay. "Go, baby!" said Fosbury, a lone voice of encouragement on the otherwise vacant inside rail. Later, Evans would jokingly blame Fosbury for inspiring him to go out too fast, though he compensated to anchor a world-record effort.

"Fosbury's two teammates, Reynaldo Brown and Ed Caruthers, spent time between jumps doing knee bends and kickups," the Associated Press said. "Fosbury sat under an umbrella and yawned."

At 2.18 meters (7'1⅞"), Fosbury flipped backward over the bar for his fourth straight make, then watched as Caruthers, Skvortsov, and Brown all missed, the latter two on their final attempts. When Caruthers cleared on his final attempt, then lay in the pit with his hands over his face in what looked to be either relief or exhaustion, only three jumpers were left: Fosbury, Gavrilov, and Caruthers. All were assured of a medal; none wanted anything but gold.

"*La barra del salto de altura de hombres acaba de subir a dos veinte,*" said the stadium announcer. ("The men's high jump bar has just risen to two-twenty.") Fosbury was first to jump at 7'2⅝", just half an inch short of his best at Echo Summit and what would be a new Olympic record. He exhaled. Hitched up his shorts. Shook his hands to his sides. Took his position and began his back-and-forth rock, almost looking mechanical.

He clenched and unclenched his fists in front of him. With his right foot forward, he rocked once, twice, three times. A smattering of clapping started to build as if an audible send-off. Some fans began counting his rocking out loud: *ocho, nueve, diez* . . .. Like a deer in the forest, Fosbury seemingly heard every snapped twig—every clap, every "Fly, Gringo, Fly!" And it empowered him. He rocked back and forth, stiffly, like the Tin Man trying to wriggle out of fast-drying concrete. By now he was on his fortieth rock forward, processing "outside" stimuli into inside fuel, waiting for the perfect moment. *Three, two, one* . . ..

Fosbury launched. Eight steps on the "J" approached, a leap, and—a collective pause from the crowd—*another make!* The crowd roared. Fosbury bounded from the pit with a boyish smile, uninhibited by any particular social protocol, thrusting an arm in the air.

Gavrilov, with no such pre-jump fanfare, wasted little time rolling over the bar as smoothly as melted butter. Soft landing. Hard look on his face. No smiles from the business-like Soviets. *Jump quickly, jump successfully, stop the momentum of your opponent.* Caruthers cleared, too, as if to suggest he'd finally come out of his funk.

"*La barra del salto de altura de hombres acaba de subir a dos veintidós,*" said the stadium announcer. ("The men's high jump bar has just climbed to two-twenty-two.") The trio had already surpassed Valeriy Brumel's Olympic record and were on the verge of becoming the first three high jumpers in history to all go beyond 7'3" in the same competition.

The new height was 7'3⅜", three-eighths of an inch higher than Fosbury and Caruthers had gone and nearly an inch higher than

Gavrilov's best. At times like this, Fosbury didn't like jumping first. To go first in a tight competition was to be like the visiting baseball team with the score tied in the top of the ninth. You batted first, but what would it take to win? You didn't know. Could you *not* score and still win? Again, you didn't know. To bat last meant knowing exactly where you stood—and exactly what you needed to win.

Fosbury put all doubt to rest with a first-jump clearance of 2.22 meters—with no brush of the bar. When his back hit the pit, it was like a finger pushing a boom-box button—the crowd instantaneously burst into a one-note song of celebration. "Even the press, which usually showed little emotion at the events they were covering, cheered at his every jump," reported *Track & Field News*.

"It had become like a home meet for Dick," remembered Caruthers. "The crowd loved the novelty of his style. Even the announcer seemed to be in his corner."

For the first time, however, Fosbury came out of the pit with what looked to be a touch of doubt on his face. He offered a token wave of acknowledgment to the fans but looked back at the bar as he jogged off, almost as if surprised it was still there. Gone was the boyish smile. Had he tweaked his injured heel? Pulled a muscle? Only later would he say that it was none of the above. Instead, it was disbelief. He had just set a personal-best 7'3⅜" in front of 80,000 people at the Olympics. And for just a moment he was like an astronaut floating in space, amazed at his position in the universe, never dreaming he would find himself in a time and place like this.

CARUTHERS'S DAY HAD gone nothing like he'd imagined: the competition had progressed slowly, meaning long waits between attempts, and he had jumped poorly, meaning he risked a late-meet energy drain. He'd already missed four times, almost unheard of for him. Still, he'd waited four years to redeem himself. Anything could happen. Look how quickly Hartfield had gone from first to fourth at Echo Summit. That could happen to Gavrilov or Fosbury, maybe both.

Indeed, Gavrilov missed his initial attempt—his first after eight straight makes. But Caruthers failed, too. Suddenly, it was advantage Fosbury.

Gavrilov missed a second time. When Caruthers cleared on his second attempt, the pressure shifted back to the Soviet jumper. With his third and final failure, the Soviets had lost an Olympic high-jump title for the first time since 1956—and not only to two Americans (reminiscent of Thomas's 1960 loss to two Soviets) but perhaps to a backward-flipping American. His coach, Vladimir Dyachkov, was not likely to be happy.

Thirty-nine high jumpers had come to Mexico City from around the world. It was now down to two: Fosbury and Caruthers. The two were studies in contrast: Caruthers, a straddler, was quick to make his attempts, slow to approach the bar, and hesitant with a smile. He was a power jumper, a pure athlete whose granite-like body reflected the considerable weights he lifted and was one of the reasons NFL teams were interested in him. Twenty-three, he could pass for thirty.

Fosbury, the Flopper, was agonizingly slow in preparing to jump but fast to the bar and quick with the smile. He was a finesse jumper, a guy who'd failed at basketball, his favorite sport, and football, but had somehow taught his gangly body—or it had taught *him*—to leap backward over a high-jump bar with incredible success. Twenty-one, he could pass for sixteen.

"*La barra de salto alto de los hombres acaba de subir a dos veinticuatro,*" said the stadium announcer. ("The men's high jump bar has just gone up to two-twenty-four.")

THE TWO WERE jumping at a height the equivalent of 7'4¼", which only two others in the world—the Soviet Union's Brumel and China's Ni Chih-Chin—had ever exceeded. In the stands, Fosbury's mother, Helen, clenched and unclenched her fists in nervous anticipation. It had been only 5½ years ago that she'd dropped Dick off at Medford High before the Grants Pass Rotary Invitational, her kid hoping he could get beyond 5'4"—and Helen hoping she could rise from her depression following Greg's death and the divorce. She and Dick had come a long way. Next to family friends from Medford, the Polks, she stood and thrust a fist in the air. "Go, Dick!"

At his home in Grants Pass, Dick's father, Doug leaned in toward the Philco with anticipation. In Eugene, where she was attending the

University of Oregon, Gail watched on a TV tucked into the student union's "Fish Bowl" eatery, certain her brother was going to win. "It was," she said later, "like a Zen thing." Less than a mile from Gail, Dick's boyhood pal Doug Sweet—he'd gotten married and detoured briefly to the University of Oregon to earn teaching credentials—sipped a beer and watched the tiny TV he had propped atop a refrigerator in UO's Amazon Married Student Housing. He could hardly believe the high jumper on TV being seen by millions around the world was the same kid who'd put Limburger cheese on the cafeteria radiator. Finally, back in Medford, where the hundreds of people who'd signed the telegram for Dick grew more tense, a light wind swept over Siskiyou Memorial Park, where Greg was buried.

The bar in front of Fosbury was more than two feet higher than that 5'4" he'd once aspired to, a foot over his head. Eighty thousand people in the stadium, and millions in front of TVs around the world, watched—until ABC cut off its live coverage to stay within its two-hour time frame. (It would show delayed highlights later that night.) Each time Fosbury prepared to jump, a *T&F News* reporter noted, coaches from the Soviet bloc fixed their movie cameras on him; in a sense, he was becoming to them what the satellite Sputnik had been to the US—a high-in-the-sky "first" from which they needed to learn—so they could reach beyond.

It was now shortly after 6 pm. The competition had gone on nearly four hours, the longest, by far, of Dick's career. The height was uncharted territory for both athletes, though each had given 7'4" an unsuccessful shot at Echo Summit. If both missed, Fosbury would win the gold medal based on one fewer miss than Caruthers had at the last height cleared; Dick had made 2.22 meters (7'3⅜") on his first attempt, Caruthers on his second. Then again, if Caruthers made this height and Fosbury could not, the gold would go to Ed and silver to Dick. As in wrestling, a high jumper could be dominating a competition, as Dick was now doing, but, in a sudden reversal of fortune, find himself lying on his back, looking upward in defeat.

As Dick stood at his mark, the murmur of the crowd spiked in anticipation. *Feed off the people's faith in you . . .* Fosbury rocked, then rolled. Up, up, up he arched, then felt the sickening scrape of metal to body. The bar fell. The crowd's anticipation turned to audible anguish. He'd cleared it with his back and butt only to catch it with his heels. A rookie mistake. Mentally, Fosbury momentarily froze; to make six jumps in a row—nine straight in two days—and then miss was to be confronted, for the first time, with a sense of vulnerability, doubt, weakness. But he quickly snapped back to the future. *Get ready for the next jump.*

He sat on the bench and watched Caruthers. Brumel, the greatest jumper in the world, would purposely not watch his competition jump. Fosbury was different. It kept him tuned in. The crowd, the competition, the atmosphere—all fed into his senses like so many electrical lines into a transformer, helping him create energy for the inches he needed.

Caruthers readied for his first attempt at 2.24 meters (7'4¼"), a red Puma on his right foot, a white Puma on his left. As was his habit, he waited only a few seconds, then began his approach. He missed. It was back to "advantage Fosbury" on fewer misses—but a tenuous advantage.

Fosbury needed a make on his second try, too. He didn't get it. He now had but one bullet left in his chamber, knowing that if Caruthers cleared, Dick would be faced with a daunting situation: in front of the largest crowd he'd ever jumped in front, he would need to clear a height he'd never cleared—just to prolong the competition.

The crowd hushed for Caruthers, who exhaled, loped toward the bar, and—missed. All even. With each having one jump left, misses for them both would mean gold for Fosbury and silver for Caruthers, the tiebreaker based on Dick's no-miss clearance—and Ed's one-miss clearance—of the last height. But who wanted to back into a gold medal? Not Fosbury.

By now, the crowd was so engrossed in the high-jump competition that when marathon leader Mamo Wolde of Ethiopa entered the stadium through a tunnel across the track from the high-jump pit, the response was underwhelming. Some hadn't even noticed his arrival.

Caruthers bent over, hands on knees. Clearly, he was gassed. The long wait. The twelve jumps. The emotional toll of always having to play catch-up to Fosbury. Still, he tried to gather himself, knowing if Fosbury missed and he made it, the four-year wait would finally be over.

"Intento final a 2,24 metros por Dick Fosbury de los Estados Unidos."

This was it. Fosbury's final attempt at 7'4¼". He walked to his mark. At that precise moment, US marathoner Kenny Moore, in fourteenth place, was nearing the stadium from outside, his body wilted from having run twenty-six miles at 7,350 feet above sea level. A murmur emanated from the crowd as Fosbury took his mark.

Moore started through the tunnel, where he glimpsed the rust-colored track, green grass, and through eyes blurred by fatigue, a high-jumper. *An American? Some white jumper. Foz?*

Meanwhile, Fosbury's focus sharpened. Anything "to fix" from the last jump? *Nope*; 7'4¼" was there for the taking. He knew it. He just needed to trust his body. *You got this.* He clenched and unclenched his hands in front of him and began his rocking, waiting for the merger of heart, mind, and soul. *Whatever it takes.* The murmur of the crowd rose a notch, then another. *Ride their energy. Can do. Must do. Will do.* Ever so subtly, the rocking back and forth intensified; there would be thirty-seven total, the crowd counting each one, the last few as if triggering a launch-pad countdown ... *three* ... *two* ... *one* ... *ignition.*

He took eight strides, each pulsing with purpose. Then came liftoff, followed by 0.9 seconds of silence—the reach for the sky, the arch of the back, the thrust of the hips, the moment of truth, the moment of relief, the softness of the Don Gordon pit on his back.

Estadio Olímpico erupted with shrieks of delight; no moment, not even Beamon's jump, had ratcheted up the roar of fans like this. When Fosbury splashed down with the bar still in place, his joy became the joy of 80,000 fans, his smile their smiles, his two-finger peace symbol their two-finger peace symbol. For the fans, the celebration only sweetened after a weary Caruthers missed his final attempt. Not that he had failed (an Olympic silver medal is no athlete's failure) but that Fosbury and the Flop had succeeded. One of the worst prep high jumpers in Oregon was the new champion of the world, an Olympic gold medalist. For the first time since the 1956 Olympic Games, an American high jumper was atop track and field's Mt. Everest.

Fosbury and Caruthers shook hands. The motor drives whirred. The crowd's roar continued, as if the fans didn't want to let go of their adopted hero. Fosbury shook hands with Gavrilov, the Soviet who eight months before in Seattle had first seen the Flop and said "it can't be done." He jogged around like a kid on stage after a school play who was waving at his parents. Moore, the US marathoner, had broken into the sunlight of the stadium just in time for Fosbury's jump. He had looked at the high-jump reader board: "2.24." *My God, Olympic record.* "Way to go!" he yelled as he began his lap on the track.

Fosbury pointed to a marathoner ahead of Moore. "Get that guy!" he yelled.

Dick's mother, Helen, hopped up and down while hugging the Polks. Wagner whooped and hollered like a school boy, pumping his fedora into the sky with jabs from his arm. In Grants Pass, Dick's father, Doug was "so thrilled I just about jumped through the ceiling," he later told the press. "Told ya, told ya, told ya!" yelled Gail, back in Eugene. Nearby, Sweet hoisted his beer bottle in the air. "To the wizard of Foz!" And 141 miles up, in outer space, Walt Schirra and the crew of Apollo 7 silently completed another lap around earth, oblivious to the madness in Mexico City.

In the press box, an Associated Press reporter typed a thirty-word message that, in minutes, chattered across thousands of teletype machines in newsrooms around the world: "Sports Bulletin. (Mexico City) --- Dick Fosbury . . . the upside-down jumper from Medford, Oregon . . . has won the Olympic high jump with a leap of seven-feet, four and one-quarter inches."

Down the row, Meyers, who back in January had called Fosbury "the funniest high jumper you ever saw" after the Seattle Invitational, placed his fingers on his portable typewriter and began his Monday story with the description that, "World records were a peso a dozen, but the glamour boy of track and field in the 1968 Olympic Games was a rawboned Oregonian who went belly-up to a Gold Medal and the most explosive ovation of the Mexico City entertainment."

Down press row, Arthur Daley of the *New York Times* started his story. "No track and field athlete at the Olympic Games drew more whoops of delight or shrieks of disbelief from the crowds—and presumably from millions of pop-eyed television viewers—than did Dick

Fosbury, the architect of an acrobatic maneuver that has become known as the Fosbury Flop," he wrote.

Once the celebration died down, Fosbury tried three times to set the world record at 7'6". He was close on the second, but it wasn't to be. No matter. With his jump of 2.24 meters (7'4¼"), Fosbury had broken the Olympic record, besting Brumel's and Thomas's 2.18 meters (7'1¾") mark from 1964. And he had jumped higher than any American in history, eclipsing Thomas's old mark of 7'3¾". He had jumped higher than all but two jumpers in the world, and with both having retired, was now the greatest active high jumper on the planet.

Soon an abbreviated Associated Press story was sent around the globe: "In an Olympic Games marred by political bickering, Black Power displays and rancor on many sides, [a] gangling 6-foot-4 college boy, a third-stringer on the U.S. Olympic team, delighted 80,000 people at Olympic Stadium by winning the high jump with one of the most unorthodox performances ever seen in bigtime sports."

Beneath the stadium, Fosbury escaped a throng of reporters—"How does it feel?" . . . "How did you come up with this style?" . . . "What were you thinking?"—and melted into a deep sense of satisfaction. Ten months of competition. Of pressure. Of expectations. Of waiting. Of wondering. It was now all over, replaced by an unfamiliar sense of relief and relaxation, which he wasn't going to let a throng of reporters spoil.

"Sorry, no interviews," he told the officials.

"But Señor Fos—."

"Sorry. I'm wiped. And wanna see my mom."

Along with the other two medal winners, he hid from the press while awaiting the medal presentation. Nearby, marathon medalists entered a room for drug testing. Finally, in the evening darkness, Foz stepped to the top perch on the podium, all smiles, for the medal presentation. The National Anthem played and the American flag rose in the Mexican night, Dick's patriotism manifesting itself not so much in a connection to a country but a city, Medford, full of flawed people like him, but folks who'd believed in him. Who sent him a telegram when he was at his lowest. All smiles, no tears. When the song ended, he flashed a quick peace sign, then spontaneously raised his right fist in solidarity with his friends Tommie Smith and John Carlos, now back in the US. Nobody booed or hissed.

Beyond a few marathon stragglers, the high jump had concluded the eight-day track and field competition. Smith, Carlos, Fosbury, and the rest of the US men's team had won fifteen gold medals and twenty-eight total, fifteen more than the Soviets' count. The US had set eight world records. Beamon had uncorked perhaps the single most amazing athletic performance in track and field history. Sprinters Smith and Carlos had defied Brundage and made a victory-stand statement about human rights that rocked the world. And Fosbury's gold-medal Flop had put an exclamation mark on it all.

The 0.9 seconds it took for him to jump, clear the bar, and land would, in a small way, change the world. And it would change Dick, in ways he would appreciate and in ways he would not. Indeed, success on the largest stage in sport, he was about to realize, came with a privilege he could never have imagined. But it also came with a price.

PART V

RE-ENTRY

Chapter 24

The toughest thing about success is that you've got to keep on being a success.

—Irving Berlin

THE NEXT MORNING, the papers were thick with Fosbury photos, headlines, and stories. "You haven't seen anything until you see skinny, tousle-haired Dick Fosbury, the new Golden Boy of the Olympics," wrote United Press International's Milton Richman. "They call it the 'Fosbury Flop' and it's a spectacle, the likes of which never has been seen in either amateur or professional athletics before." *Lo nunca visto!* ("Never seen anything like it!") trumpeted a headline in a Mexican paper.

While Dick was on his way to breakfast, reporters flocked to him. "What were your emotions when hitting the pit after going 7'4¼"?"

"I figured I'd make it . . . just the same I was surprised when I looked up and saw the bar was still on."

"What did you think of the facilities?"

"Best I've ever seen."

"Why did you skip the press interviews last night?"

"Too tired," he said. "I took my mom to dinner."

"How did you invent this style of yours?"

"I was a sophomore in high school and one of the worst high jumpers in the state . . . ."

Some, in print, chided him for skipping the post-event interview. "He pleaded exhaustion," wrote Leo Davis of *The Oregonian*. "Nobody bought [it]. After all, Bob Seagren pole vaulted for six hours and invited interview. Mamo Wolde ran 26-plus miles and had breath enough for conversation . . . ."

It was a lesson Dick would learn the hard way in months to come: no matter what he did or didn't do, he couldn't please everyone. Wear a sombrero for the photographers, and they think you're great; decline an interview, and they think you're rude.

In Medford, plans were already underway for a parade. Requests for magazine interviews and speeches came fast and furious. Fans thrust newspaper photos of him for autographs. Dick was thrilled with the attention—and drowning in it. When Stenlund suggested they escape with the swimmers to a resort in the mountains, Dick was quickly on board. Mexico City was fun, but he'd had enough. He wanted to get away from the throngs. And did so. A few days in the mountains became a few more. And before Dick knew it he had book-ended his Olympic experience by not only missing the opening ceremonies but the closing ceremonies as well. But the girls were cute, the beer was cold, the pool refreshing, and the reporters—thank God—far, far away.

AFTER THE TEAM flew to LA, John North, a Medford high-roller who owned North's Chuck Wagon, had his private jet dispatched to pick up Dick and his mother. Some 800 people greeted them at the Jackson County Airport, twice that number lining the streets for the ticker-tape parade that followed. It was "Dick Fosbury Day" in Medford. Fosbury, in his official Olympic uniform featuring a navy-blue sport coat, waved from the back of a slow-rolling convertible. Confetti floated down from atop buildings, which meant for a fast float; the highest building was three stories. Signs were sprinkled throughout the crowd. Among them: "Ole Ricardo Fosbury." "Up, Up and Away." "You put Medford on the Map." And "Flip it to 'em, Foz." City officials gave him the key to the city. He gave the city a signed Olympic flag. "He often flashed his now-famous grin," wrote AP, "gave autographs liberally and kissed a number of girls."

Dean Benson, his old coach, stepped to the outdoor podium. "Just who would believe six years ago that this scrawny kid could be an American record holder? This boy—he just did it!"

Sports Illustrated sent a reporter to trail his every move. Athletic journals delved into the intricacies of the biomechanics of the Flop. In a cartoon, the *Christian Science Monitor* showed presidential candidate Hubert Humphrey Flopping over the "Nixon poll." With Fosbury now an Olympic champ, some reporters thought "Flop" was inaccurate, so started calling it the "Fosbury Flip." It didn't catch on, which was fine with Dick, who liked the irony of "Flop."

In Corvallis, each day Wagner dumped Dick's mail in his OSU locker, which was getting harder and harder to shut. Amid the flurry of appearances, the media had neatly framed Fosbury as a true-blue American hero, the feel-good alternative to what *Chicago American* columnist Brent Musburger had called the "black-skinned stormtroopers"— Smith and Carlos. "After the fuss stirred by the black athletes," wrote George Pasero of the *Oregon Journal,* "this Olympics needed something that emphasized once more what the Games are all about." Fosbury, he believed, was that "something." Pasero pictured Dick " . . . standing alone, reaching for the moon along with a fellow named Walter Schirra . . . just a man and his talent pitted against a bar that seemed as high up as the Empire State building . . . ."

But if that was the press's narrative, it wasn't necessarily Dick's. In early November, at a Medford Linebackers Club meeting, Fosbury defended Smith and Carlos. "The IOC," he said, "acted quite irrationally." In the audience, some people looked at each other, wondering if they'd just heard what they thought they'd heard. Was he actually supporting these two?

IN NOVEMBER, RICHARD Nixon beat Hubert Humphrey to replace Lyndon Johnson as president. The Beatles released "Revolution." And shortly before Christmas, Apollo 8 became the first US spacecraft to orbit not the Earth, but the *Moon*. While some members of the 1968 team were lavishly feted—double-medal winner Larry James (gold in 400-meter relay, silver in 400 meters) was honored with his own "day" in his hometown of White Plains, New York—the cheering stopped in a hurry for others. The US Army, as was the deal, came for Kenny Moore; he was off to boot camp. Steeplechaser Bill Reilly and sprinter Mel Pender returned to Vietnam.

Meanwhile, Oregon State's marching band spelled out "D-I-C-K" at a football game. In Medford, a scholarship fund was established to help him pay for his remaining schooling at OSU. He sipped milk cheek to cheek with Oregon's Dairy Princess for a promotional ad. Flew to Berlin for a demonstration of his high-jumping style. Dined at the home of Adidas founder Adolf "Ad" Dassler. Was honored—along with Schirra and his Apollo 7 crew, Andy Warhol, Dustin Hoffman, and Janis Joplin—at a New York party hosted by *Life* magazine publisher Jerome Hardy. Went on TV's *The Dating Game* with decathlete Bill Toomey. (Neither was chosen for the date.) And, during an appearance on *The Tonight Show* with Johnny Carson, slipped while attempting a 6'8" jump on stage. Wrote Carson: "Glad to hear the x-rays were negative."

Back home, at Wagner's insistence, Fosbury met with Berny to map out a plan for the winter indoor season. The coach—as with the straddle/Flop experiment—was more eager to do so than Dick. Once a doubter, Wagner now bathed in the Fosbury spotlight, knowing, among other things, the notoriety could only help recruiting. Berny predicted a new world record in 1969. (Fosbury avoided predictions, thinking them counterproductive.) Berny predicted there would soon be "a big swing to the Fosbury style." (Only two years earlier, Wagner had said the Flop may "just be a shortcut to mediocrity.")

"Berny had a grand plan," remembered Fosbury. "Me? I hadn't thought it out much." But how was it portrayed in the press? "Dick wants a fairly heavy indoor meet schedule," Wagner told the *Gazette-Times*.

Wagner had clearly been energized by Dick's gold-medal win and saw it as a step to even greater things. Fosbury, on the other hand, was exhausted. "You're going to have to learn to say no," his father, Doug, cautioned him. Between ten months of high-scale competition and three months of post-Olympic appearances, the last thing Dick wanted was another second in the public eye. What he really wanted, more than anything, was to be just a regular guy—specifically, a civil engineer. Indeed, the most accurate headline that he'd seen since getting home was in the *New York Times*: HIGH JUMPER BACKS INTO OLYMPIC GLORY, BUT SAYS HE WORRIES ABOUT RE-ENTRY.

WHEN DICK RETURNED to school at OSU in January 1969, it began a season of change in his life like no other since the loss of his brother and divorce of his parents. He transferred to sociology and began taking classes in philosophy and religion; "I was curious about stuff like that—man's belief systems." (And, if he wanted to be eligible for the spring outdoor season, he desperately needed some credits.) He moved into a former nunnery with a handful of other guys, including his best buddy, Terry Rosenau; sprinter Willie Turner; and a soccer player known only as "Pig Pen." (It was, perhaps, the only former nunnery that featured blacklight rooms, Jimi Hendrix posters, and kegs of beer.) And he found himself involved in a controversy involving a black OSU athlete that forced him, for the first time, to decide what he really stood for.

In February, Dee Andros, OSU's popular football coach—and a Marine who had fought at Iwo Jima—dismissed a black player from the team for having grown a thin mustache and goatee during the offseason. Fred Milton argued that Andros had violated his human rights. Though he knew of Andros's no-facial-hair rules, this was the offseason—and plenty of white players, Milton pointed out, were sporting facial hair far thicker in the form of sprawling sideburns. Wasn't this an overreaction? Andros said no.

Encouraged by the Black Student Union, the nearly sixty African American students on campus—about .41 percent of the 14,500 enrollment—called for a boycott. The BSU argued that the Milton case was only a symptom of deeper grievances blacks on campus had experienced but had little chance to express. Among them: blacks were given inferior housing to whites, the athletic department had an unwritten policy that African American athletes could not date white women, and they were called to higher standards, such as the "facial hair" ban, than their white counterparts.

Andros and the athletic department wouldn't budge. School president James Jensen tried to play peacekeeper but offered little support for Milton; after all, this was staid Corvallis, a conservative engineering/agricultural/forestry school that drew many of its students from rural farm communities. This wasn't San Jose State, whose president, Robert D. Clark, had defended Olympic protesters—and SJS students—Tommie

Smith and John Carlos as "honorable young men . . . dedicated to the cause of justice for the black people of our society."

The OSU incident exploded like a lightning strike to a tinder-dry forest and spread nationwide with media-whipped winds. On February 26, dueling rallies took place on campus. A few thousand people showed up on the main quad of the Memorial Union in support of Andros. Among them was a huge contingent of athletes, led by All-American football center John Didion, who earlier had presented to Jensen a petition with the names of 173 OSU athletes supporting Andros. Meanwhile, not far away, about a thousand students rallied in favor of Milton and the BSU. Among them were Carlos, the black sprinter who had thrust a defiant glove in the air at the 1968 Olympics, and Dick Fosbury.

Fosbury? The gold-medal winner? The kid Pasero had held up as the righteous alternative to Smith's and Carlos's tainting of the Games? Fosbury had never voiced a political or social opinion to speak of—at least publicly. He was the happy-go-lucky kid whose wacky high-jump style had leavened the more serious '60s with a touch of lightness. He was the kid rooted in a community with a sundown law suggesting African Americans weren't welcome overnight. When competing in the NYAC event that many black athletes boycotted in New York, Fosbury said he "didn't really understand the issue."

But with nearly all OSU athletes and coaches supporting Andros and while knowing that doing so would—as it had for Smith and Carlos—trigger a backlash against him, Fosbury was among only a handful of white athletes who stood with Milton and the BSU. His photo appeared in the *Corvallis Gazette Times*. FOSBURY APPEARS IN SUPPORT OF STAND OF BLACK STUDENTS read a bold headline in the *Medford Mail Tribune*.

"That moment," Dick said, "was a turning point for me in my life." When Smith and Carlos had made their stand in Mexico City, it hardly registered with Dick; at the time, three days before the high-jump competition had begun, he was in "the zone." Now, he was starting to realize the courage it took for them to make their statement about racial inequality. And how so many white people refused to see beyond the black glove and *own* the racial inequalities that led to it being thrust into the air in the first place.

"Dick's response at OSU was a latent response to Mexico City," said Smith, nearly half a century later. "He was a deep thinker and wasn't trying to make trouble. He was on the quiet side. But this was a human-rights issue, and he'd come to see if you don't stand up for something you'll fall for anything."

As expected, he was roundly castigated my many. Folks who might have bought his beer at the Beaver Hut before the rally now glared at him in contempt. Hate mail poured in, many people saying he was being unfaithful to OSU. Football players who'd proudly seen him as part of the Beaver sports family now ostracized him. They didn't care whether he'd won a gold medal or not—in their book Fosbury was a traitor, plain and simple. (Bill Enyart, Fosbury's friend from Medford and an All-American on OSU's football team, refused to take sides on the issue.)

"After that I was either loved or hated," said Fosbury. "There wasn't much in between."

In retrospect, Fosbury saw his stance as symbolic of his coming of age. "In a sense," he said, "I became an adult that day." In the last few years, he'd competed with, and against, blacks, befriended blacks, lived with blacks (Turner). But even as he'd come to see life more clearly through their eyes—as opposed to eyes of a person from all-white Medford—he'd kept quiet about a newfound empathy he'd developed for African Americans.

"Mexico," he said, "set me up to do what I did that day. Everything changed that day Tommie and John did what they did. I felt connected to those guys. It affected my life." Even if he didn't express it at the time and even if he didn't agree with Smith and Carlos using the backdrop of the National Anthem for their protest, he had come to understand why they felt a need to make a statement. America, he realized, was full of good-hearted, well-meaning people who nevertheless had blind spots when it came to understanding oppression from a black perspective. Why did an otherwise good place like the Medford of the 1960s perpetuate racism? Because, in essence, nobody had dared stand up against it, allowing it to quietly entrench itself all the deeper. Fosbury was no longer willing to go with a flow that decreed a certain righteousness to white people.

Later, Fosbury realized his standing up for Milton symbolized something else: an affirmation of himself, to himself, as more than a gold-medal winner. With the public, that wasn't often the case. "You get placed on this pedestal," said Fosbury. "When I got back from Mexico City, everybody wanted to buy me a drink, be my friend. To them, I'm an Olympic athlete. But I'm a college kid. I'm more than an Olympian. I'm just an ordinary person who happened to win a gold medal."

IN AN *OAKLAND Tribune* photo from the Athens Invitational in January 1969, Dick Fosbury was sitting cross-legged, just off the track, sweats on, head down, autograph hounds—a gaggle of little girls—closing in. What's striking about the photo isn't what's seen, but what's *not*: the Fosbury smile. Gone. MIA. He had failed three times at his opening height of 6'6" and was out of the competition. In the photo, he was staring down with an expression on his face that few fans had seen before.

"I had problems with my steps," he later told a *Tribune* reporter. "I didn't jump high enough. I didn't feel like jumping."

"Why not?" asked the reporter.

"I don't know why. Sometimes I just feel that way."

Wagner, Fosbury's coach jumped into the conversation.

"I'll tell you what's wrong," he said. "He's looking forward to four straight weekends and two meets in each one."

The Wagner interjection was awkward, its meaning unclear. Was the suggestion that Dick should put on a happy face and look forward to the next night's meet in Seattle? Or was Wagner using a touch of sarcasm to empathize with Fosbury and suggest Dick had a rugged schedule ahead of him? In either case, this indoor dog-and-pony show was reminiscent of Wagner's decision to deprogram Dick of the Flop: the idea had been Wagner's, but Fosbury the pleaser was entering into the agreement with less enthusiasm than Berny.

After the Friday night meet in Oakland, fans poured out of the stands and pushed toward Fosbury for autographs. Two security guards had to step forward to give him some breathing room. He signed for fifteen minutes, then went to his hotel for a quick few hours of sleep before flying to Seattle for a Saturday night meet. He didn't even place.

In fact, as winter 1969 deepened and Fosbury grew wearier, he didn't win a single meet of the handful he entered. He never cleared 7'0". In the previous few years, a go-to headline on sports pages across America was "Fosbury Flops to success" or some derivation thereof. Now, the go-to headline was simply "Fosbury Flops"—period. Stories were full of the phrase "failed to . . ." and "couldn't clear . . ." and "far short of his Olympic jump of . . . ." In February, he couldn't make 6'10" in New York Friday, nor in Portland the next night after a red-eye, cross-country flight.

Enough. "I'm done," Fosbury told Wagner, despite there being a few more meets on Berny's schedule for him. To his credit, Wagner did not argue. He'd seen the results. He realized Fosbury was mentally and physically shot. Wagner told the press a doctor had advised Dick to take a break. "There's no physical problem but he is suffering from mental exhaustion and lack of sleep," said Wagner. "He's been doing too many things."

Wagner hoped Fosbury would return for the NCAA indoor championships in Detroit. He did not. In late spring, Fosbury did bounce back to win his third Pac-8 title (7'0") and second NCAA outdoor title (7'2½", a new NCAA record). But the victories proved to be the athletic equivalent of light bulbs suddenly growing brighter just before they burn out. Fosbury would never rediscover the magic of Mexico City, nor, frankly, lament it.

He finished second in the AAU meet in Miami at 7'1", not bothering to take a third try to make 7'2". And in a three-way meet in LA against the Soviet Union and the United Kingdom in July, he managed only 6'8¾". In a what-have-you-done-for-me-lately world, this was, as *Gazette-Times* columnist Chuck Boice wrote, "far below his Olympic mark of 7'4¼"." NCAA championships with national records were now yawners; every jump he made was compared to his mountaintop experience in Mexico City. Not that Fosbury was the first athlete to be pressured for more—or punished for what the public saw as "less." After heavily favored John Thomas lost to two Soviets in Rome in 1960 in what some papers called "Black Thursday," he got hate mail for years.

Fosbury's AAU finish qualified him for an all-expenses-paid trip for a handful of meets in Europe, where he'd never competed before. "It could be a chance of a lifetime," wrote Boice. "And they want him. Oh, how those Europeans want him, no matter how he feels." Boice's final five words hammered home the overlooked person in this equation: " . . . no matter how he feels." Everyone wanted a piece of Fosbury, everyone wanted results, everyone wanted him to be the second-coming of Bob Richards, the squeaky clean athlete on the front of their morning Wheaties. But what about Dick? Didn't anyone care how *he* felt?

Fosbury turned down Europe. Instead, he chose to come home to Oregon to work, start making some money, and get out of the public eye. Meanwhile, his political and social consciousness expanded, in part because of classes he was taking, in part because of more broad-minded people he was getting to know, and in part because, for the first time, he was taking time to put his life in perspective, to understand white privilege. "Looking back on my days in Medford: I had no idea I was coming from a racist community. I thought I was coming from simply a white community. But when I got beyond the college competition and into the indoor meets, that changed. And I changed. I started to understand a larger world. All these things they had faced as blacks— the discrimination—I had never faced any of that."

He volunteered to work with the Special Olympics program. While his friend Sweet, with a mimeograph machine and unbridled energy, rallied students for marches, sit-ins, and teach-ins, in the spring of 1969 Fosbury joined an anti-war march from campus to downtown—not as Dick Fosbury, gold medalist, but as just another person against the war. From his house near 9th Street in Corvallis, he'd walk the railroad tracks—not drive the main streets—to get to campus. "Hard to believe that long-haired freak just won a gold medal," muttered the owner of a business along his route.

"What's the matter with Dick?" people kept asking Wagner and the press.

Berny's answer to the *Gazette-Times'* Boice showed he'd developed a new empathy for, and sensitivity to, Fosbury's post-Olympics plight. "You can't believe the pressure. Dick is one of the greatest attractions in track and field in the world. [Meet promoters] all feel they have to have him, even if he isn't ready. Would he just come and try? He was cajoled, bludgeoned, enticed, and generally persuaded to compete. Then, when he did not do well, many were critical of him. They do not seem to understand athletes and championship performances. You do not just go out and achieve record-approaching performances anytime regardless of how you feel physically and mentally. A lot of things have to be right."

If Fosbury appreciated Wagner defending him, if he credited him for teaching him to train seriously as an athlete, the two had their moments. One came in late spring 1969 at OSU's season-ending track and field banquet at the Memorial Union. Dick showed up in a pair of bright yellow bell-bottoms he'd bought at Macy's in New York after the Millrose-Wanamaker Indoor Meet in February. Dick was getting a lot of good-natured kidding from teammates for the groovy and gaudy pants when Wagner interrupted with a quick head nod suggesting the two needed to chat. *Now.*

"I can't believe you're wearing those," Wagner huffed. "You look like a clown. This is *unacceptable.*"

Fosbury was speechless. People were looking their way. Dick was embarrassed. He quickly weighed his options, then turned and walked out the door. "I couldn't tolerate that kind of criticism," he later said. "That was probably the low point of our relationship."

"Ending well" had never been Fosbury's strong suit. He, of course, blew off the post-event press conference after his Olympic victory, missed the closing ceremonies in Mexico City, and, now, had done an about-face at his final banquet as an OSU athlete. "I can be stubborn and a little hard to get along with," he admitted. But to suggest that he hadn't "ended well," in general, after his Olympic gold medal was to be shortsighted. Canadian Debbie Brill, the first female backwards-over-the bar jumper with her "Brill Bend" in the early- to mid-'60s, was among those lamenting Fosbury's fall from prominence after the 1968 Olympics.

"It was sad that, despite all that wonderful raw ability, Fosbury slipped into obscurity soon after winning Olympic gold in Mexico City the following years," she wrote in her 1986 memoir, *Jump.* "I've seen him quite often at the meets in Eugene, Oregon, and he's a charming guy. For him it was a case of everything coming in one quick rush. It was like *kapow!*—and then a vacuum. People expected him to proceed effortlessly from one success to another but, of course, it doesn't always work out like that."

Fosbury would be the first to admit that, in terms of high jumping, he tanked the post-Olympics indoor season; "in 1968, I basically folded three years of jumping into a single year," he said. But he hardly disappeared into a vacuum. More accurately, he broadened a life that had been narrowly focused on high jumping. He returned to OSU so he could finish his degree. He expanded his educational horizons with forays into the studies of religion and philosophy. And he took a gutsy public stand on a race-related issue. Amid it all, the more surprising thing might not have been his lack of success indoors, but that he was able to bounce back to defend his Pac-8 and NCAA crowns, the latter with an NCAA record.

Again, Fosbury was true to form: when a meet mattered to him, he rose to the occasion. From Fosbury's days at Medford High, what had fueled him was a passion—a desperation—to jump higher. He jumped best when he could wrap himself emotionally around the significance of winning and jumped worst when he could not. Obviously that competitive spirit, after Mexico City, was absent on the indoor circuit. But what some seemed to miss—the press and perhaps Brill among them—was the idea that high jumping, to Fosbury, had never been his lifeblood. It was always a *means* to greater end: A way to feel good about himself in the wake of a little brother's death. A way to *belong* after feeling orphaned in the wake of his parents' divorce. A way to build a sense that he *mattered*. But never the endgame.

High jumping for Fosbury had been like a solid-rocket booster that powers a space craft into the heavens: it was the propulsion to send him where he needed to go, on the trajectory he needed to follow, to a destination no American had reached before. But once he was on his way, the spent booster detached and fell away; its job was done. "High jumping took me out of my house, out of my neighborhood, and beyond my town," he said. "It exposed me to different communities and cultures. It taught me that we may look different, speak differently and believe differently, but we all have the same desire to test ourselves on the field. I have met presidents and kings, seen the world, shared my life with wonderful people. That's what high jumping did for me."

The irony is that just as he was realizing that he was more than an Olympic champion with a new high-jump style, the world seemed all the more intent on pigeonholing him as nothing more. The press was relentless. "What happened in your indoor season?" "Can you break the world record?" "What about Munich in 1972?"

Meanwhile, Fosbury, only twenty-two in the spring of 1969, was trying to stay centered on the "regular guy" stuff and resist what so many athletes did—believe that the only way they could stay relevant was by jumping higher or running faster. In essence, conform to the world's standards, meet the world's demands. "I was fulfilled from Mexico City," said Fosbury, "and finally relieved after the 1969 NCAA victory. I'd won three straight Pac-8 titles, two NCAA titles, and an Olympic gold medal. I didn't need the Pan Am Games. I didn't need Europe."

IN SPRING 1969, something happened that forced Fosbury to decide how serious he was about the "regular guy" stuff. George Gleeson, the dean at OSU's School of Engineering, called Dick into his office and offered him a chance to finish his work for a degree. Fosbury was stunned. Intrigued. Grateful. He wanted to accept the offer on the spot.

"There's just one catch, Mr. Fosbury," said Gleeson, who'd been at OSU since the end of World War II.

"What's that?"

"No high jumping, Dick. The demands of the program are incompatible with a life spent training on week days and jetting around the country on weekends. You've already failed once. We don't want you to fail again."

Dick didn't need to be reminded that he'd flunked out of the School at the end of his junior year. Now, he was getting a second chance. But Munich was coming—and the Olympic Trials, in Eugene only forty miles away, couldn't be more convenient.

"Well," said Gleeson, "what do you think?"

Fosbury exhaled. "Thanks for the offer," he said. "I accept." Dick's smiled beamed with the handshake.

For the next two and a half years, he steeled himself to the task of making right what he'd gotten wrong before. In March 1972, six and a half years after he'd enrolled at OSU, Fosbury graduated with a bachelor of science degree in civil engineering technology. The certificate came in the mail. He didn't attend the ceremony, feeling embarrassed about how long it had taken, but treasuring it almost as if it were Olympic gold.

In the spring, with the late-summer Olympic Games in Munich approaching, Fosbury tried to round himself into shape for a shot at the Olympic Trials that would be held in June. The team would be chosen in a much simpler way than in 1968: Meet the qualifying standard for your event—for the high jump, that meant 7'¼"—and you could compete in the Trials. Finish in the top three at the Trials and you were on the team. But with only an abbreviated training opportunity, Fosbury couldn't meet the standard just to get into the Trials. His Olympic career was over. Short and sweet.

Two years later, he took a brief stab at the International Track Association—a new pro circuit—but found himself unsuccessful and unfulfilled. He started teaching children in track clinics about the benefits of healthy living, exercise, and sports. He ultimately got involved with a number of Olympic organizations, rising to president of the World Olympians Association, promoting the same "Olympism" spirit he'd first discovered when practicing with the Soviet's Valentin Gavrilov in Mexico City. But he never jumped in open competition again—nor, frankly, regretted it. Never regretted that his top-echelon career had but a butterfly's life. Fosbury's four hours in Mexico City marked the only true international outdoor meet he ever competed in.

Fosbury looked upon high jumping as Kenny Moore suggested Steve Prefontaine looked upon distance running in his last few years. After Pre's death in an auto accident in 1975, Moore told mourners at Hayward Field how Pre had encouraged prisoners, spoken to youth groups, and sought justice for athletes against the AAU. "He conceived of his sport as a service," said Moore, "in a way an artist serves." Likewise, Fosbury painted with a style all his own, then shared what he'd learned with the world.

"High jumping was a gift I received, and it was never about money," said Fosbury. "I never jumped well professionally because I was not, nor am I now, motivated by money. My motivation was the challenge of competition. I didn't want to lose."

In 1977, with his new wife Janet, he moved to Ketchum, Idaho, for a fresh start. He couldn't have been more thrilled. He loved living far from the hub-hub of more populated places. Loved the fresh air. The mountains. The snow. The cross-country skiing. And, eventually, the new job.

He was a civil engineer.

Chapter 25

In trying to make something new, half the undertaking lies in discovering whether it can be done. Once it has been established that it can, duplication is inevitable.

—Helen Gahagan Douglas

IN A SOUTHERN California office in the spring of 1969, Dr. Harry J. Silver wrapped the 8½"-by-11" flier around the drum of a Ditto machine, flicked the "On" switch, and watched as the purple-inked pages spit off the drum, each with a toxic scent. Silver, a member of the board of directors of a track and field team known as the Southern California Striders, was no spoilsport. But he'd been so frightened by an article he'd read in a medical journal, he vowed to send a warning to every high school in the area. Its theme? The dangers of a new high-jump style known as the "Fosbury Flop."

Silver's warning was hardly the first, nor would it be the last. In the wake of Fosbury's gold-medal jump—beamed by TV to millions of homes—such threats of doom came from doctors, mothers, even from the head of the U.S. Olympic track and field team himself. Only days after Fosbury's victory, a concerned Payton Jordan told the *New York Times*: "Kids have a tendency to emulate champions, and I hope that Dick's wonderful victory doesn't start a trend. If it does he's liable to wipe out an entire generation of high jumpers. They'll all have broken necks."

In Waynesboro, Virgina, Dr. J. Tracy O'Hanlan had watched Fosbury's victory with a touch of admiration and a ton of horror. A noted lecturer in orthopedic surgery at the University of Virginia

School of Medicine, O'Hanlan further studied Fosbury's style and wrote a highly critical article for the March 6, 1969, issue of the *Medical Tribune*. "Dick Fosbury has opened a door for high school boys to imitate him and has, thereby, set the stage for possible severe injuries to the cervical vertebrae and the spinal cord with resultant quadriplegia."

It was a more medically sound way of saying exactly what Jordan had said: kids are going to break their necks doing the Fosbury Flop on anything but first-rate foam landing pits. "The style may be copied by high school boys this spring and encouraged by their coaches. These boys, their parents and their coaches must be apprised of the inherent dangers in this style of jumping. It is the duty of all team physicians to be aware of the hazards of the jump and to warn high school principals of them."

Silver and O'Hanlan were not alone in their concern. "To the frustration of track coaches and mothers everywhere, thousands of kids are following Dick Fosbury over the bar," wrote Neil Amdur of the *New York Times*.

OSU Coach Berny Wagner started getting letters of worry; "you're going to kill my boy," wrote one mother. Fosbury, too, got letters. "I happened to see a television picture of your high jump—and it scared the devil out of me," wrote Eugene R. Erickson, head of the Rancho Los Amigos Hospital in Downey, California. "I have seen a great number of young men with broken necks at this hospital from high jumping, water skiing, surfing, diving, etc. and your technique certainly doesn't look good to me. The slow-motion TV pictures appeared to me that you were landing on your head and neck, not on your shoulders."

Fosbury thought the doctors were being alarmists. Coaches would be foolish to have their jumpers try the technique on sand or hard-packed sawdust. "I'm not stupid," he told the *Los Angeles Times*. "I wouldn't dream of jumping the way I do into sand." (Though, in Pullman, Washington, he did jump 7'0" onto wood chips, not that he was bringing it up amid the dissent.)

"The Wagner hackles rise over any hint of outlawing the unique 'Fosbury Flip' style as 'too dangerous' or 'too different,'" said the *Gazette-Times*. "But Fosbury had never been hurt. Dick lands exactly the way vaulters land coming down from sixteen or seventeen feet, but nobody seems to worry about them."

With all the hubbub, the American Medical Association's commission on the medical aspects of sports retained Dr. Donald Slocum, a prominent Eugene, Oregon, physician to examine Fosbury, evaluate his style, and see if the Flop was, indeed, dangerous. His conclusion? "The Flop is no more dangerous than pole vaulting, other styles of high jumping or some forms of gymnastics." And in the months and years after Fosbury won a gold medal, no reports of serious injuries from it made the newspaper.

Meanwhile, Don Gordon's Port-a-Pit business was ramping into overdrive. Part of that was a post-Olympic comment of Fosbury's on TV that he couldn't have won his gold medal without the Port-a-Pit's assurance of a safe landing. And part of it was fear triggered by the Associated Press article featuring Dr. O'Hanlan. Gordon had more orders than he knew what to do with.

BEFORE FOSBURY'S OLYMPIC victory in October 1968, a smattering of youngsters was trying the technique, particularly in Corvallis and Medford, where Fosbury was well-known. After his victory, the popularity of the style was like microwave popcorn—a pop here, a pop there, then mad popping everywhere. Suddenly, kids around the country were flopping—on couches, on beds, on stacks of pillows.

From coast to coast, high schools started replacing sawdust and woodchip pits with net-bound foam rubber, often stacked atop old tires. It was particularly popular among young jumpers uninhibited by years as straddlers or by coaches who, through no fault of their own, only taught the straddle. Fosbury came to believe girls picked it up faster because, with little in the way of high school sports available to them, they weren't restricted by coaches steeped only in the straddle. "At the club level, they didn't have coaches saying 'you can't do that.'"

Moms weren't thrilled by it. "My son," they'd write, "is Flopping on the couch, ruining the furniture." Read an *Oregonian* headline: "Mothers 'cry' to Fosbury." But in a world with worse to worry about—like a war in Vietnam that dragged on like a dark movie with no ending—the "Flop" was America's new feel-good fad. It was like real-life "Flubber," its birthplace of Medford High deliciously close in name to the movie's Medfield College. And if not vaulting athletes above basketball rims as in *The Absent-Minded Professor*, certainly helping kids jump higher than they ever had before.

"Fosbury Flop better'n rock 'n' roll," read a headline in the *Kokomo Tribune* in Kokomo, Indiana. In South Lake Tahoe, middle-school teacher Les Wright had long taught his students the straddle, then saw Fosbury's new style while he was running the nearby long-jump event at Echo Summit. "I shut my mouth and taught them to do the Flop," he said.

"Nothing electrified the general US sports fan in 1968 more than the Fosbury Flop," said *Track & Field News*. "The event will never be the same."

Mexico City was Fosbury's moon landing. "His victory, in an Olympic- as well as American-record height, totally validated his style as a legitimate technical breakthrough and not just an oddity performed by one outlier athlete," said Hendershott.

Still, early on, elite jumpers were hesitant to even attempt the Flop. Most had honed their straddle for years, if not more than a decade. Like rock climbers, they were hesitant to let go of a "hold" with one hand without the certainty of a secure grasp to something else with the other. But gradually the shift to the Flop began. A jumper from the University of Texas, Bill Elliott, was among the first to find success at the collegiate level. In the spring of 1969, he cleared 7'3¼", more than a foot higher than his straddle best. The same year, in South Africa, Emile Rossouw went 7'0" at age sixteen.

Fosbury's gold-medal jump was similar, in some respects, to Roger Bannister's four-minute mile in 1954—not that he broke a measurable barrier but that he told the world: *this is possible*. Runners had been running the mile for more than three centuries, but prior to Bannister's 3:59.4 race, many thought a sub-four was physiologically impossible; Australia's John Landy described it as a "brick wall." But within a year of Bannister breaking the barrier, four other runners did it, including Landy himself, suggesting the barrier was far more psychological than physiological.

Likewise, within two years of the '68 Games, five jumpers around the world had already reached 7'1¾" or better with the Fosbury Flop. Among them was the Soviet Union's Kestutis Sapka, who, in 1972, became the first flopper to equal Fosbury's 7'4¼" mark. Later that year, twenty-eight out of forty competitors in the men's Olympic high jump in Munich had flipped to the Flop. The Soviet Union's Jüri Tarmak's victory in Munich (2.23 meters, 7'3¾") in 1972 marked the last time any male would win an Olympic high-jump event with anything but the Fosbury Flop, which has now produced ten straight gold medals. Jacek Wsola of Poland was the first jumper since Fosbury to win a gold medal using the Flop, going 2.25 meters (7'4½") in Montreal in 1976, narrowing eclipsing Dick's Olympic record.

Starting in 1973, *Track & Field News,* when compiling its yearly lists of world rankings, put an "f" by the names of those jumpers who employed the Flop. By 1978, so many jumpers were Flopping—twenty-seven of the top forty-one jumpers whose style the magazine could determine—that they started also listing the straddlers, as if *they* were the oddity. In 1979, the magazine stopped designating styles altogether because the exception had now become the rule, flummoxing those who, as Al Moss of the *Los Angeles Times* had written in a pre-Olympics column, "regard it as a freak—something that undeniably works for Fosbury but will never catch on generally."

Among the "conversion" stories, perhaps the most amazing belonged to Fosbury's old OSU teammate and friend John Radetich. A straddler, he had blown into Corvallis with rock-star bravado, called Dick's style "goofy," and boasted he'd be out-jumping Fosbury by season's end. In fact, at OSU Fosbury improved 9¼" with the Flop in a little more than three years (6'7" to 7'4¼") while Radetich improved only 3¼" (6'9¾" to 7'1") with the straddle in four years. Frustrated with his lack of improvement, Radetich converted to the Flop at the end of his senior year. In March 1973, at an International Track Association pro meet in Pocatello, Idaho, he set the first world record with the Fosbury Flop (7'4¾")—as Dick himself cheered him on with an occasional, "Go, Rat!" In 1976, Radetich soared 7'6" in Salt Lake City to up the world indoor mark. The painful kicker? Dwight Stones Flopped 7'6¼" later that night, so Radetich held the new record for less than an hour.

Stones, in July 1973, had been the first to set a world outdoor record, 7'6½", with the Flop. That same year, Oregon State's Tom Woods, a Flopper, broke Fosbury's 7'4¼" school record when he went 7'4¾".

Would any of this have happened if Valeriy Brumel, the world-record holder, hadn't had the motorcycle accident in 1965 and, thus, had competed in the '68 Games—and perhaps beaten Fosbury? After all, a gold medal gives an athlete credence that silver and bronze do not. But given his propensity to jump just as high as necessary, who knows what Fosbury might have done if Brumel had been around to force the issue?

"Dick still would have won," said *T&F News'* Hendershott. "No pun, but he was on a roll. He was naïve; it was almost as if he didn't know what he was doing but was doing it well. He was like the Beatles, breaking new ground. In 1968, all the stars lined up for him. It was his year."

What if, even without Brumel in the competition, Fosbury had *not* won—would the Flop have become the go-to style? "My guess is the Flop would have eventually caught on," said Hendershott. Remember, too, that Brill was soon competing at a world-class level with her "Bend" so the world takeover might have been accomplished from a two-front, two-gender pursuit.

At any rate, the straddle did not go gently into the good night, nor, frankly, were some glad to see it pass. (And, technically speaking, it hasn't completely "passed," as some jumpers on the master's circuit still employ the style.) On the world level, in 1978, Vladimir Yashchenko, a member of the Soviet team, went 2.35 meters (7'8½"), the highest straddle-jump ever. The last straddler—male or female—to win an Olympic gold medal in the high jump was East Germany's Rosemarie Ackermann in 1976. All subsequent Olympic high-jump medal winners have Flopped.

Some Baby Boomers who grew up with the straddle still lament its passing, considering it a piece of athletic art. In their eyes, it is a classic wood sailboat, the Flop a gaudy Jet Ski driven by an interloper. Said a post on *T&F News'* online forum: "My onetime Santa Ana JC teammate Ed Caruthers settled for silver in Mexico City and many of us thought after years of paying his dues and perfecting his technique he was robbed by a newcomer with a fluky, awkward style—an outlier who got massive elevation from a junk style he developed because he was too uncoordinated to jump the elegant way, the 'right' way, and who risked paraplegia with every attempt."

Beauty, of course, is in the eyes of the beholder. "The Flop executed properly is a thing of beauty," read another *T&F News* post. "The straddle is clumsy, awkward, and made athletes look like herniated crabs with hemorrhoids . . . ."

"I hate the Fosbury Flop," said another poster. "It uglified a beautiful event."

"It *athleticized* it," countered someone else, pointing out that the straddle was "like a ballet leap."

If not necessarily "raging," the debate has abided quietly in bars, locker rooms, and the back eddies of *T&F News'* forum for decades. Regardless of what it looks like, the Flop has clearly won the test of time, even if some are still not convinced it's a better way to jump. Jesus Dapena, a biomechanics expert and professor emeritus in Indiana University's Department of Kinesiology, studied the two styles for years and concluded that each favors a particular type of athlete—the straddle, the powerful, athletic jumper and the Flop, the faster, quick-footed jumper.

The Flop's main advantage, Dapena argues, is the simplicity of learning it—a few months instead of a few years. Nobody denies that. But plenty dispute that the straddle is as efficient as, or more efficient than, the Flop. If the straddle were even *as* efficient as the Flop, wouldn't a jumper here or there, at the world-class level, have won an Olympic medal or set a world record in the last forty years? With the exception of East Germany's Christian Schenk, who straddled amid his decathlon gold-medal performance in the 1988 Olympics in Seoul, that hasn't happened. And whereas most particular high-jumping styles dominated—if weren't used exclusively—for roughly thirty to forty years each, the Flop has been the go-to method of high jumpers around the world for nearly fifty years. If the world high-jump record set by Flopper Javiar Sotomayor, 8'½", of Cuba in 1993 hasn't been improved upon for nearly a quarter of a century, it is still four inches beyond what a straddler has done.

"Without question, the Flop is more efficient," said *T&F News'* Hendershott. "Time has proven that. The proof is in the pudding."

The most telling measure of comparison between jumping styles might be "height over the jumper's head." By that standard, the Flop is completely dominant; no straddler is ranked among the Top 50. (Fosbury, at 14.25" over his head, is far from the record of 23.3" held jointly by Floppers Franklin Jacob of the US and Stefan Holm of Sweden.)

In 1978, a decade after his gold-medal jump, Fosbury predicted an 8'4" jump—virtually a foot above his 1968 Olympic record—within his lifetime. At present, Sotomayor's mark is 91 percent there. It's possible that 8'4" will be achieved by some now-sixteen-year-old girl or boy who's concocting a better style than the Flop; after all, nobody in the 1960s foresaw Fosbury revolutionizing the world with his style. But until then, the revolution still belongs to him.

"It's funny," he said, "but when I came home from the Olympics a few of my friends said to me that I would go down in history. I couldn't imagine what that meant. But it has been amazing to see the revolution of the event. I was the right person at the right time."

Had Fosbury's 5½" improvement in less than nine months— 6'10¾" prior to the Athens Invitational in Oakland to 7'4¼" at Mexico City—come a year earlier or a year later, who knows if, without Dick winning Olympic gold, the Flop would have become the sensation it did. "I'm proud of my achievement; it changed my life. And I'm incredibly fortunate, because, well, I got the naming rights."

That said, Fosbury never clung to the style with a sense of me-first selfishness. "I've never had pride of ownership," he said. "I've never tried to 'sell' my style, to convince anyone that they had to use it. If they were curious, I was happy to share and help. But to each his or her own."

He has never doubted that others developed similar styles while, or before, he was developing his, notably Quande in Missoula, Montana, in the early 1960s and Brill in British Columbia in the early-to-mid-1960s. He has never resisted the idea that others—for example, Dwight Stones—have improved it to make it more efficient than what Dick used. "What amazes me now is how jumpers fling their heads back and are looking straight up in the sky," he said. "I went over looking at the bar over my left shoulder."

Despite the Flop abiding for half a century, its roots have all but been lost now on nearly two full generations of high jumpers. In 1988, twenty years after Fosbury won his gold medal, Corvallis High track and field coach Steve Locey folded himself neatly over the bar with the old straddle method during a practice—just to see the reaction.

"Now *that* is goofy!" said one of his jumpers.

"What in the world is that?" said another.

"I've got fifteen high jumpers—all use the Flop—and I'll bet twelve don't have a clue where the Flop came from," said Locey at the time. "They think it's just some method that's been around forever."

Now, with another thirty years having passed, even fewer have a clue where, or how, it came from—or who Dick Fosbury was, and is. In 2017, when a writer stopped at a drive-up coffee hut en route to hear the gold medalist speak in his hometown of Medford, the teenage barista asked him where he was headed.

"I'm going to a banquet," he said, "to hear Dick Fosbury talk."

"Oh," she said, "do you know someone in the band?"

But those who remember the darkness of the '60s remember the Flop as a touch of light, a feel-good story about a boy and his imagination. "That's what makes this whole story so beautiful," his old coach, Dean Benson, said in 1988. "He was just an everyday kid who devised a method that caught on with the whole world."

Fosbury won his gold medal for myriad reasons, from genetics to Medford's pulsating athletic environment to Don Gordon's timely invention of the foam pit to high-flying teammates who brought out the best in him to, yes, luck; at Echo Summit, had the high-jump officials not impeded on Hartfield's approach and he not lost his concentration, might John have cleared 7'3" and Dick not made the Olympic team?

But beyond all this, what, in the end, made Dick Fosbury a world champion was something else: like *Harold and the Purple Crayon*, the imagination to draw, in his mind, whatever it was his new style needed to become the efficient technique it did; the desire to refuse to conform when there was pressure from coaches to do so; and the doggedness to simply not quit.

"Steve Prefontaine was the greatest competitor on the track I ever saw," said Wagner. "Dick Fosbury was the greatest I ever saw on the field. When it mattered, he just didn't lose."

History will forever remember Fosbury for his winning jump in the Olympics, but he was leading that competition and, as it turned out, would have won, on fewer misses, even if he'd failed at 7'4¼". But the Echo Summit clearance of 7'2" with two misses—knowing a miss would leave him off the team—and the subsequent first-jump clearance of 7'3": that was the essence of Dick Fosbury the high jumper. That was desperation at its deepest. That was what drew Fosbury back to Echo Summit in September 2017, at age seventy, to remember, amid the mountains, trees, and granite boulders, his defining moment as a jumper.

In the wake of his brother's death and parents' divorce, the Flop warmed in an incubator of Dick's desperation to belong, was hatched at a time when JFK had America dreaming about going to the Moon, and took flight in a decade that beckoned people to question the old ways and consider the new. But after the Olympics, Fosbury's taking a stand for Fred Milton, the black OSU athlete, suggested his was a life destined to stretch beyond fame and fortune, to the deeper things that matter, to higher aspirations than high-jump bars. In so doing, Fosbury, a young man who'd once struggled to find his place in the world—a place to belong, to be accepted, to be valued—was standing up for black people simply seeking the same: a place to belong, to be accepted, to be valued.

And it all began by Dick literally turning his back on the establishment. "Has there ever been an athlete who epitomized American imagination better than Fosbury with his revolutionary flop?" asked Moore, the Oregon marathoner who entered the stadium just as Fosbury broke the Olympic record—and went on to an illustrious career with *Sports Illustrated*.

Most athletes' legacies are locked in performances of the past. But Fosbury's imprint is the rare case of sustainability in sports achievement, evident every time an athlete bends backward over a high-jump bar. Whether at a youth camp Dick is teaching in Maine or at a high school in LA; whether in an Olympic high-jump final in front of nearly 100,000 or in a poor neighborhood in Havana where a lone Cuban girl emulates national hero Javier Sotomayor, a part of Fosbury sails over the bar with each athlete's jump.

"Fosbury expressed what a lot of people were trying to reach for back in the 1960s," said Tom Greerty, a dorm mate of Fosbury's at OSU. "He expressed himself with athletic art—and he was a Picasso. Everyone was talking about revolution but there was this herd mentality of copycats; one guy grew his hair long so everybody else did. But he had something truly different. Dick Fosbury was the only true revolutionary I ever met."

EPILOGUE

IN JULY 1969, nine months after the Olympic Games in Mexico City, the US made good on JFK's 1961 challenge to go to the Moon. Once the US beat them to it, the Soviets lost interest in the space race. They never got to the Moon.

Dick's mother, Helen Fosbury, remarried twice and remained in Medford, working as a bookkeeper. She died of cancer in 1982. She was fifty-eight.

In 1988, the men's track and field program at Oregon State was discontinued because of budget shortfalls. Three decades later, an effort is underway to revive it.

Berny Wagner not only became the first coach of three 7'0" jumpers at the same time—Fosbury, Kelly, and Radetich—but coached seven high jumpers who cleared 7'0" or better in his ten years at OSU. In addition, he coached Joni Huntley, the first American woman to clear 6'0". He helped Corvallis become known as the "high jump capitol of the world." He coached twenty-five All-Americans and placed four teams in the top ten in the NCAA Championships. Wagner died in 2013. He was eighty-eight.

Bill Bowerman served as head coach of the US men's track and field team in the 1972 Olympics in Munich. He led Oregon to four NCAA championships and trained thirty-one Olympic athletes, twelve American record holders, and sixteen sub-four-minute milers. He was the co-founder, along with Phil Knight, of Nike. He died on Christmas Eve 1999. He was eighty-eight.

Dean Benson, head track and field coach at Medford High when Dick developed the Flop, served thirty-two years in that position. He retired in 1989 after winning numerous Southern Oregon Conference championships and one state title—Fosbury's junior year, 1964, though Dick didn't qualify for the meet. Benson died in 2005 at seventy-one. He was best remembered for being Fosbury's coach.

Fred Spiegelberg, Medford high jump and football coach, led the school to 253 wins and four state titles over his thirty-one-year career. In 1971, he was named National Coach of the Year. He died in 1996 at age seventy-six. MHS's stadium is named in his honor.

Ed Caruthers, who dueled with Dick for the gold medal in Mexico City, was drafted by the Detroit Lions but released after he was injured. He spent thirty-nine years as a teacher and coach before retiring. Still friends with Fosbury, he contends Dick isn't the athlete Ed was. "But he found his niche, and I take my hat off to him."

Reynaldo Brown, Dick's other teammate in Mexico City, became one of the most consistent 7'0" jumpers in the 1970s, winning five national titles. For his work with youth he received, in 2015, the Athletes in Excellence Award from the Foundation for Global Sports Development. A photographer, his work has been featured in the Art of the Olympians program.

John Hartfield, the odd-man out in the 1968 Olympic Trials at Echo Summit, remained one of America's top jumpers through 1971. He spent most of his life as a high school track and field coach, and held the Master's world record in the high jump. He died in 2012 from cancer. He was sixty-seven.

Toni Hartfield, John's wife of forty-four years, is retired and living in Missouri City, Texas. The couple's daughter, Jami, with whom she was pregnant at Echo Summit, is now forty-nine and lives nearby. Toni said John never mentioned the incident involving the official who broke his concentration. "He was disappointed about losing," she said, "but never bitter. He never jumped better than he did that day at Echo Summit."

Tommie Smith, who broke the world record in winning the 200-meter dash at the '68 Olympics, played briefly in the NFL, taught in Oberlin College's physical education department, and is now a public speaker. Because of his black-glove fist protest, he's also received death threats, been passed up for jobs, and been called a traitor to his country.

In 1993, he was awarded the California Black Sportsman of the Millennium Award and was, along with Carlos, honored with a statue at his alma mater, San Jose State.

Carlos fell on hard times in the 1970s; his ex-wife committed suicide, leading him to a period of depression. In 1985, he became a track and field coach at Palm Springs High and later worked as a counselor there. Along with Smith, he received an Arthur Ashe Courage Award at the 2008 ESPY ceremony. In 2006, after the death of Australian Peter Norman, the runner-up in the 200 meters who was ostracized for wearing a human-rights badge in solidarity with the two on the Olympic podium, Carlos and Smith served as pallbearers at the man's funeral.

Doug Sweet became OSU's student body president in 1970. He taught thirteen years at Santa Clara University and ended up as director of rhetoric and writing studies at Chapman University in Orange, California. He now lives in the woods along the North Santiam River in Oregon.

Steve Davis, Fosbury's high-jump rival at Medford High became a special agent with the US Secret Service, with responsibilities for protecting presidents Jimmy Carter and Ronald Reagan. He lives in San Diego, California.

In 1979, Debbie Brill was ranked the top female high-jumper in the world. Her Canadian outdoor (6'6", 1984) and indoor records (6'6", 1982) still stand today. At forty-six, she broke the world master's record (age forty-five-plus) when she cleared 5'9¼". In 1982, *T&F News* asked her if she was sorry that the backward style ultimately was referred to as the "Fosbury Flop" and not the "Brill Bend." "No, I've never felt that way," she said. "I want to be great at what I do but I don't care if I'm not really well-known for it."

Don Gordon, inventor of the Port-a-Pit, was so overwhelmed with orders after Fosbury's victory in 1968 that he sold the company to Leisure Enterprise in San Francisco. It was, he said, "the biggest business mistake I ever made." The founder of AirPlay, Gordon went on to invent, and have patented, more than 300 products, including many of the "Moon Bounce" inflatable houses for children. He died in 2016 at eighty-four. Fosbury never met him but always felt indebted to him.

More than half a century after the Civil Rights Act went into place, a black man, Barack Obama, spent two terms as president. However, a 2017 CNN poll showed two-thirds of blacks believe prejudice against minorities to still be a "very serious" problem—almost twice the ratio of whites. In June 2015, nine black people were massacred during a prayer service in Charleston, South Carolina, by an avowed white supremacist. In August 2017, one person was killed and thirty-four injured in a "Unite the Right" march by white supremacists in Charlottesville, Virginia. In September 2017, when NFL football players began kneeling during the National Anthem to protest racial discrimination, the response from some Americans was hauntingly similar to the response Smith and Carlos got after making their stands in Mexico City. President Donald Trump said NFL owners should react by saying: "Get that son of a bitch off the field right now. He's fired."

Medford's "sundown law" faded in the 1970s. Fifty years after the 1960 census reported six blacks in Medford, the city was home to 699. One third of Medford School District students are now children of color, the largest ethnic group Hispanics. Combined, the two Medford High football teams—in 1986, the city finally added a second high school—had nearly two dozen players who were minorities. All things being equal, the district said, "[we] will give employment preference to applicants of color and bilingual applicants."

In Corvallis, the Fred Milton incident led to OSU creating the Office of Minority Affairs in 1970. Five years later, a cultural center was opened for the Black Student Union. By 2010, nearly one fifth of the Oregon State University enrollment of 23,763 was comprised of minority students. Like most universities in America, black athletes now comprise a good share of OSU's football and basketball teams.

American's nearly twenty-year involvement in Vietnam ended with the fall of Saigon in April 1975. US casualties included 303,644 wounded and 58,318 killed, twenty-three of whom were from Dick's hometown, Medford. Dan Shepard, the Grants Pass athlete who had written Dick from Vietnam, was not among the casualties.

At the forty-year reunion for the 1968 Villanova track team in 2008, former Olympic Track and Field Coach Payton Jordan, then ninety, made a surprise appearance. He said he and the USOC had made a mistake in not including Dave Patrick on the 1968 Olympic team and, retroactively, was making him an honorary member. Jordan died the following year. He was ninety-one.

The 1968 US Olympic men's track and field team is still remembered as perhaps the finest in the history of the Games—and, despite the controversy over how its members were chosen, perhaps the most closeknit. "There was a brotherhood on that team," said *T&F News'* Hendershott, "like no other." Team members have gathered for a handful of reunions, including a thirty-year celebration in New Orleans in 1998 and a fifty-year celebration in Colorado Springs in 2018.

In 2014, through the tireless efforts of former *Sacramento Bee* sportswriter Bob Burns, the state of California recognized Echo Summit as a California Historic Landmark with a plaque installed on a granite boulder near the gravel-road entrance to the here-and-gone track facility.

Soon after the Olympic Trials were held at Echo Summit, the Tartan track was moved to what is now South Tahoe Middle School. After falling into disrepair, it was replaced in 2008. The Olympic Trials site—"the most bizarre location for an Olympic Trials ever," according to Wikipedia—is now home to Adventure Mountain, a sledding park. Though part of the old track has become a parking lot, two of the turns are still recognizable, particularly from high on the mountains that rise above it or from the air.

In February 2017, Doug Fosbury, ninety-five, heard, for the first time, his son Dick speak at a banquet—in Medford. Grainy movies his dad had taken in 1964 and 1965 were shown of Dick jumping backward into woodchip pits. For the first time, Dick honored his father publicly. Doug Fosbury died five months later. Among the items he had never thrown out: a photograph of son Greg's mangled bicycle.

Dick Fosbury moved from Oregon to Idaho in 1977. He now lives with his wife, Robin Tomasi, on a twenty-acre horse farm in Bellevue, near Sun Valley. His son, Erich, thirty-five, lives in Redmond, Oregon; Stepdaughter Stephanie, forty-nine, in Orange, California; and Kristin, forty-five, in Albany, Georgia.

Fosbury has been inducted into the US Olympic Hall of Fame, the Oregon Hall of Fame, the USA Track and Field Hall of Fame, the National High School Hall of Fame, and the World Humanitarian

Hall of Fame located in Boise, Idaho. He founded the Idaho Chapter of Olympians in 2007. In 2011, in Dubai, he was presented the Mohammad bin Rashid Al Maktoum Creativity in Sport Award.

Fosbury is past president of the World Olympians Association and current president of the United States Olympic and Paralympic Association.

He has been teaching at clinics and track camps around the world for more than forty-five years and has been chairman of the Simplot Games held in Pocatello, Idaho, each February for the past twelve.

In 1998, he won a bronze medal in the World Masters Track and Field Championships in the high jump, clearing the same height he was stuck on as a high school sophomore—5'4"—at age fifty-one. In 2014, he lost when, as a Democrat, he ran for a seat in the Idaho Legislature.

Fosbury has happily appeared in a Burger King ad ("I ate my burger upside down") and done commercials for such companies as Pepsi, 3M, Xerox, Visa, and Mazda. As "the Uber of high jumping," he has spoken to numerous US businesses about thinking outside the box. And is a big fan of "Broken Arrows," a video by the late Swedish record producer Avicii that mythologizes how the Flop is instrumental in turning a man's life around.

In 2008, Fosbury was diagnosed with stage one lymphoma. He beat it, thanks to being physically fit, to chemotherapy and radiation, and to having a father-in-law who's a cancer researcher at the University of New Mexico Medical Center.

Half a century after winning at Mexico City, the still-laid-back Fosbury keeps his gold medal in an old sock. Over the years, he has happily signed autographs for anyone who recognized him in an airport or hotel, but his Olympic fame never became his calling card; he enjoys "just being a regular guy." Once, he competed in the televised Converse Veterans Superstars competition in Florida. Hearing this, a neighbor looked puzzled. "Why?" she asked, "would they invite a surveyor?"

Besides operating his own civil engineering firm for four decades, Fosbury served as city engineer for the cities of Ketchum and Sun Valley. In that capacity, he oversaw the design and construction of the Wood River Trails and Sun Valley Trails. The thirty-six-mile system is a paved bike and running path, separated from roads, that allows people of all ages to enjoy the outdoors, get exercise, and not have to worry about the dangers of traffic. "Having a safe place to ride bikes was my life's dream," said Fosbury. "I was inspired to do that by my brother." In his mind, Dick thinks of it as "Greg's Trail."

Appendixes

by Tom Penix

Fosbury High-Jump Progression by Years

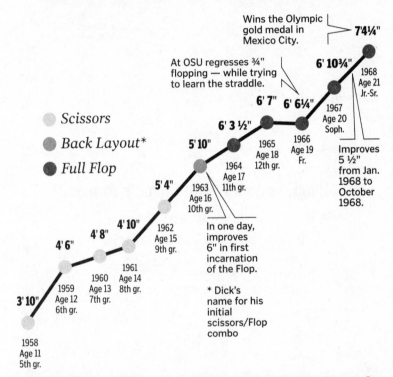

Wins the Olympic gold medal in Mexico City.

7'4¼"

At OSU regresses ¾" flopping — while trying to learn the straddle.

6' 10¾"

1968
Age 21
Jr.-Sr.

○ Scissors

◐ Back Layout*

● Full Flop

6' 7"   6' 6¼"

1967
Age 20
Soph.

6' 3 ½"

1966
Age 19
Fr.

Improves 5 ½" from Jan. 1968 to October 1968.

5' 10"

1965
Age 18
12th gr.

5' 4"

1964
Age 17
11th gr.

4' 10"

1963
Age 16
10th gr.

4' 8"

1962
Age 15
9th gr.

In one day, improves 6" in first incarnation of the Flop.

4' 6"

1961
Age 14
8th gr.

1960
Age 13
7th gr.

* Dick's name for his initial scissors/Flop combo

3' 10"

1959
Age 12
6th gr.

1958
Age 11
5th gr.

High-Jump Styles Commonly Used, By Decade

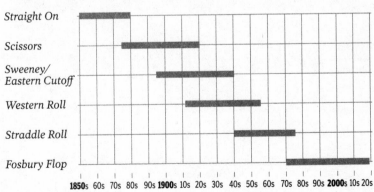

Straight On

Scissors

Sweeney/
Eastern Cutoff

Western Roll

Straddle Roll

Fosbury Flop

1850s 60s 70s 80s 90s 1900s 10s 20s 30s 40s 50s 60s 70s 80s 90s 2000s 10s 20s

Jump-by-Jump 1968 Olympic Trials

Final Olympic Trials, South Lake Tahoe, Calif., September 16, 1968

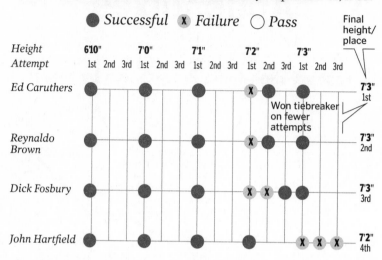

Jump-by-Jump 1968 Olympic Games

Olympic Games, Mexico City, October 20, 1968

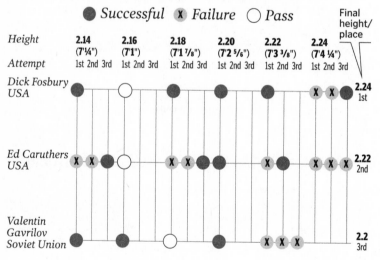

AUTHOR'S NOTE

CONFESSION. I WAS the kid in Chapter 13 who busted his bed while Flopping in his bedroom. I grew up in Corvallis and, in 1967, at age thirteen, first saw Dick Fosbury flip backward over a high-jump bar at Oregon State's Bell Field, a fifteen-minute bike ride from my house. My bedroom was literally wallpapered in color *Sports Illustrated* photos, among them shots from the 1968 Olympic Men's Track and Field Trials at Echo Summit. I was fascinated by the woodsy Trials at Tahoe. I was fascinated by the Flop. And, of course, by Foz.

In 1988, at age thirty-four, I first met, and interviewed, Fosbury in Ketchum, Idaho. It was for a freelance piece that was published in *Sports Illustrated* on the twenty-year anniversary of his gold-medal jump. In the time since, I was always surprised at how many people I came across who had heard of Fosbury and the Flop but how few really knew his deeper story. I also realized something else: *I* didn't really know his deeper story—at least all of it. For example, I did not learn about the death of his brother until he volunteered that information in January 2017 when I first called him to propose the book project. But as a journalist—and as a kid with Fosbury's photo slapped onto the bedroom wall of my youth—I had a thirst to discover his fuller story and tell it.

The Wizard of Foz is a braiding of Dick's personal remembrances of the way things were with my cultural interpretations of the way things were. Together, with the help of people more expert than ourselves, we plumbed the depths of Dick's childhood wounds of losing a brother and having his parents' marriage breakup within a year of each other.

As much as possible, I've tried to recreate Dick's journey through his eyes and through those who shared the journey with him. Dialogue in quote marks is either taken from written records or is presented as the best recollection of what was said, according to Dick. Anecdotes are based on eyewitness reports, written accounts, or records. Some less significant contextual detail is based on recollections of those who encountered experiences similar to Dick's or on reasonable assumptions given time, place, and circumstances.

The informational lake for the book was fed by ten major tributaries:

1) Countless interviews with Dick himself. From February 2017 to September 2017, we e-mailed, texted, and talked over the phone weekly, culminating with a weekend in South Lake Tahoe on the forty-ninth anniversary of the Trials. I saw where, deep in the woods, he'd won his spot on the Olympic team; where he almost drowned in Emerald Bay; and where he read the note saying the USOC was changing its mind on how the team would be chosen.

2) Interviews with people who knew Dick: Doug, his father, who died three months after we talked; Gail, his younger sister; and Doug Sweet, his closest boyhood friend who, like Dick, attended OSU. I spoke with nearly a dozen people who attended Medford High at the same Dick did, including Scott Spiegelberg, son of MHS football coach Fred Spiegelberg, Bob Haworth, Ron Wallace, Bill Foulon, Marc Bayliss, and Jack Mullen. I interviewed high jumpers Dick was teammates with and/or competed against in his seven-year career, including Steve Davis, Bob Shepard, John Radetich, and "Big Ed" Caruthers. I interviewed Chuck McNeil, a former OSU track and field assistant track coach when Dick was going to school. Among US Olympic teammates I talked to were: Kenny Moore, Tommie Smith, Wade Bell, Bill Clark, Roscoe Divine, Ralph Boston, and Bill Toomey. I interviewed people from the press who were at Echo Summit: reporter Blaine Newnham of the *Oakland Tribune* and photographer Rich Clarkson, who was shooting for *Sports Illustrated*; media aide Dave Kayfes; and Les Wright, who ran the long-jump event. I talked to track and field experts Jon

Hendershott, with *Track & Field News*; Joe Henderson, who was with *T&F News* and *Runner's World*; and Richard Hymans, editor of *The History of the United States Olympic Trials: Track and Field*. I was constantly bouncing questions off former high jumpers and current high-jump experts Joe Cantrell and John Dobroth. I explored the physical properties of the Flop with Jesus Dapena, a retired biomechanics expert in Indiana University's Department of Kinesiology. Finally, I interviewed sports psychologist Steven Ungerleider; nationally known grief expert Debra Alexander; Oregon State alumni magazine editor Kevin Miller; Grants Pass Athletic Director Clay Rounsaville; *Medford Mail Tribune* sports editor Tim Trower; and JoAnne Gordon, the widow of Port-a-Pit founder Don Gordon, who shared with me a detailed account her husband had written about how he'd invented the foam pit.

3) The Berny Wagner Scrapbooks, 1966–1975, at the Special Collection and Archives Research Center, OSU Libraries and Press, Oregon State University. These were Wagner's personal scrapbooks, full mainly of clippings from West Coast newspapers, many regarding Fosbury.

4) *Track & Field News.* The so-called "bible of the sport" was invaluable for not only the most minute statistical details but for sharing myriad perspectives on the human-rights issues that nearly led to a black boycott in 1968.

5) Internet sites. Thirty years after my *Sports Illustrated* article on Fosbury, I found it mindboggling how much information unavailable back then is now easily accessible: high-jump discussions on *T&F News'* forum, Google Earth perspectives of Echo Summit from the air, slideshows on the history of high jumping, the shape of the Moon in the sky over Medford Stadium on May 14, 1965, and far more. In particular, a searchable index of newspapers across the country proved valuable.

6) Photographs and videos. From Doug Fosbury's grainy Bell & Howell movies of Dick jumping as a high school kid to the

Olympic high-jump finals, they provide much insight into the Flop.

7) The microfiche department at the University of Oregon's Knight Library in Eugene. Nothing is more "old school" and yet these windows into newspapers provided information that the search-only online sites could not.

8) A trip to South Lake Tahoe and Echo Summit. The challenge of writing about history is trying to capture what it was really like in a single place at a specific time. The trip helped me do just that. And, when a handful of hikers—near where Dick had jumped forty-nine years ago—asked for his autograph, I was reminded me of how his legacy lives on, even in the middle of nowhere.

9) The Medford Branch Library of Jackson County Library Services, for yearbooks and city directories.

10) Books. Many, many books. See the bibliography on the next page.

BIBLIOGRAPHY

Baum, Kenneth, with Richard Trubo. *The Mental Edge: Maximize Your Sports Potential with the Mind-Body Connection.* New York: TarcherPerigee Books, 1999.

Bowerman, Bill, and William Freeman. *Bill Bowerman's High-Performance Training for Track and Field.* Monterey, California: Coaches Choice, 2009.

Chronicle of the 20th Century. New York: Chronicle Publications, 1987.

Brewster, Todd, and Peter Jennings. *The Century.* New York: Doubleday, 1998.

Brill, Debbie, and James Lawton. *Jump.* Vancouver/Toronto: Douglas & McIntyre, 1986.

The Diagram Group. *The Sports Fan's Ultimate Book of Sports Comparisons.* New York: St. Martin's Press, 1982.

Doherty, Ken. *Track and Field Ominbook.* Los Altos, California: Tafnews Press, 1976.

Gambetta, Vern. Editor. *The Athletic Congress's Track and Field Coaching Manual.* Champaign, Illinois: Leisure Press, 1989.

Gillon, Steve. *Boomer Nation: The Largest and Richest Generation Ever and How It Changed America.* New York: Free Press, 2004.

Guttmann, Allen. *The Olympics: A History of the Modern Games.* Urbana and Chicago: University of Illinois Press, 2002.

Hoffer, Richard. *Something in the Air.* New York: Free Press, 2009.

Hymans, Richard. *The History of the United States Olympic Trials—Track & Field.* Indianapolis, Indiana: USA Track & Field, 2008.

Kurlansky, Mark. *1968: The Year That Rocked the World.* New York: Random House, 2004.

Johnson, Crockett. *Harold and the Purple Crayon.* New York: HarperCollins, 1955.

Johnson, Paul. *A History of the American People.* New York: HarperCollins Publishers, 1997.

Keating, Kevin. *Medford: Images of America.* Charleston, South Carolina: Arcadia Publishing, 2011.

Large, David Clay. *Nazi Games: The Olympics of 1936.* New York and London: W.W. Norton & Company, 2007.

Maraniss, David. *Rome 1960: The Olympics That Changed the World.* New York: Simon & Schuster, 2008.

Moore, Kenny. *Bowerman and the Men of Oregon.* Emmaus, Pennsylvania: Rodale, 2006.

Pearson, Carol S. *The Hero Within: Six Archetypes We Live By.* New York: HarperCollins, 1998.

Oregon Blue Book, 1963–1964. Salem, Oregon: State of Oregon, 1963.

Oregon Blue Book, 1965–1966. Salem, Oregon: State of Oregon, 1965.

Pender, Mel, and Debbie Pender. *Expression of Hope: The Mel Pender Story.* Meadville, Pennsylvania: Christian Faith Publishing, Inc., 2017.

Redihan, Erin Elizabeth. *The Olympics and the Cold War, 1948–1968: Sport as Battleground in the U.S.-Soviet Rivalry.* Jefferson, North Carolina: McFarland & Co., Inc.

Smith, Tommie, with David Steele. *Silent Gesture: The Autobiography of Tommie Smith.* Philadelphia: Temple University Press, 2007.

Steben, Ralph E., and Sam Bell. *Track and Field: An Administrative Approach to the Science of Coaching.* Hoboken, New Jersey: John Wiley & Sons, Inc., 1978.

Strauss, William, and Neil Howe. *Generations.* New York: Quill, William Morrow, 1991.

Taylor, George, and Ray Hatton. *Oregon Weather Book.* Corvallis, Oregon: Oregon State University Press, 1999.

Ungerleider, Steven, and Jacqueline Golding. *Beyond Strength: Psychological Profiles for Olympic Athletes.* Dubuque, Iowa: Wm. C Brown Publishers, 1992.

Webber, Bert and Margie Webber. *The Lure of Medford.* Medford, Oregon: Webb Research Group Publishers, 1996.

Zang, David W. *Sports Wars: Athletes in the Age of Aquarius.* Fayetteville, Arkansas: The University of Arkansas Press, 2001.

Zinn, Howard. *A People's History of the United States.* New York: Perennial Classics, 2003.

ACKNOWLEDGMENTS

BOB WELCH:

My deepest thanks to:

Sally Jean Welch, without whose patience and encouragement I would not have cleared the opening height on this book.

Also, thanks to:

My agent, Greg Johnson, who fought hard to make this project happen.

Skyhorse Publishing, which believed in Fosbury's story.

Julie Ganz, my editor at Skyhorse, who always put the book, not herself, first.

Ann Petersen, editor extraordinaire, for saving me from myself time and again. (But I take responsibility for any and all errors in the book.)

Doug Sweet, a longtime Fosbury friend, for being a deep source of insight into Dick and for playing the role that Aubrey Montague plays in *Chariots of Fires*: a fellow athlete with the subject(s) of the story whose keen insight helps tell a deeper, richer story.

Track and field experts Joe Henderson (*Track & Field News* and *Runner's World*) and Jon Hendershott (*Track & Field News*), for superb fact-checking, reading the original manuscript, and answering more e-mail questions than there are grains of sand in a long-jump pit. Sadly, Hendershott, only a month after my last e-mail exchange with him, suffered a stroke and died unexpectedly at age seventy-one.

High-jump experts—and proud straddlers—Joe Cantrell (6'8¼") and John Dobroth (7'2⅝"), for the detailed nuances of the event.

Michael Dicianna, with Oregon State's Special Collections and Archives Research Center, for going out of his way to point me to newspaper stories and photos regarding Fosbury.

Kenny Moore, for inspiration, insight, and perspective, the latter shared so wonderfully in *Bowerman and the Men of Oregon.*

Wade Bell, for perspective on Echo Summit, photos, and more time than I deserved.

Tom Penix, friend and graphic designer, whose charts helped put Dick and his style in perspective.

Bob Goodwin and Jonny Mills, for help on Spanish translations.

Jack Wilson, editorial page editor at *The Register-Guard,* and Ilene Aleshire, associate editor, for flexibility in my work schedule.

Kevin Miller, editor of the *Oregon Stater,* for perspective from one of the best storytellers and editors on the planet.

B.G. Gould, director of football operations for the Medford School District, and Natalie Hurd, communication and public relations specialist for the Medford School District, for tracking down information.

The Medford High Class of '65 dinner group that played host to me at the lovely home of Bob and Meri Haworth: Sandy Darland, Tim Darland, Gibb Mitchell, Ron Wallace, Judy Wallace, Marc Bayliss, and Rob Rector. Besides being with Dick at Echo Summit, my favorite moment on the Fosbury journey was listening to Kingstron Trio member Bob Haworth sing "Today" in his living room before my long drive back to Eugene.

Others who put pieces in the puzzle were Carl Davaz, Curtis Anderson, Steve Locey, and Kelly Fenley.

And, my greatest thanks to Dick Fosbury, who created the story and helped recreate the story not only through the answering of hundreds of my questions but through the courage it took to answer the painful ones.

DICK FOSBURY:

Thanks to:

Terry Rosenau, for laughing at my jokes.

Willy McCarty, for training me up every mountain.

Kerry Eggers, *Portland Tribune* journalist, for always listening.

The late Jim Dunaway, journalist, who watched me arrive on the scene and always cared.

My good agent, Ray Schulte, who has always had my perspective to make the right move.

And the ultimate Robin Tomasi, for guiding my slow feet, holding my frame, and being my best partner for life.

I suffered to be born, practiced to breathe easy, and came to understand the One.

INDEX

California Black Sportsman of the
  Millennium Award, 227
California Democratic Primary, 1968, 108
California Historic Landmark, 229
Cal State-Los Angeles, 33
Campbell, Joseph, 89
Camus, Albert, 81
Canada, 227
Cantrell, Joe, 237
Cape Kennedy, 81, 172
Carlos, John, 136, 147, 151, 175-76,
  193, 199, 202-03, 227
Carpenter, Scott, 112
Carson, Johnny, 200
Carson, Rachel, 40
Carter, President Jimmy, 227
Caruthers, Ed ("Big Ed"), 92-93, 95,
  101, 124, 151, 158-64, 167, 178,
  181, 183-90, 218, 226, 236
Cascade Mountains, 3, 4
CBS, 134
The Century, 138
Cerutty, Percy, 171
Chaffee, Roger 80
Chambers Brothers, 134
Chaplin, John, 79
Chapman University, 227
Charleston, South Carolina, 228
Charlottesville, Virginia, 228
Chicago American
"Chicken Fat," 5
Chih-Chin, Ni, 187
Christchurch, New Zealand, 107
Christian Science Monitor, 106, 125, 199
Civil Rights Act (1964), 64
Clare, Cassandra, 157
Clark, Bill, 126, 128, 141, 144, 168, 236
Clark, Robert, 201
Clarkson, Rich, 148-49, 163, 236
Cluff, Carl, 128
CNN, 228
Coast Range, 4

College Inn (Corvallis), 103, 115
College of San Mateo, 72
Colorado Springs, Colorado, 181, 229
Colton High (Colton, Oregon), 6
Columbia University, 105
Commerce High (Portland, Oregon)
communism, 5
Compton High (Los Angeles), 127, 152,
  160
Converse Veterans Superstars competition,
  230
Cooper, Dr. Donald, 177
Cortez running shoes, 149-50
Corvallis High, 221
Corvallis, Oregon, 16, 60, 72, 74, 89,
  102, 105-07, 111, 114, 121, 201,
  215, 217, 225, 235
Cosell, Howard, 174
Cousteau, Jacques, 84
Cox, Jim, 54
Crater Lake, 6, 137
Crater Lake Avenue (Medford), 21,
  48-49
Creedence Clearwater Revival, 93
Cronkite, Walter, 50, 90
Crosa, Giacomo, 179
Cuba, 5, 219, 222
Cuban Missile Crisis, 5, 94, 112
Curry, Stan, 158
Czechoslovakia, 90

D

Daegu, South Korea, xi
Daley, Arthur, 93, 191
Daley, Richard, 138
Dapena, Jesus, 59, 219, 237
Dassler, Adolf "Ad," 200
The Dating Game, 200
Davis, Leo, 174, 183, 197
Davis, Miles, 24
Davis, Steve, 8, 53, 60, 63-64, 66,
  74-75, 124, 227, 236

Florida, 230
Flubber, 53, 216
"Fools Rush In," 5
Ford Motors, 59
Fosbury, Dick,
adult children of, 229; and breakup of
his parents' marriage, 22-24; as a
"disruptor," 95; as Ashton Eaton's
inspiration, xi-xii; as one of worst
high jumpers in Oregon as a high
schooler, 5-6, 68, 190, 197;
breakthrough high-jump performances by, 27-30, 61-62, 82-83,
93, 162-166, 183-191; competitive
nature of, 63-66, 69, 122, 210; civil
engineering pursuits of, 114, 200,
209-211, 230; and death of brother,
Greg, and aftermath, 21-24, 47-50,
57-59, 187, 201, 229; and desire to
belong and prove himself worthy, 5,
8, 18, 24, 54, 153, 181, 208; and,
following death of brother and
divorce of parents, desire to risk,
57-59, 187, 201; and desire to be
accepted beyond high-jumping
accomplishments, 193, 203-04,
207-09; and difficulty of first two
years at Oregon State, 75-76,
80-82; at Echo Summit training
camp, 132-34, 136, 139-40, 145;
and earliest high-jump attempts,
7-8; and failed attempt at football,
44-45; and high-jump records
(American, 192; collegiate, 164;
Medford High, 61-62, 67; NCAA
Championships (outdoor), 114;
Olympics, 192; Oregon State
University, 83, 84, 164); and
inception, and evolution, of what
became the Fosbury Flop high-
jump style, xiii, 27-30, 51-52,
64-65; and media's misspellings,

and other inaccuracies, of name, 30,
67, 83; and mental intensity during
competition, 110-111, 121-24, 222;
and missing 1968 Olympic closing
ceremonies, 198; and missing 1968
Olympic opening ceremonies, 172;
near-drowning of, 137-38; at 1968
Olympic Trials at Echo Summit,
150-169, 222; at 1968 Olympic
Trials in Los Angeles, 126-28; at
1968 Olympic Games in Mexico
City, 171-74, 176-93; physical
attributes of, 5, 9, 79, 122; and
post-Olympic burnout as high
jumper, 204-09; and race relations,
97, 100, 102, 176, 199, 201-04, 222;
and rank in the world prior to 1968
Olympics, 122, 181; and realization
that he had not, as he had assumed,
made 1968 Olympic team, 139-140;
and recommitment to academics at
Oregon State University after the
1968 Olympics, 201, 208-210; and
relationship with Berny Wagner, 68,
71-76, 79, 81-83, 85, 140, 204, 207;
and relationship with media, 197-98;
and relationship with hometown of
Medford, 172, 177, 192, 198,
199-200; and struggles with
academics at OSU, 76, 86, 91,
114-15; and struggles as high jumper
in college, 75-76; and struggles as
high jumper in high school, 5-6; and
survivor's guilt, 50, 58; and training
at OSU, 79-80; and Vietnam War
draft, 82, 91, 102-06; 114-15
Fosbury, Doug, 6, 7, 21-24, 26, 28, 44,
49-50, 54, 68, 82, 187, 191, 200,
229, 236-37
Fosbury Flop
and advantages of, 104, 122, 219;
competition's reaction to, 26, 53,

Nobel Peace Prize, 64
Norman, Peter, 175, 227
North's Chuck Wagon, 16, 42, 198
North Santiam River, 227
North Vietnam, 64

O

Oakland, California, 91, 93, 121, 168,
    204, 220
Oakland Coliseum, 91
Oakland Tribune, 83, 93, 157, 163, 204
Obama, President Barack, 228
Oberlin College, 226
O'Brien, Parry, 106
Oerter, Al, 175
Office of Minority Affairs (Oregon
    State), 228
O'Hanlan, Dr. J. Tracy, 213-14
Olympic Games (summer), xi, 63, 112,
    128, 131, 191; of 1936, Berlin, 97,
    101, 171; of 1948, London, 117; of
    1952, Helsinki, 117; of 1956,
    Melbourne, 117, 178, 180, 190; of
    1960, Rome, 33, 64, 109, 117, 123,
    173, 178, 205; of 1964, Tokyo, 63,
    96, 117, 119, 125, 152, 161,
    178-79; of 1972, Munich, 17,
    209-10, 225; of 1976, Montreal,
    217; of 1988, Seoul, 219; of 2012,
    London, xii; of 2016, Rio, xii
Olympic Games of 1968 (summer),
    Mexico City xii, 73-74, 90, 92,
    122, 125, 171-93, 218, 220, 225;
    altitude factor of, 117, 125, 143,
    175; competition of, 174-75; dates
    of, 139; high-jump competition of,
    178-93 (jump-by-jump breakdown
    of leaders, in graphic); pre-Games
    violence of, 171
Olympic Project for Human Rights,
    145, 175

Olympic Stadium (Mexico City), 192
Olympic Village (Mexico City), 139,
    174-75
Olympism, 173, 210
Olympus, Mt., 132
Orange, California, 227, 229
Oregon (state), xi, 3, 4, 6, 26, 129, 143,
    151, 179, 206
Oregon Coast, 6
The Oregonian, 69, 84, 129, 174, 183,
    197, 215
Oregon Dairy Princess, 200
Oregon Hall of Fame, 229
Oregon Journal, 85, 128, 151, 174, 199
Oregon Junior Chamber of Commerce
    Track and Field Meet, 68
Oregon Democratic Primary, 1968, 108
Oregon Republican Primary, 1968, 59
Oregon Sportswriters and Sportscasters, 101
Oregon State Class A-1 Track and Field
    Championships (boys'), 1965, 68
Oregon Stater, 57, 95
Oregon State University (OSU), 16, 44,
    51, 57, 67, 71, 73-74, 79, 81-83,
    89-90, 100, 102, 122, 124, 129,
    133-34, 141, 150, 158, 164, 181,
    199-201, 203, 218, 222-23, 225,
    227-28, 235-36
Oregon State University School of
    Engineering, 209
O'Rourke, Meghan, 21
Oswald, Lee Harvey, 100
Owens, Jesse, 97

P

Pacific Crest Trail, 119, 134
Pac-8 Conference (and equivalent league
    prior to 1968), 74
Pac-8 Track and Field Championships
    (men's), 1967, 85, 209; 1968, 107,
    121, 209; 1969, 208-09